PERGAMON RUSSIAN CHESS SERIES

THREE STEPS
TO
CHESS MASTERY

PERGAMON RUSSIAN CHESS SERIES

General Editor:
Kenneth P. Neat

Executive Editor:
Catherine Shephard

THREE STEPS
TO
CHESS MASTERY

BY

A. S. SUETIN

International Grandmaster

Translated by

KENNETH P. NEAT

PERGAMON PRESS

OXFORD · NEW YORK · BEIJING · FRANKFURT
SÃO PAULO · SYDNEY · TOKYO · TORONTO

U.K.	Pergamon Press, Headington Hill Hall, Oxford OX3 0BW, England
U.S.A.	Pergamon Press, Maxwell House, Fairview Park, Elmsford, New York 10523, U.S.A.
PEOPLE'S REPUBLIC OF CHINA	Pergamon Press, Room 4037, Qianmen Hotel, Beijing, People's Republic of China
FEDERAL REPUBLIC OF GERMANY	Pergamon Press, Hammerweg 6, D-6242 Kronberg, Federal Republic of Germany
BRAZIL	Pergamon Editora, Rua Eça de Queiros, 346, CEP 04011, Paraiso, São Paulo, Brazil
AUSTRALIA	Pergamon Press Australia, P.O. Box 544, Potts Point, N.S.W. 2011, Australia
JAPAN	Pergamon Press, 8th Floor, Matsuoka Central Building, 1-7-1 Nishishinjuku, Shinjuku-ku, Tokyo 160, Japan
CANADA	Pergamon Press Canada, Suite No. 271, 253 College Street, Toronto, Ontario, Canada M5T 1R5

English translation copyright © 1982 K. P. Neat

First edition 1982
Reprinted 1983
Reprinted 1988

British Library Cataloguing in Publication Data
Suetin, S. A.
Three steps to chess mastery. —
(Pergamon Russian chess series).
1. Chess
I. Title
794.1'2   GV1445

ISBN 0-08-024139-5 Hard cover
ISBN 0-08-024138-7 Plexi cover

Printed in Great Britain by A. Wheaton & Co. Ltd., Exeter

CONTENTS

Contents

Contents

FOREWORD TO THE ENGLISH EDITION

This book sees the combination of two of my works: *The Chess Player's Laboratory* and *The Path to Mastery*. The earlier of these, the *Laboratory*, was written back in the early seventies, while *The Path to Mastery* was compiled much later, at the end of the seventies. But, as I pointed out in the Russian foreword to the second work, these books are closely linked to each other, both ideologically, and as regards their content. Moreover, *The Path to Mastery* is virtually a continuation of the *Laboratory*, and is a consistent extension of its main theme, aimed at the player who has already reached a fairly high standard*: questions of how he can improve, and the problems and methods of independent work on his own game.

This, incidentally, has been one of the main themes in my methodological literary activity, and it is on this that I have been working for the past decade, the fruit of which is the book *The Path to Mastery*.

I consider the decision of Pergamon Press to combine my two works in one publication to be perfectly justified. I should like to emphasize certain basic points which will be examined in the present book:

1. The basic factors of a chess player's thinking (evaluation of position, specific calculation of variations, choice of move, etc.).

2. Typical mistakes and narrow thinking tendencies.

3. Psychological factors. Problems of intuition. The two basic types of thinking: inductive and deductive.

4. Individual and general playing styles.

5. Methods of home preparation (opening preparation, study of typical positions, work on analysis, etc.).

And much more besides, to which I hope that the reader will direct his attention. I should like to wish my readers success in grasping the laboratory secrets of work on chess. For it is this, together with practice, that constitutes the path to mastery.

A. SUETIN

---

* In the text the author refers to various Soviet grades, for which the approximate equivalent ratings are: Candidate Master — 200-220 (BCF), 2200-2360 (Élő); 1st Category — 180-200 (BCF), 2040-2200 (Élő); 2nd Category — 160-180 (BCF), 1880-2040 (Élő) [Translator's note].

PART I

The Chess Player's Laboratory

1

WAYS AND MEANS OF IMPROVING

The alpha and omega of a chess player's thinking

In accordance with our aims, we will first attempt to establish what components make up the concept of 'a chess player's thinking'. Let us, however, begin with a position and the calculation of variations.

Two young players of master standard—A. Karpov (the future World Champion) and I. Miklayev—had just adjourned their game in a deciding match for first place between 'Burevestnik' and the Central Army Sports Club in the USSR Team Championship in Riga (1968). The Army representative, Karpov, went home in a very cheerful mood. Indeed, the position of Miklayev, who was playing Black, appeared to give serious cause for alarm.

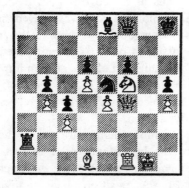

The move **43 Ng3!** suggests itself, after which the black pawns come under attack.

The resumption of the game seemed to serve as a demonstration of White's excellent technique. Black was reconciled to the inevitable, and his resistance, although prolonged, was of a formal nature:

43...Qg7 44 Q×f6 Q×f6 45 R×f6 Ra1 46 Rf1 Rc1 47 Ne2!

The commencement of a winning manoeuvre by the knight, which heads with gain of tempo for the square f5.

47...Ra1 48 Nd4 Kg8 49 Nf5! Ra6 50 Kf2.

And now the white king comes into play with decisive effect.

50...Bg6 51 Ke3 B×f5 52 e×f5 Ra2 53 Kd4 Ra1 54 Be2! Ra2 55 B×h5.

White already has a decisive advantage. Against the advance of the pawns Black is helpless.

55...Rh2 56 Rf4 Rd2+ 57 Ke4 Rd3 58 f6 R×c3 59 Kf5!

An instructive moment. White's king penetrates into the black position, and takes an active part in the decisive attack.

59...Re3 60 Rf1 Nd7 61 Rg1+ Kf8 62 Ra1 Re5+ 63 Kg6 Re8 64 Ra7 Rd8 65 Rc7!

An essential piece of accuracy. White deprives his opponent of the slightest hope of counter-play, associated with the advance of his c4 pawn.

65...Kg8 66 Kg5 Kh8 67 Bg6 Kg8 68 h5 Kh8 69 h6 c3 70 R×c3 Rf8 71 f7 Resigns.

White convincingly realized his advantage, but we now want to talk about something else. Let us return to the initial position.

Is Black's position really so hopeless? Is he indeed doomed to a slow and agonizing defeat? After all, in White's position too there are many weak points. His pawns may come under attack. At the same time White must reckon with the possibility of a counter-attack on his king, since Black's rook controls the dangerous second rank. With the inclusion of the black queen in the play, the counter-attack would become very real.

"This is all very well", the reader will object, "but for the moment these are general considerations, and how after 43 Ng3 is Black to parry the very direct threat of **44 Q×f6+?**".

But even so Black had an interesting possibility of creating counter-play by 43...Ra3!, immediately attacking the most vulnerable link in White's pawn chain—his c3 pawn.

If now White withdraws his queen to the defence of c3 by 44 Qd2, Black promptly activates his queen by 44...Qg7!, threatening to seize the initiative.

The main, crucial variation arises after 44 Q×f6+ Q×f6 45 R×f6 Bd7!

The first tactical subtlety. 45...R×c3 is less clear on account of 46 Kf2!.

46 Rh6+.

Before capturing the d6 pawn, White lures the black king to g8 or g7, where it comes under attack by the white knight.

46...Kg8 47 R×d6 R×c3 48 N×h5 Rc1! 49 Nf6+ Kf7!

An interesting tactical point. In the event of 49...Kg7 50 N×d7 R×d1+ 51 Kf2 c3 52 N×e5 c2 the natural 53 Nd3? fails to

the combinative blow 53...Rd2+!, when White loses (*54 Ke3 R×d3+!*, or *54 Ke1 R×d3*, and White is defenceless against the threat of ...*Rd1+* and ...*c1 = Q*). But even so, the variation with 49...Kg7 is unsatisfactory. Instead of 52 Nd3 White should play 52 Rc6! c1 = Q 53 R×c1 R×c1 54 Ke3, when the resulting ending is hopeless for Black.

50 N×d7 R×d1+ 51 Kf2 Ke7!

All this is forced and exactly calculated (the analysis is by Geller and Furman).

52 Re6+ K×d7 53 Ke2!!

Already it is White who has to think in terms of saving the game. 53 R×e5 is bad in view of 53...c3!, when the black pawn queens.

53...Rd4 54 R×e5 c3 55 d6 etc., forcing a draw.

From this example it is apparent that one can penetrate into the heart of a position only by combining the specific calculation of variations with an evaluation of the position (weak points and pawns, activity of the pieces, etc.).

Black's position proved to be defensible not thanks to some accidental subtlety, which one player might think up, and another might not. It was defensible thanks to the rich resources of defence and counter-attack, which were latent in the positioning of his pieces. Thus in his correct plan of counter-play, an important role was played first by Black's strong rook, and then, in the ending, by his passed c4 pawn. The centralized position of the knight at e5 was also an important factor in the defence. It was these objective positional factors which were reflected in the analysis given.

This example demonstrates in the first instance the importance of a correct 'diagnosis', reached as a result of a thorough evaluation of the position. Incidentally, from this same example it is apparent that formal logic on its own would be insufficient for this.

In complicated situations it is important to sense the hidden subtleties of a position. It is this that the player with Black was lacking. Only a subtle 'positional feeling' would have enabled Black to find the manoeuvre 43... Ra3!, and then consistently to disentangle the mass of variations given above.

Positional feeling is a category which is by no means mystic. It is acquired by experience, and the degree of its keenness is an indication of the talent of a player. It is no accident, for example, that the wonderful positional intuition of Capablanca became proverbial.

Of course, it should on no account be thought that the correct evaluation of a position will automatically and invariably ensure the finding of the best move. Not at all. It happens that a player will grasp correctly the essence of a position, but fail to take account of some 'trifle' in a specific variation. The sad consequences of this may be seen even more quickly than after a mistake in evaluation.

Here is an example, taken from the game **Kupreichik–Tal** (Sochi 1970).

White's attack hardly compensates for the sacrificed piece. Black established this fairly quickly, and this evaluation is correct. But in the tactical sense Black probably thought his defensive task to be simpler than was in fact the case.

White's latent threats should on no account be underestimated, and perhaps the most forceful measure was the counter-sacrifice 22...Qb6!?. In the event of 23 B×b6 B×b6 Black has the strong threats of 24...Ng4, or 24...B×b3 and 25...Nd5, which give him the better prospects.

The game in fact continued **22...Qb7 23 Rg3 Nc5?**

The critical point of the game. The position is so full of combinative motifs that the question of evaluation is pushed into the background. While considering his 22nd move, Black had intended playing 23...Bb6, but then, on closer examination, he saw the following fantastic variation: 24 Re7! B×b3 25 B×g6 B×d4+ 26 Kh1 Kh8 27 B×f7! Ne4(?) 28 Q×h7+!! K×h7 29 Bg8++! and 30 Rh7 mate!

It was this factor which led him to choose 23...Nc5?, which led directly to disaster. Nevertheless, 23...Bb6 was correct, only on his 27th move Black should play not 27...Ne4, but 27...Ng4!, so as on 28 Bg6 to reply 28...Rf7! 29 R×f7 N×h6 30 R×h7+ Kg8 31 Be4+ Kf8 32 B×b7 R×c2, when Black has every chance of winning.

After 23...Nc5? Kupreichik brought his attack to a spectacular conclusion: **24 N×c5 d×c5 25 f5! c×d4 26 f×g6 f×g6 27 B×g6 Kh8 28 Q×f8+ Ng8 29 Bf5! Rb8 30 Re8 Qf7 31 Rh3!! Resigns.**

This example shows that there is a large number of positions, in which the main role is played not by the weighing up of positional factors, but by the art of deep calculation of variations and by combinative vision.

Thus the thinking of a chess player consists of two basic components: calculation of variations and evaluation of position, which are determined by the content of the game—its strategy and tactics.

The connection between strategy and tactics

Chess *strategy* comprises questions of the general interaction of the forces for the attainment of the most important goals at various stages of the battle. The basis of strategy is a *plan*—a purposeful method of action. As the art of chess develops, strategic plans are constantly enriched by new types, many of which become typical.

The plan in a chess game is always based on an *evaluation* of the initial position, taking account of its important peculiarities. A plan in a game is a kind of guide line, which is followed depending on conditions. If the conditions of the game change, the plan also changes. After all, every change in the position, sometimes even an insignificant one, demands new strategic solutions.

A plan accompanies a chess game from the first to the last move, as though illuminating its course. In practice, strategy is sometimes very prominent, while at other times it becomes as though invisible. The plan 'recedes' when *tactics*—the second integral component of the game—begin to play the predominant role.

While strategy gives a player the principles of how to handle his forces in general, tactics demands a concrete approach to the solution of a particular position, and demands that the specific nature of conducting the struggle is approached as closely as possible. As Dr Euwe picturesquely remarked, "strategy demands reflection, tactics demands a penetrating glance".

Tactics in chess is the art of conducting the struggle. It takes account of the fighting properties and pecularities of the pieces and pawns, and of the various forms of interaction between them. Projected ideas are put into action by means of specific devices and operations.

The basic tactical operation is the threat in the broadest sense of the word. Threats can be highly diverse in character: a threat to the enemy king, a threat of gaining a material advantage, a threat to seize space and restrict the mobility of the opposing pieces, a threat to create weak points or squares in his position, a threat to exchange the opponent's attacking pieces, with the aim of easing the defence, etc. Thus, in their content and form threats are unusually diverse.

Among the numerous and diverse tactical devices, a special place is occupied by the combination. A combination invariably involves a sacrifice of material, and leads to unusual, at times quite fantastic, situations. And it is this factor which makes chess so enormously attractive. The combination is also one of the most dangerous and common stratagems in a chess game. We will examine this question in practice.

The calculation of variations and combinations

Even players who have little experience very quickly begin to realize that, first and foremost, one has constantly to battle against tactical threats by the opponent, and to create similar threats of one's own. In other words, in practice the players' efforts are mainly directed towards the calculation of variations (incidentally, this is directly apparent from the examples given above).

Even the most simple, at times purely mechanical, calculation of variations (say, in an elementary pawn ending) has its intrinsic themes, the mastery of which is a very important step on the road to improvement.

Calculation is usually associated with combinative creativity. The latter demands great imagination.

Let us take, for example, an episode from the game **Tal–Gligoric** (Candidates' Match, 1968).

A very sharp combinative situation has arisen. White's next move, **31 Qh5**, appears crushing, but Black finds a brilliant counter-combination, which was not foreseen on this occasion even by Tal.

There followed **31...Q×c1+ 32 Kh2 Bd6+! 33 R×d6 Qf4+ 34 Rg3 Q×d6 35 Nf5 R8e1!!**

A tactical blow of fearful strength. Only now does it become apparent that even such a virtuoso of combinations as Tal made an irreparable mistake on move 31 (correct was *31 Nb3!*, with winning chances for White).

36 Q×f7+ K×f7 37 N×d6+ Ke6 38 Rg6+ Kd5 39 Nf5 Rb7! 40 Ne3+ R×e3! 41 f×e3 Rc7!

It is readily apparent that Black's position is easily won.

42 Kg3 c4 43 Kf4 c3 44 e4+ Kc4 45 Ra6 c2 46 Ra1 Kd3 White resigns.

Even the strongest players, endowed with combinational talent, sharpen their calculating skill in their everyday training.

Methods of training one's calculating ability have been fairly well studied. Lack of space prevents us from dwelling here in detail on this complex question. To anyone wishing to study these methods, I can recommend the writings of Botvinnik, Blumenfeld, Romanovsky, Kotov, Averbakh and others.

Here we will dwell only on certain points of a general nature. It is customary to think that the art of making combinations depends in the main on native talent, and this can hardly be disputed. But even so, it has long been known that a whole series of elements, out of which various combinations are formed, are constantly repeated. And it is for this reason that an ability to make combinations depends to a considerable extent on correct tuition.

A great deal was done for the systemization of combinations by the outstanding Soviet specialist Romanovsky. In his book *Mittelshpil* he singles out three basic features which accompany a combination: *idea*, *theme* and *motif*.

Romanovsky takes the idea of a combination to mean the ways and methods of realizing combinational plans. One can single out, for example, elementary ideas such as diversion, decoy, interference, blocking, square-vacating etc.

The action of the pieces, characterizing the combinative achievement, is called by Romanovsky the theme of the combination, examples of which are: double attack (perhaps the most frequently occurring theme), pin, discovered check, smothered mate, pawn promotion etc.

In practice, elementary ideas and themes rarely occur in their pure form. More often than not they are interlaced one with another. It is the disentangling of this mass that comprises the essence of a combination. And it is by no means always that the existence of all the factors indicated enables a combination to be carried out. Its realization depends on numerous, at times barely perceptible peculiarities of the position—combinative motifs. What Romanovsky calls a motif is the sum total of circumstances assisting the creation of a combination, for example: a particular piece arrangement, the existence of weak points etc.

The following example, taken from the game **Karpov–Velimirovic** (Skopje 1976), is an excellent illustration of both the origin, and the exploitation, of combinative motifs.

In the diagram position there appears to be no herald of an imminent combinative storm.

Black continued:

19...Rad8?

The first inaccuracy. In the tactical sense (as soon becomes clear!) d8 is an unfortunate square for Black's rook. 19...Rae8 was correct, when a manoeuvring battle could have developed. With the aim of increasing the pressure on Black's castled position, White would probably have had to double rooks on the g-file: 20 Rg2 Re7 21 Rcg1 Ref7. In view of the possibility of 22 Ng4, with the threat of Nh6+, White's positional advantage is undisputed, but the realization of this advantage is still a lengthy and difficult matter.

20 b3 c6?

This further mistake, this time a serious one, meets with a swift refutation. It was not too late to play 20...Rde8, transposing into the variation given above.

21 d×c6 b×c6 22 Nf5!

The start of a spectacular, and deeply and accurately calculated combination, which breaks up Black's fortress on the K-side. One of its important motifs is the unfortunate position of the black rook at d8.

22...g×f5.

Black has little choice. 22...B×f5 23 e×f5 g5 is decisively met by 24 N×g5 f×g5 25 Q×g5 Rd7 26 f6 etc. On 22...Be8 there follows simply 23 Ne7+, when Black inevitably loses material.

23 R×g7+! K×g7 24 Rg1+ Kf7.

Forced, since 24...Kh8 is met by 25 Ng5 f×g5·26 Q×g5, when Black does not have the move 26...Rf7 because of 27 Q×d8+! (This is where the unfortunate position of the rook at d8 tells!)

25 Qh5+ Ke6.

Of course, not 25...Ke7? 26 Rg7+!

26 Q×f5+ Kf7 27 Qh5+ Ke6 28 Qf5+ Kf7.

After 28...Ke7 29 Rg7+ Rf7 30 R×f7+ K×f7 31 Ng5+ White's attack is irresistible.

29 Ng5+ Ke8 30 Ne6 Rf7 31 Rg7! Rc8.

After 31...R×g7 32 N×g7+ Kf7 33 Q×h7 Black has no defence against the threats of Nf5+ and Nh5+.

32 R×f7 K×f7 33 Ng5+ Ke7 34 Q×h7+ Kd8 35 Qh8+ Kc7 36 Q×f6.

This is the position that White had in mind when he began his combination. Although Black has a rook and two minor pieces for White's queen, his position is very difficult, if not hopeless. The point is that Black's forces are lacking in harmony (as before, his knights are playing a pitiful role). White, on the other hand, has the 'mercurial' h-pawn, which will soon cost Black one of his pieces.

36...Re8 37 h4 Nc5 38 h5 Ne6 39 h6 Nf8 40 b4 Nc8 41 Kd2 Ne7 42 h7 N×h7 43 N×h7 Nc8 44 Nf8 Re7 45 a3 Be8 46 Ne6+ Kd7 47 Ng7 Kc7 48 Nf5 Rd7 49 a4.

The realization stage commences, which first and foremost demands good and accurate technique. White's problem is to shatter Black's final fortress. The organic weaknesses in Black's position at a7 and c6 foreshadow his defeat.

49...Bf7 50 Kc3 Ba2 51 a5 Rf7 52 Qh6 Rd7 53 f4! e×f4 54 Q×f4 Rf7 55 Qh6 Rd7 56 Qh2 Be6 57 Qh6 B×f5.

On 57...Ba2 there could have followed 58 Nd4, when against the threat of e4–e5 it is difficult to find a defence.

58 e×f5 d5 59 Kd4 Nd6 60 Qf4 Kb7 61 Qe5 Nf7 62 Qe8 Kc7 63 Qa8!

The queen's lengthy manoeuvre comes to a successful conclusion. Now it penetrates by force to c5, attacking simultaneously the pawns at a7 and c6, which immediately decides the game.

63...Kd6 64 Qf8+ Kc7 65 Qc5 Nd6 66 Q×a7+ Kc8 67 Qa6+ Resigns.

Apart from its fine combination, this game was also instructive for the subsequent battle with unbalanced material, and for the fine technique of White's lengthy queen manoeuvres, which completed the realization of his advantage.

But let us not be diverted from the basic theme of this section, which is combination.

It can be verified that a player, who has consciously acquired elementary combinational skill, has in this way created the preconditions for the development of his *combinational vision*. No less important is the development of combinational flair, which enables one to 'feel' the harmonious co-ordination of the pieces, to sense in time the existence of a combinational threat, and as a result to find a way of implementing the combination.

It is only after undergoing such a training that a player can approach that which is called the art of analysis. In his writings (for example, the article 'On the improvement of a chess player', *Shakhmaty v SSSR*, 1939 No.9) grandmaster A. Kotov indicates the following factors, which a player should aim to achieve in his everyday work on the art of calculation.

1. Aim to penetrate as deeply as possible into the subtleties of the position, and examine variations as far ahead as possible.

2. The art of 'selecting' variations for analysis; determine the optimum number of variations which are of practical value.

3. Calculate the variations in the minimum length of time.

The acquiring of these qualities depends to a great extent on purposeful training. The best method of developing these qualities lies in the specific analyses of positions, the various forms of which will be dealt with in chapter two.

For the moment we will remark that, for the practical player, analytical training involving the moving of the pieces is inadequate. After all, during a game one has to work out variations in the mind, and using a minimal amount of time. Therefore one's training should be in mental analysis, with the aim of making the calculation rapid and accurate. During analysis one should polish the technique of calculation; to do this fix in one's mind the most important positions which arise in the course of the calculation, and take the calculation as far as possible.

A player differs from a chess computer in his ability to select for analysis an optimum number of variations, which are of practical value. For such analysis one should choose positions which are rich in combinational possibilities.

Good ways of developing one's calculating ability are the analysis of positions from diagrams in books without a board, the 'blindfold' analysis of positions, and so on.

Apart from the analysis of games, the solving of problems and studies from diagrams (again mentally) can also be recommended. This is a good method of training. We wish particularly to emphasize the importance of solving studies. A study normally contains a whole complex of tactical problems, and in addition its analysis is useful for the study of the endgame.

Here is an example.

G. Nadareishvili

White to play and draw

The black pawn at a2 appears bound to queen, but White's position is perfectly viable.

1 Bc4!

White loses after 1 Kc2? Rc5+ 2 Kb3 Rc3+ 3 K×b4 Kb2, or 1 Rb8? Kb2 2 R×b4+ Ka3 etc.

1...Rc5! 2 Bg8!!

The only way! After 2 B×a2? K×a2, or 2 Rf4? R×c4 3 R×c4 b3 4 Rc1+ Kb2, Black wins.

2...Kb1 3 Rb8! Rc1+ 4 Kd2 Rc2+ 5 Kd1 a1=Q 6 R×b4+ Rb2 7 Rc4! Rc2 8 Rb4+ Rb2 9 Rc4. Draw!

Thus the art of rapid calculation is the first necessity for the practical player. Only in this case can the preconditions be created for the development of specific thinking, without which quality a present-day master is inconceivable.

I recall an episode from my work with Petrosian. On completing his preparations for the 1966 World Championship Match, he once said: "You know, all these lofty matters we have been studying—strategy and endless opening subtleties—are not the main thing. The match will be decided, first and foremost, by our calculation reflexes during play, or, as they say, who is better at doing 'you go there, and I go here'... And no one knows how his mind will 'behave' ".

Methods of evaluating a position

In mathematics there exists an incontestable statute about qualities which are essential, but not yet sufficient for the achievement of a goal. In the same way, the art of calculation, and, closely linked to it, the development of combinational vision, are qualities which are essential, but which are not yet sufficient for the forming of genuine mastery.

In practical play, it is by no means always that one can embark on a path of endless specific analytical searchings. On the other hand, it is always necessary to make a sober assessment of the course of the struggle, and to find sensible plans.

It is customary to make an evaluation of a position based on its apparently static features (material balance, and positional factors, such as: position of the kings, central formation, strong and weak points and pawns, open lines and diagonals, and so on).

Such an evaluation is a prelude to the main, dynamic evaluation of a position. The dynamic evaluation is invariably accompanied by the specific calculation of variations, in which the relative possibilities are weighed up in perspective. Only a dynamic evaluation gives the possibility of penetrating into the latent possibilities of a position.

In books on the middlegame, one frequently comes across a more detailed exposition of the successive methods (or steps) for evaluating a position.

Thus, for example, in his book *Mittelshpil*, Romanovsky suggests the following approximate stages in the evaluation of a position:

1. Take into account the material balance.
2. Take into account positional factors.
3. Take into account the basic principles of strategy and tactics which operate in the given situation.
4. Study combinational motifs.

Of course, the separation of the evaluation process into these stages is highly arbitrary. But it is correct that a position should be evaluated by a definite method, in which it is essential to take account of both material and positional factors, as well as all possible combinational motifs. Only the possession of such a method enables one to avoid impulsive decisions, whereby moves are chosen for random reasons.

It goes without saying that there are many positions which comparatively easily lend themselves to evaluation. Some are easy to 'weigh up' on the basis of general positional considerations, while others, in contrast, can be exhausted only by analytical means (take, for example, any endgame study). But more often than not the position on the board can be exhausted neither by specific calculation, nor by general evaluation. In complex situations of this type, apart from stable factors, an important role is also played by dynamic, highly mobile factors, such as the co-ordination of the forces, and their positioning at the given moment. A major role in the evaluation of such positions is frequently played by individual peculiarities, which are characteristic only of the position in question (this was seen in the Kupreichik–Tal game, p.5).

Let us examine a position from the game **Szabó–Sigurjonsson** (Reykjavik, 1968).

We will begin with a static evaluation. Material is equal. There have been hardly any exchanges. The pawn formation looks more favourable for White. His pawn chain on the K-side is very flexible, and in addition he potentially has an extra pawn in the centre. In Black's position, on the other hand, there are distinct pawn weaknesses. Two white pawns—at a3 and b4—securely hold back Black's pawn trio. The backward pawn at c6, which seems securely fixed, gives cause for concern.

How are the pieces of the two sides positioned? If one counts the relative number of tempi spent, Black has a slight lead in development: White has 12 tempi, and Black 14. But the position is of a closed nature, and it is unlikely that this factor will play a significant role.

Let us examine more closely the character of the disposition of the forces, and in particular the question of king safety. Although the positions of both kings are unweakened, the white king experiences the pressure of the enemy pieces, whereas the black king does not. Black's pieces are unequivocally trained on the opposing castled position.

But even so, a careless evaluation of the position may give the impression that White's position is fairly favourable. Black's white-squared bishop is lacking in mobility, and it only needs White to play 22 Nc5 for any possible activity by Black to be paralyzed.

But it is Black's turn to move, and a deeper, more dynamic study of the position reveals that things are by no means so favourable for White. Moreover, Black has at his disposal a forcing combinational way of exploiting the latent dynamic advantages of his position. At the same time we wish particularly to draw the attention of the reader to the inharmonious positioning of White's pieces, which hinder one another in their actions. All this goes to explain a sensation—an unexpected break-through by Black, 21...c5!!, involving brilliant sacrifices, and undertaken for the sake of activating the white-squared bishop.

Events develop by force.

22 N×c5 R×c5! 23 b×c5 Nf3+!

A fresh surprise. 24 g×f3 is decisively met by 24...Qh3!

24 B×f3 B×f3 25 Ne2.

The only defence against an immediate rout. After 25 g×f3 Black wins by 25...Qh3!

26 f4 Ng4. Note the exceptionally important role played by the activated bishop at b7.

25...Ne4 26 Ng3.

On 26 Bc1 there could have followed 26... Ng5, when it is not apparent how the threat of 27...Qh3!! can be parried.

26...N×d2 27 g×f3 N×f3+ 28 Kg2 Qc6 29 e4 N×e1+ 30 R×e1 B×g3 31 h× g3 Re5 32 Rd1 R×c5.

The storm has subsided. The position is considerably simplified, but White's lot has not improved. The heavy-piece ending is easily won for Black, who has an extra pawn and a big positional advantage.

33 Rd8+ Kh7 34 Qe2 f5 35 Rd4 Rc4!

An elegant solution, taking play into a pawn ending.

36 R×c4 Q×c4 37 Q×c4 b×c4 38 Kf3 g5! 39 e×f5 h5! 40 Ke4 c3 White resigns.

Thus it is very important to develop a correct feeling for position, which is a first step towards the skilful exploitation of strategic elements.

Planning

A plan in chess is not an invariable concept. The times when it was considered proper that a plan should run through an entire game have long since passed.

Back in the mid 1920s, such dogmatic ideas about plans, 'created on move four for the rest of the game', were aptly criticized by Emanuel Lasker. For example, in his article 'Capablanca and Alekhine' in 1926 he wrote: "Learn carefully to work out strategic plans, like Capablanca, and you will laugh at the plans told to you in ridiculous stories. Indeed, it was difficult to avoid laughing, when at the very end of the afore-mentioned game, with its renowned and unusually deep strategy, I found a saving manoeuvre for the opponent, refuting the entire unprecedentedly devised strategy, and, obviously, overlooked by the author of over-deep plans".

This relates even more to the present-day dynamic struggle, where over the course of the game the centre of battle very frequently switches from one part of the board to another.

This position arose after 16 moves in the game **Silman–Smyslov** (Lone Pine, 1976).

Glancing at the external structure, it is difficult to imagine that the game will soon end in a debacle for White on the K-side. After all, the field of battle appears to be the Q-side, and that is how it was up to a certain time.

The game continued: **17 Qa4 Bd7 18 Qb4 Rfe8 19 Qd6** (this unwieldy queen manoeuvre merely facilitates the development of Black's initiative over the entire front) **19...Qb7! 20 Rfe1 Nd5 21 Nf4 Nf6 22 f3 g5! 23 Nfe2 Nd5 24 Qg3 h6 25 Qf2 b5.**

This looks like a localized offensive. But, in opening up the game on the Q-side, Black is guided in the first instance by the further activation of his forces, and by his sharp-sighted perception of the weakness of the a7–g1 diagonal, in combination with threats against f2.

26 Ng3 b4 27 c×b4 N×b4 28 R×e8+ R×e8 29 Ndf5 Nd3!

The decisive manoeuvre. It now becomes clear that the game will be decided by a swift attack on the white king.

30 Qd2 Qb6+ 31 Kf1 c3 32 b×c3 Bb5 White resigns.

On examples such as this, it is very good to develop one's positional feeling, which is essential for the rapid evaluation of non-standard situations.

In practical play, a rapid change of plan is very often required, depending on the actions of the opponent. Here it is not normally a matter of studying static features. What is important is the dynamic development of the struggle, and an evaluation based on general positional considerations can merely reinforce one's calculations.

In connection with this, I should like to dwell on certain points from one of my own games.

Suetin–Polugayevsky
34th USSR Championship 1967

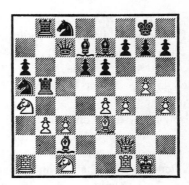

Virtually the most critical moment of the strategic battle has been reached. I think that only the players themselves can fully sense this. And, of course, the analysis of such a position is very important not only for understanding the game, but also for studying the peculiarities of one's own thinking.

In this sharp position, with attacks on opposite flanks, the possession of the initiative is of paramount importance. For this reason I was most afraid of the positional exchange sacrifice: 23...N×b3!? 24 N×b3 R×b3 25 B×b3 R×b3. After 26 f5 Bf8 27 g6 a very sharp battle develops, where the advantage is still with White, although Black's pieces have been markedly activated.

Black in fact continued 23...Bf8.

Now at any rate White has a firm hold on the initiative, and Black's chances are purely tactical in nature.

24 f5 e5 25 h5 Bc6 26 h6! g6 27 f×g6 h×g6 28 b4 Nc4 29 Bd3 Be8 30 Nb3 R5b7 31 Bc1 Ra7 32 Nb2 N×b2 33 Q×b2 Nb6 34 Be3 Raa8 35 Na5 Na4 36 R×a4!

By sacrificing the exchange, White sets up a dangerous attack on f7.

36...B×a4 37 Bc4 Be8 38 Qf2 Rd8 39 Bb6 Qd7 40 B×d8 R×d8 41 Qh4 Rc8.

This last move was sealed by Black. At home I mainly analyzed the ending which could have resulted after 41...Qa7+ 42 Qf2 Q×f2+ 43 K×f2 Be7. By playing 44 Rg1 Rc8 45 Rg3 Bb5 46 Bd5, White retains the advantage.

But how many times did I reproach myself for my haste! After all, 41 Qh4 was played after the time control, and it should not have been difficult to find the stronger continuation 41 Qe3. (I should, incidentally, remark that it is essential that you should condemn yourself for such omissions, but the vexation caused by them should on no account be allowed to interfere with your adjournment analysis and subsequent play.)

The subsequent play deviated from my analysis, and was impromptu in nature. But nevertheless, the analysis was not in vain, since it enabled me to penetrate fairly deeply into the peculiarities of the position.

Perhaps it was thanks to this that White's tactical play was accurate.

42 Rf3! Qd8 43 Bd5 Be7 44 Qf2 Qd7 45 Qg3 Rc7 46 Nc4 Qa4 47 Qf2 B×g5.

Now White wins by force.

In this game there were numerous combinational subtleties and specific variations. It is hardly expedient to publish them all. But for oneself it is beneficial to take the trouble to write down all the specific calculations, both one's own and the opponent's, however many there may have been.

In the book I will restrict myself to an analysis of the move 47...Qd1+, after which my opponent was of the direct impression that he had drawing chances.

Variations show that this evaluation is incorrect. Even then White wins, for example: 48 Kg2 Qc1 49 R×f7 Q×g5+ 50 Kf1 Qc1+ 51 Ke2 Qc2+ 52 Nd2 Bb5+ 53 Kf3 Qd1+ 54 Kg2 Qg4+ 55 Qg3 Q×g3+ 56 K×g3 Bh4+ 57 K×h4 R×f7 58 h7+ etc.

Returning to the move in the game, I should remark that it can be decisively refuted only by 48 N×d6 Bf4 49 N×e8 Q×e8 50 Qb6!, as was in fact played.

When, as I was calculating the variations before playing 48 N×d6, at the last moment, in time trouble, I espied the double attack on c7 and g6, I experienced that amazing joy, which is understandable only to a chess player.

These infrequent moments of pleasure are particularly precious, for the reason that they are achieved as a result of hard work, and at a cost of much searching and uncertainty.

50...Qa4 51 Q×g6+ Kf8 52 Qg7+ Ke7 53 h7 Qd1+ 54 Kg2 Resigns.

It is clear that the development of flair is assisted by the ability to discern the most imperceptible peculiarities, which are present only in the given position. In such cases the evaluation of the position is normally closely linked to the calculation of variations.

The next example we will consider is from the game **Tseshkovsky–Vasyukov** (USSR Zonal, 1975), where after Black's 16th move the following position was reached:

White's next move had been carefully prepared: **17 Nd5!**

In this way the defects of Black's position are revealed. The tactical point of this move is that, after the enforced acceptance of the sacrifice, Black's knight at b4 and bishop at c6 are 'hanging'.

17...e×d5 18 c×d5 Ba4.

When embarking on this position, White had to calculate and judge accurately that in the event of 18...Nb×d5 19 e×d5 B×d5 20 B×a6 Ra7 21 Bc4 the advantage would be on his side.

19 b3 a5 20 b×a4 N×e4 21 Qe3 f5?

This impulsive move creates a serious weakening on Black's K-side, which subsequently proves fatal. Better was 21...Nf6, with an inferior, but still solid position.

22 f3 Nc5 23 Nb5 N×a2 24 R×c5!

The start of a lengthy and accurately calculated combination. But in finding it, a far from minor role was played by positional feeling. In the end, it was Black's weakened squares on the K-side which stimulated White's searchings. We would advise the reader to note the masterful way in which White constantly finds the best moves. Without this ability, it is impossible to carry out a single chess operation!

24...b×c5 25 Qe6+ Rf7 26 B×d6 B×d6 27 N×d6 Nc3.

A beautiful variation results after 27... Rbe7 28 N×f7! R×e6 29 d×e6 Nc3 30 Rd8+ Q×d8 31 N×d8 N×e2+ 32 Kf2 Nd4 33 e7, and White wins.

28 N×f7 R×f7.

After this the end is close, but even in the event of 28...N×e2+! 29 Q×e2 R×f7 30 d6 Qd8 31 d7 it is not difficult to judge that the passed pawn is bound to decide the game.

29 Bc4! N×d1 30 d6 Nc3 32 Q×f7+ Kh8 33 Qg8+! Q×g8 34 B×g8 Ne2+ 35 Kf2 Nd4 36 Bd5 Resigns: the d6 pawn queens.

Digressing from the purely chess outline of the examples given, we can assert that the common method in them is a search for deep and original ways to win. After all, in the end, what chess creativity consists of is non-routine thinking.

We will merely remark that it is non-routine thinking that not only allows a deep solution to be found to the problem each time, but also brings into being new ideas, and a fresh approach to things.

The choice of move

Calculation and evaluation are not abstract concepts. It is they that determine the choice of each move.

Of course, there are numerous positions where the choice is not difficult, and where the moves suggest themselves, since they are determined by the plan, or by the development of a forcing variation. Such simple cases arise, for example, in various exchanging operations, in the parrying of obvious threats, in the playing of well-known opening variations, and so on.

But at the same time there are numerous positions in which the choice of move is a very difficult problem.

Em. Lasker–Capablanca
Match 1921

White has emerged from the opening with a better development, and with his pieces more actively placed. But how is he to exploit this advantage? The question demands an immediate decision, since apart from 17...N×c3 Black also threatens to consolidate his position by 17...Rfe8 or 17...Rfd8.

The search for the correct decision obviously had to be directed towards forcing matters, and that is how Lasker operated by continuing **17 B×d5 N×d5 18 B×e7 N×e7 19 Qb3.** But after **19...Bc6! 20 N×c6 b×c6**

21 Re5 Qb6 22 Qc2 Rfd8 23 Ne2? (23 Na4 was more consistent) **23...Rd5 24 R×d5 c×d5!** not a trace remained of White's advantage.

And yet in the critical position White had the possibility of gaining a big, virtually decisive, advantage. This is shown by the following analysis by Breyer: 17 B×f6! N×f6 18 Ng6! f×g6 19 R×e6!, or 17... B×f6 18 B×d5 e×d5 19 Ng4 Bg5! 20 f4 B×f4 21 Qf5 Bc7 (*21...Bg5 22 Q×d5 a6 23 a4* loses material) 22 N×d5 Kh8 23 N×h6 g×h6 24 Nf6 Kg7 25 Nh5+!, and White mates.

Thus the correct choice of move depended mainly upon a deep and accurate calculation of variations.

Let us now consider another position, outwardly similar to the previous one. It arose after 16 moves in a game between two Dutch players—**de Groot** (White) and **Scholtens** (1938).

During the famous 1938 AVRO-Tournament, one of these players, professor de Groot, carried out an interesting experiment. He invited several grandmasters and, at the same time, some ordinary chess enthusiasts, to find the best move for White, and in each case recorded the time spent on the search.

The enthusiasts were guided mainly by general principles, and suggested a variety of continuations, such as 17 Rfe1, 17 Bh6, 17 Bb1, 17 h4?, and on average spent 15–20 minutes in thought.

The grandmasters, Alekhine, Keres, Fine and Euwe, were more in agreement. On the basis of a definite calculation, they evaluated the position as won for White, giving as strongest the forcing continuation 17 B×d5!.

Here is the approximate analysis, made in nine minutes, by Alekhine: "...17 B×d5!. Now 17...B×d5 is not good, therefore 17...e×d5. There can follow 18 Ng4, 18 Re1, or 18 N×c6 and 19 Re1, or perhaps 18 Qf3. The move 17 B×d5 is certainly tempting...

17 Ng4 must be considered, but it doesn't look good.

17 N×d5, and then perhaps 17...N×d5 18 B×d5 B×g5, with numerous, but not very convincing, possibilities.

17 N×c6. At first sight there follows 17... b×c6, which reinforces Black's d5 square. A pity. But at any event, White stands better. I would be happy to have such a position in a tournament.

Are there any other forcing moves, apart from 17 B×d5? It looks very strong.

Let's compare: 17 N×c6 b×c6: pressure on c6, the bishop pair, its very pleasant, but the position demands more. Let's check 17 B×d5! again."

Grandmaster Flohr made a curious oversight, after spending ten minutes in thought. He considered 17 B×d5 e×d5 18 Qf3 but, after failing to find a direct solution, placed his choice on 17 N×c6, having in mind the variation 17...b×c6 18 B×d5 c×d5 19 B×f6 and 20 Nd7?—an hallucination. The knight on e5 had already been exchanged three moves earlier!

The continuation **17 B×d5!** is undoubtedly the strongest, as was confirmed by the de Groot–Scholtens game. After **17...e×d5 18 Qf3 Qd8 19 Rfe1 Kg7 29 Ng4 N×g4 21 B×e7 Qd7 22 B×f8+ R×f8 23 Qf4** White won.

Thus here too the choice of move depended mainly on accuracy of calculation.

At the same time it is very frequently not easy to choose the best move, because it is difficult to evaluate the positions reached at the end of the variations calculated.

R. Byrne–Uhlmann
1968

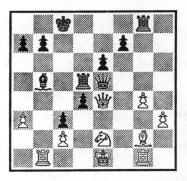

The position is very sharp, and, in view of the unbalanced material, difficult to evaluate.

Black finds the correct path, forcing matters in the centre, and creating sharp threats against the white king.

22...d3! 23 Q×e5 R×e5 24 R×b5.

The critical point. Black is faced with a difficult problem: what should he take, the rook or the knight? The difficulty lies not only in the necessity for a lengthy calculation, but also in the correct evaluation of the positions reached as a result of forcing play.

In the heat of the battle, even such an experienced player as grandmaster Uhlmann was unable to make the correct choice. He played **24...R×b5.**

Black captures the piece on the principle of 'seniority', and maintains the material balance. But it is precisely this that leads him into difficulties. Meanwhile, in the variation 24...R×e2+! 25 Kd1 Rd2+ 26 Kc1 R×c2+ 27 Kb1 Rd8!, Black, despite being a piece down, has the better chances. His strong passed pawns soon force White to return the material, and to seek drawing chances. After the possible 28 B×b7+ Kc7 29 Be4 Re2 30 B×d3 R×d3 White has only slight hopes of saving the game. In the given instance Black was unable to overcome a formal barrier in his evaluation of the variations: in particular, material balance.

The game continued **25 N×c3 d×c2 26 Kd2 Rb2 27 Be4 c1 = Q++ 28 K×c1 Rb3 29 Kc2 R×a3 30 Rf1 Rg7 31 Rf4 Kb8 32 Bd3 Ra1 33 h4 Rh1 34 g5 Rh2+ 35 Kb3 Kc7?**

By playing 35...a6 and then ...Kc7, Black would still have retained every chance of a draw. Instead, an obvious oversight, leading to the loss of an important pawn. After first losing his orientation in the evaluation of the position, Black now fails to cope with the tactical difficulties.

36 Nb5+! Kd7 37 N×a7 e5 38 Rb4 b6 39 Bf5+ Kc7 40 Rc4+ Kb7 41 Nb5 Ka6 42 Nd6 b5 43 Rc6+ Ka7 44 N×b5+ Kb7 45 Rc4 Resigns.

Thus, in the problem of choosing a move, positional evaluation and deep calculation are closely interwoven.

But it would be incorrect to assume that the problem of choosing a move is associated only with the evaluation and calculation of variations.

In a number of cases, choosing a move is not at all easy, even if in general the player senses correctly the direction for the strategic blow.

Just as in life it is sometimes more difficult than anything to overcome oneself, so in choosing a move it is not easy to get away from certain habits in one's style of play. In general, his style of play is the strength of a player, but who does not have an 'Achilles' heel'? Thus players of combinational style, which in general is not only a very attractive,

but also a promising one, are sometimes carried away by tempting combinational ideas. And this leads to an unreal evaluation of the position, i.e. to a conflict with objective factors.

At the same time, how often do strict 'rationalists' fail to display due audacity in sharp positions, where every tempo is worth its weight in gold!

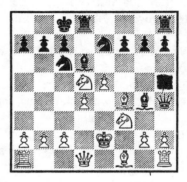

This position arose in the game **Spassky–Furman** (Tallinn, 1959). White's opening play has been eccentric, and the storm clouds are gathering over his king. He continued **10 c4?!**. Furman, who in general certainly had an excellent positional understanding, was nevertheless unable to overcome his leaning towards rational thinking.

Of course, this wasn't necessarily bound to happen. Rather the opposite. Possibly on that day Furman was unwell, and in such situations any deficiencies in style are as though 'uncovered'. At any event, he continued **10...Nf5?**, and after **11 e×d6 Nf×d4+ 12 Kd3!** soon White easily realized his advantage. But the outcome could have been different, if instead of 10...Nf5? Black had made the unusual move 10...Bb4!! etc.

The choice of move is also influenced by all kinds of psychological turns during a game. They as though test the flexibility of a player's thinking in rapidly changing situations. In short, 'his majesty' the move is a highly capricious 'person'.

We have examined the basic, I would say, synthetical problems of the practical thinking of a chess player. After all, it is assumed that we are dealing with a fairly advanced, well-prepared audience, possessing a considerable store of elementary skill and knowledge.

And even so, just as, for example, a specialist in higher mathematics, commanding all the 'secrets' of the Maclaren series etc., must be completely familiar with the ancient laws of elementary mathematics, so any chess player who is striving for mastery of the game, for the solving of synthetical problems, must have an impeccable command of a whole complex of elementary, and a variety of auxiliary, knowledge.

A game—a single process

During the battle of tactical ideas and plans in a chess game, there is a constant changing of situation. Apart from the slight, frequently insignificant changes in position, which are bound to occur with each move of the game, there are several important key moments. In particular, these are the transitional phases between stages (between opening and middlegame, middlegame and endgame), various combinations, complicated exchanging operations, sharp attacks, etc.

Such metamorphoses are not accidental, but stem naturally from the course of the game.

The connections considered between strategy and tactics find their application mainly in the middlegame, where the main chess battle takes place. But it would be incorrect to assume that they do not operate in the opening and the endgame. Let us dwell in more detail on these subtle problems.

The connection between opening and middlegame

We will examine several characteristic instances.

Undoubtedly, one of the most important strategic elements of the coming middlegame, which influences the plan of mobilization, is the plan of an attack on the king. The forms taken by this plan can be highly varied.

Of course, particularly frequently there is a risk that a king which is stuck in the centre will come under attack.

In this position from the game **Boleslavsky-Ravinsky** (Leningrad 1949), White, in spite of the position in the centre being closed, found an effective way of attacking the black king. He continued **8 b4!**.

A routinely-thinking player would have placed his choice on the manoeuvre Nbd2–f1–e3, satisfying himself with a minimal advantage.

8...c×b4 9 c×b4 N×b4 10 Nc3 Nf6 11 Qb3 Nc6 12 d×e5 d×e5 13 Rd1! Nd4.

It turns out that 13...Bd6 is bad in view of 14 Ba3 Qe7 15 R×d6 R×d6 16 Nb5 N×e4 17 N×d6+ N×d6 18 Rd1 Nd4 19 N×d4 e×d4 20 Qb4! etc. Both in this variation, and in the subsequent development of the game, it is instructive to follow how dynamically White's attack develops.

14 N×d4 e×d4 15 e5 Ng4 16 Nb5 Bc5 17 Ba3 b6 18 Nd6+ Kf8 19 R×d4!

And this is already a decisive combination.
19...B×d4 20 N×f7+ Bc5 (20...Ke8 is more tenacious, although even then after 21 Nd6+ Kf8 22 Qf3+ Nf6 23 Re1! White is bound to win) **21 B×c5+ b×c5 22 N×d8 Q×d8 23 Qf3+ Nf6 24 Rd1,** and White wins.

Many modern opening systems are characterized by castling on opposite sides, which normally leads to subsequent attacks on the respective flanks.

Such a situation is typical, for example, of the numerous variations of the Rauzer Attack in the Dragon Variation of the Sicilian.

Karpov–Gik
Moscow 1969

1 e4 c5 2 Nf3 d6 3 d4 c×d4 4 N×d4 Nf6 5 Nc3 g6 6 Be3 Bg7 7 f3 Nc6 8 Bc4 0–0 9 Qd2 Qa5 10 0–0–0 Bd7 11 h4 Ne5 12 Bb3 Rfc8.

In this variation the chief aim of each side is an attack on the king, and the quicker the better!

13 h5 N×h5 14 Bh6 B×h6 15 Q×h6 R×c3 16 b×c3 Q×c3.

This move allows White to build up a decisive and very fine attack. 16...Nf6 was more tenacious.

17 Ne2! Qc5.

17...Nd3+ is not good on account of 18 R×d3 Qa1+ 19 Kd2 Q×h1 20 g4!, and Black loses material.

18 g4 Nf6 19 g5 Nh5 20 R×h5! g×h5 21 Rh1 Qe3+ 22 Kb1 Q×f3 23 R×h5 e6.

Black had no doubt pinned his hopes on this move, and considered his position to be perfectly defensible.

24 g6! N×g6.

On 24...f×g6 White wins easily by 25 Q×h7+ Kf8 26 Qh8+ Ke7 27 Rh7+ Nf7 28 Q×a8 etc.

25 Q×h7+ Kf8 26 Rf5!

The point of White's combination.

26...Q×b3+ 27 a×b3 e×f5 28 Nf4 Rd8 29 Qh6+ Ke8 30 N×g6 f×g6 31 Q×g6+ Resigns.

In the examples given, the plan of attack stemmed from the peculiarities of the play in the opening. This plan naturally involves the adoption of strong tactical measures. An apparently similar picture can be seen in those instances when one of the sides, thanks to a mistake by his opponent, gains an advantage from the opening, which, however, can be consolidated only by tactical means.

What is more, sometimes this is the only way of realizing an advantage.

The tactical exploitation of an opening advantage

Gufeld–Petrosian
37th USSR Championship 1969

1 e4 e5 2 Nf3 Nc6 3 Nc3 g6 4 d4 e×d4 5 Nd5 Bg7 6 Bg5 Nce7 7 N×d4 c6 8 Nc3 h6 9 Be3 Nf6 10 Bc4 0–0.

White, failing to sense the danger and hoping for the initiative, is tempted by a pseudo-active queen move.

11 Qf3.

This surprisingly allows Black not only to seize the initiative, but even to gain a won position virtually by force.

11...d5 12 e×d5 c5!

It was this move that White overlooked. It turns out that the white pieces are in one anothers' way.

13 Ndb5 (White also stands badly after 13 Nde2 Bg4 14 Qg3 Nf5!) **13...a6 14 d6 Nf5 15 Nc7 N×d6!**

This decisively refutes the raid by the white knight. In the event of 16 N×a8 Black wins two pieces for a rook, by continuing 16...N×c4 and 17...Bg4.

16 0-0-0.

In search of counter-chances, White sacrifices a piece, but this brings him no relief.

16...Q×c7 17 Bf4 Bg4 18 Qd3 b5! 19 Bd5 Rad8 20 f3 b4 21 Q×g6 Kh8 22 Qd3 b×c3 23 f×g4 Qb6 24 b3 Qb4! White resigns.

Often the tactical exploitation of an opening advantage involves the determined and swift storming of the enemy king position. The essential difference between the plan of attack considered earlier, and the given case, is that here the attack can be calculated out to the end.

Faibisovich–Lomaya
Grozny 1969

1 e4 e5 2 Nf3 Nc6 3 Bb5 Nf6 4 0-0 N×e4 5 Re1 Nd6 6 N×e5 Be7 7 Bd3 N×e5 8 R×e5 0-0 9 Nc3 c6 10 b3 Ne8 11 Bb2 d5 12 Qh5.

Here, instead of the essential 12...Nf6, Black incautiously played **12...g6?**. The retribution was swift.

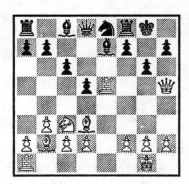

13 N×d5! Q×d5.

Forced. After 13...c×d5 14 Q×h7+!!, or 13...g×h5 14 N×e7+! Kg7 15 R×h5+, Black is mated.

14 Qh6 Be6 15 R×d5 c×d5 16 Re1 Bf6 17 Ba3 Bg7 18 Qf4 Rc8 19 h4 Nc7 20 B×f8 B×f8 21 h5 Be7 22 Qd4 b6 23 Qa4 Resigns.

Of course, the tactical way of exploiting an opening advantage is not the only one. The logical, slow, strategically well-founded consolidation of the gains made in the opening is perhaps a more characteristic phenomenon in chess.

There are many typical plans for the development of an opening initiative, depending on the peculiarities of the position.

The reader will be familiar, of course, both from his own experience, and from the games of others, with the typical plans for exploiting an advantage in space (in the centre and on one of the wings), pressure on pawn weaknesses, the seizing of an open file, and the transition into a better ending.

We should particularly like to draw the attention of young players to this last plan.

Transition into a complicated endgame

Modern practice not only does not spurn, but even confirms more and more the importance of the early transition into an endgame (sometimes even by-passing the middlegame), in cases, of course, where it is appropriate.

Polugayevsky–Ivkov
Belgrade 1969

1 Nf3 Nf6 2 c4 c5 3 Nc3 Nc6 4 d4 c×d4 5 N×d4 N×d4 6 Q×d4 g6 7 e4 Bg7 8 Be3 d6 9 9 f3 0–0 10 Qd2 Be6 11 Rc1 Qa5.

Now White forces a transition into an endgame.

12 Nd5 Q×d2+ 13 K×d2 B×d5 14 c×d5 Rfc8 15 Be2 a6 16 b4!

In the resulting ending White has a whole series of slight but significant advantages: the two bishops, a spatial advantage in the centre, and finally, an active plan of play on the Q-side.

Black is unable to find an adequate counter, and White strengthens his position unhindered.

16...Kf8 17 a4 Nd7 18 a5! Bb2 19 Rc2 R×c2+ 20 K×c2 Bg7 21 Kb3 Rc8 22 Bd2 Bd4 23 g4 Kg7 24 g5!

Having tied down Black's forces on the Q-side, White begins a decisive offensive on the K-side.

24...Rc7 35 Rd1 Kf8 26 f4 Rc8 27 Bg4 Ke8 28 Rf1 Rc7 29 h4 Bg7 30 h5! Bd4 31 Rh1 Bg7 32 Rh3 Kf8 33 h6.

An important stone in the winning foundation. The h6 pawn is destined to decide the game.

33...Bd4 34 Rd3 Ba7 35 Bh3 Bg1 36 Bc3 Ke8 37 e5 Bh2 38 e×d6 e×d6 39 Re3+ Kd8 40 Re4 Bg1 41 B×d7 Resigns.

On 41...R×d7 White wins by 42 Bf6+ Kc7 43 Re8 followed by Rh8 and R×h7.

Positional equality on reaching the middlegame

We have examined several instances where one of the sides has emerged from the opening into the middlegame with a certain advantage, or with a dangerous initiative. But how do events develop if neither side has succeeded in gaining an advantage? Of course, there are a number of variations, where at the start of the game the position is simplified to such an extent that the subsequent play does not require any particular explanation... But, as a rule, equality of chances in the opening merely emphasizes the interesting nature of the subsequent struggle in the middlegame. In this case positional play frequently begins, in which the players are required to show great skill in patient manoeuvring, and in the accumulation of small advantages.

Very necessary for this type of play is a knowledge of *typical pawn structures*: the open centre, or, in constrast, blocked pawn chains, or cases where one side has a pawn majority in the centre, and the other has one on a wing. Many typical positions of dynamic equilibrium are characterized by the existence of a pawn weakness in the centre, which is compensated by good piece play.

Becoming more and more characteristic in the present-day opening are doubled-edged positions, full of tactical points. In them there is no quiet struggle for equality within a framework of positional manoeuvring. In such positions one must pay particular attention to variations in plan, justified by rapid changes in situation. What become of paramount importance are tactics, and a study of the combinational features of the position. The following is an instructive example.

Keres–Smyslov
The Hague 1948

1 c4 Nf6 2 Nf3 c6 3 Nc3 d5 4 e3 g6 5 d4 Bg7 6 c×d5 N×d5 7 Bc4 0–0 8 0–0 b6.

More active is 8...Nb6 followed by ...N8d7 and ...e5, aiming for pressure on the centre.

9 Qb3 N×c3 10 b×c3 Ba6 11 Ba3 B×c4 12 Q×c4 Re8 13 e4 b5 14 Qb3 Nd7 15 c4 Rb8 16 Rad1 Qa5.

With his last few moves Black has been preparing the freeing advance ...c6–c5. This plan appears to have succeeded, since White cannot maintain his pawn centre (*17...b×c4* is threatened, while if *17 c×b5*, then *17...R×b5* and then ...c5). But White has at his disposal an interesting plan. He ignores Black's counter-play in the centre, and begins an energetic attack on the K-side.

17 c5!

This energetic move demanded deep calculation. The evaluation of White's plan depends on whether the tactical advantages of the advance c4–c5 outweigh its positional drawbacks.

17...b4 18 Bb2.

More accurate was 18 Bc1!, but to take account at this point of all the consequences of the bishop's retreat was extremely difficult.

18...e5 19 Ng5! Re7 20 f4 e×d4 21 f5 N×c5?

The decisive error. Essential was 21...Q×c5!, with a satisfactory game.

22 Qh3 h5 23 f6 Bh6 24 f×e7 B×g5 25 Qf3! f6 26 B×d4 Nd7 27 h4 Resigns.

In the very general case, when making the transition from opening to middlegame, a player must set himself the aim of working out a specific plan for the subsequent conduct of the game, or, more precisely, make a choice of a definite strategic character for the battle. It should be mentioned that, in a number of cases, the transition from opening to middlegame requires very subtle play. The art of conducting the game at such 'delicate' moments was, and still remains, a criterion of genuine mastery. It is no accident that Alekhine, when preparing for his match for the World Championship with Capablanca, over a period of several years in his practical play developed with particular thoroughness his skill in this stage of the game. At the same time, Alekhine devoted particular attention to such latent factors as the evaluation of the coming endgame, questions of very subtle technique, the realization of small advantages, and so on.

Once more on the basic principles of the opening

Playing the opening correctly is a great art. In order to master it, one should always remember the basic opening principles, and remember that, for the successful execution of any plan in a game of chess, a sensible mobilization of the forces is necessary.

Apart from real possibilities of seizing the initiative from the first few moves, there are also numerous tempting, pseudo-active possibilities lying in wait for a player. In understanding when a path is true, and when it is false, one is helped by opening principles.

The deliberate adoption of opening principles is also necessary for the acquisition of skill in thinking. From his very first steps a player should penetrate into the logic of the opening battle, avoiding random decisions, and 'off-chance' actions.

The mastery of opening principles allows one to 'control' successfully the numerous variations, and enables one to avoid drowning in them. It is for this reason that experienced players are able, as though of their own accord, to remember new variations, sharply outlining the range of possibilities, and eliminating unreasonable continuations.

An important indication of the correct mastery of opening principles is correct orientation in an unfamiliar opening situation.

Take, for example, an instance where at an early stage your opponent begins unexpected and sharp activity. You are convinced that his action is unfounded, but it is no good arguing in general terms. You have to play. It is essential to investigate deeply into the tactical course of the struggle, into its specific peculiarities, and at the same time, while remaining cool, you should not forget about the principles of mobilization.

Of course, it is not easy playing according to the given prescription. It is much easier to be guided by general principles of development in a quiet situation. But it is the analysis of positions similar to the one considered that are very useful for the development of chess intuition.

Here is an example of the creative adoption of opening principles, this time taken from a well-known game, where, incidentally, a sharp gambit variation, which later became known as the 'Marshall Attack', was first employed.

Capablanca–Marshall
New York 1918

1 e4 e5 2 Nf3 Nc6 3 Bb5 a6 4 Ba4 Nf6 5 0–0 Be7 6 Re1 b5 7 Bb3 0–0 8 c3 d5?! 9 e×d5 N×d5.

10 N×e5.

On this, Capablanca made the following comment:

"I thought for a little while before playing this, knowing that I would be subjected thereafter to a terrific attack, all the lines of which would be of necessity familiar to my adversary. The lust of battle, however, had been aroused within me. I felt that my judgement and skill were being challenged ... I decided that I was in honour bound, so to speak, to take the pawn and accept the challenge, as my knowledge and judgement told me that my position should then be defendable".

10...N×e5 11 R×e5 Nf6 12 Re1 Bd6 13 h3 Ng4 14 Qf3 Qh4 15 d4 N×f2 16 Re2!

The point of White's plan. There was a clever trap concealed in the variation 16 Q×f2 Bh2+ (but not immediately *16...*

24

Bg3? because of *17 Q×f7+!!*) 17 Kf1 Bg3 18 Qe2 B×h3 19 g×h3 Rae8, and Black wins. It should be mentioned that another strong retort has since been found—16 Bd2!

16...Bg4 17 h×g4 Bh2+ 18 Kf1 Bg3 19 R×f2 Qh1+ 20 Ke2 B×f2 21 Bd2 Bh4 22 Qh3 Rae8+ 23 Kd3 Qf1+ 24 Kc2 Bf2 25 Qf3 Qg1 26 Bd5 c5 27 d×c5 B×c5 28 b4!

At last White has seized the initiative. Now the game concludes quickly.

28...Bd6 29 a4 a5 30 a×b5 a×b4 31 Ra6 b×c3 32 N×c3 Bb4 33 b6 B×c3 34 B×c3 h6 35 b7 Re3 36 B×f7+! Resigns.

Thus the ability to put into effect correctly the opening principles is the first essential condition for the perfecting of one's play in the opening.

The above example showed how a premature, incorrect attack was refuted. But sometimes it may be necessary to play actively at a very early stage. In this case the attack must be begun before the completion of mobilization, and such an attack can in no way be called premature or incorrect.

Essentially, the mobilizing moves can be regarded as only the first few, when the forces of the two sides can physically not yet come into contact. But as soon as this happens, the development of the pieces is inevitably combined with an attack on the king, or with other active operations.

A little example given by Réti is instructive. After **1 e4 e5 2 Nf3 Nc6 3 Nc3 Bc5 4 N×e5! N×e5 5 d4 B×d4? 6 Q×d4** Black might be tempted by the pseudo-active move **6... Qf6,** with the threat of **7...Nf3+.** Now the mechanical developing move **7 Be3** would be a weak counter. A deeper study of the position shows that White has the possibility of resolutely refuting his opponent's play by **7 Nb5!**

Only this move (with an already-developed piece!) allows White to punish his opponent. It is not difficult to see that material losses for Black are inevitable. On 7...Kd8 there follows 8 Qc5!, with a decisive double attack on c7 and f8.

One is forced to the conclusion that it is not always necessary to follow the rule 'in the opening don't move one and the same piece several times'. On the contrary, it may happen that the opponent can be punished for his fanciful play only by energetic manoeuvres by the same pieces.

Back in the 1920s such examples were a comparative rarity. At the present time every experienced player easily masters this method of play in opening set-ups where the balance is disturbed.

Suetin–Bondarevsky
31st USSR Championship 1963

1 e4 e5 2 Nf3 Nc6 3 Bb5 a6 4 Ba4 d6 5 0–0.

Here Black chose an eccentric plan, beginning a diversion on the K-side by **5...g5?!** In the event of slow play by White, after 6 c3 g4 7 Ne1 Bg7 followed by ...h7–h5–h4, Black might possibly have gained real counter-play. But White finds an energetic reply.

6 d4! g4 7 B×c6+ b×c6 8 Ne1 e×d4 9 Q×d4 Qf6 10 Qa4!

It is only this manoeuvre, in connection with White's 12th move, that underlines Black's opening difficulties.

10...Ne7 11 Nc3 Bd7 12 Qa5!

Completing the queen manoeuvre. To avoid loss of material, Black is forced to give up the right to castle.

12...Kd8 13 Nd3 Bg7 14 e5 Qf5 15 Re1 d5 16 Ne2 Ng6 17 Ng3 Qe6 18 Bg5+ Kc8 19 Nc5 Qe8 20 Nh5!

It is not difficult to see that White has a completely won position. And yet out of the 20 moves he has made, 11 have been with his queen and knights!

Why did this happen? The point is that in the opening Black chose a fanciful plan with 5...g5. His play could be refuted only by unusual, very determined measures.

In the examples considered we have seen not so much an exception to the rule, but rather a creative application of the rule. Of course, it merely emphasizes that, in the opening, time should be valued very highly.

Such an approach—creative, and not dogmatic—should also be applied to the other rules and principles of opening strategy.

On open and closed openings

There are more than 50 different openings in existence, all of which are separated into three basic groups: open, semi-open and closed.

A study of games by present-day masters reveals that the majority of them are of a manoeuvring, positional character. Modern strategy was preceded by a whole epoque of 'open' battles, where particular attention was devoted to the attack on the king. It was obviously for this reason that the first openings to be developed were those where there is an early opening of the centre, which favours attack.

For a long time players aimed to play actively from the very first moves, without paying any particular attention to mobilization.

To support sharp and risky attacks in the opening, the players willing went in for sacrifices of material, the acceptance of which was considered a matter of honour. Methods of defence were more weakly developed than methods of attack.

Here is one such example in the classical style.

Anderssen–Zukertort
Barmen 1868

1 e4 e5 2 Nf3 Nc6 3 Bc4 Bc5 4 b4 B×b4 5 c3 Ba5 6 d4 e×d4 7 0–0 Bb6 8 c×d4 d6 9 d5!?

A decision characteristic of Anderssen. Later 9 Nc3 came to be preferred.

9...Na5 10 Bb2 Ne7 11 Bd3.

11 B×g7 is not good, in view of 11... Rg8 12 Bf6 N×c4 13 Qa4+ Qd7 14 Q×c4 R×g2+ 15 Kh1 Qh3 16 Nbd2 Bg4 17 Qb3 0–0–0!, when it is difficult to repel Black's attack.

11...0–0 12 Nc3 Ng6 13 Ne2 c5 14 Qd2 f6 15 Kh1 Bc7 16 Rac1 Rb8 17 Ng3 b5 18 Nf5 b4 19 Rg1 Bb6 20 g4!

White carries out the correct plan. With the centre closed, he prepares for a decisive storming of the enemy castled position.

20...Ne5 21 B×e5 d×e5?

A serious error. Better was 21...f×e5, averting the g4–g5 breakthrough. Now a debacle is inevitable.

22 Rg3 Rf7 23 g5! B×f5 24 e×f5 Q×d5 25 g×f6 Rd8.

Both 25...R×f6? and 25...e4 fail to 26 Bc4!

26 Rcg1 Kh8 27 f×g7+ Kg8 28 Qh6!

A deadly blow; the threat of 29 Q×h7+! is inavertable. Now comes a very fine finish, in which the main heroes are the white pawns.

28...Qd6 29 Q×h7+! K×h7 30 f6+ Kg8 31 Bh7+! K×h7 32 Rh3+ Kg8 33 Rh8 mate!

Of course, in our day opening theory has markedly changed and become more complicated. Such gambits, and the ideas associated with them, have become merely a pleasant memory, and when they occur nowadays from time to time, they are taken to be an anachronism.

However, for developing players the ancient open games still are of considerable practical interest. It is on such material that it is best to sharpen one's combinational skill.

At the same time I should like to warn against a one-sided view on closed games, which are sometimes contrasted with open games. Open games are described in romantic terms, with spectacular attacks on the king and beautiful combinations. Modern opening systems are represented as much more prosaic: in them the main theatre of battle rarely becomes the K-side, and in the main there is an unintelligible manoeuvring battle in the centre and on the Q-side, lacking in sharp situations.

Unfortunately, in the majority of openings books written today, the authors, who are occupied with the scrupulous compilation of endless subtleties, demonstrate insufficiently clearly the diverse and attractive strategic ideas. But meanwhile, for example, in the new gambits there is ample romance, although their strategy has changed; now the most important problem is the rapid switching of action from one part of the battlefield to another, and the life of a king is by no means quiet. In essence, the scope for combinational creativity in modern openings is much wider than in the majority of the ancient ones, where from our present-day point of view, the complications often resemble a storm in a tea cup.

To illustrate the combinational potential of closed games we will first examine the following example.

Breyer–Esser
Budapest 1917

1 d4 d5 2 c4 c6 3 e3 Nf6 4 Nc3 e6 5 Bd3 Bd6 6 f4!? 0–0 7 Nf3 d×c4 8 Bb1?!

A paradoxical decision, the point of which was not guessed by Black. White plans a pawn storm on the K-side, and voluntarily concedes Black superiority on the Q-side.

It should be mentioned that in the event of 8 B×c4 b5 9 Bd3 b4 followed by 10...Ba6, Black would have had good counter-play.

8...b5? (correct was the timely undermining of White's central d4 square by 8...c5!, when Black gains sufficient counter-play) **9 e4 Be7 10 Ng5 h6 11 h4 g6 12 e5 h×g5.**

12...Nd5 fails to ease Black's position. For example, 13 h5 N×c3 14 b×c3 h×g5 15 h×g6! f×g6 16 B×g6 Kg7 17 Rh7+! K×g6 18 Qh5+ Kf5, and Black is effectively mated: 19 g4+ Ke4 20 Qh1+ Kd3 21 Rh3+ Kc2 22 Qg2 mate!

13 h×g5 Nd5 (13...Nh5? 14 R×h5!) **14 Kf1!**

A quiet move, by which White prepares the following amazing combination, crowning his attack on the king.

14...N×c3 15 b×c3 Bb7 (better defensive chances were offered by the counter-sacrifice of a piece—15...f5 16 g×f6 B×f6 17 e×f6 R×f6, although even then White's attack is very dangerous) **16 Qg4 Kg7 17 Rh7+!**

A brilliant combinative blow, which might be envied by the most celebrated knights of the King's Gambit or the Evans Gambit! White carries out a decisive combination, which he had planned back on his 14th move.

17...K×h7 18 Qh5+ Kg8 19 B×g6 f×g6 20 Q×h6+ Kh8 21 Qh6+ Kg8 22 g6!

This is where the point of 14 Kf1 is revealed. If the king were still at e1, Black would have a defence: 14...Bh4+ and 15...Qe7!

22...Rf7 (otherwise mate is inevitable) **23 g×f7+ K×f7 24 Qh5+ Kg7 25 f5! e×f5 26 Bh6+ Kh7 27 Bg5+ Kg8 28 Qg6+ Kh8.**

Here the quickest way to win was by 29 Bf6+ B×f6 30 e×f6 Qg8 31 Qh5+! Qh7 32 Qe8+ Qg8 33 f7! etc.

But, perhaps, such attacks were possible only at the start of this century? Not at all. One of the main features of the modern opening is the sharp reappraisal of many 'closed' set-ups, and a sharp growth in the sharpness of the tactical struggle.

It is true that in the 1930s gambits in closed openings were rather rare. One such example was the sensational 6th game from the **Alekhine–Euwe** return match (1937), where White employed the following gambit: **1 d4 d5 2 c4 c6 3 Nc3 d×c4 4 e4 e5 5 Nf3 e×d4 6 B×c4?** Although Euwe thought for about an hour, he was not only unable to find a refutation of White's plan, but promptly committed a decisive error, by playing 6...b5?, on which there followed 7 N×b5!, when 7...c×b5 fails to 8 Bd5, winning the rook. So great was the psychological effect at that time of employing unexpected gambits in orthodox openings.

It is interesting that, in their analysis of this game, researchers endeavoured in the main to find a refutation of the gambit, regarding White's idea as an 'unlawful' attack on their harmonious positional conceptions. The ways in which theory develops are complex, and these researchers achieved their aim: the variation 6...d×c3! 7 Qb3 c×b2! 8 B×f7+ Ke7 9 B×b2 Qb6! was found. After

much analytical work, it was established that the gambit was dubious.

But even so, such experiments were to play their innovatory role. Now, when gambits of the type 1 d4 d5 2 c4 c6 3 Nf3 Nf6 4 Nc3 d×c4 5 e4 b5 6 e5 Nd5 7 a4 N×c3 8 b×c3 Bb7 9 Ng5!?, or 1 d4 d5 2 c4 e6 3 Nc3 c6 4 e4 d×e4 5 N×e4 Bb4+ 6 Bd2! Q×d4 7 B×b4 Q×e4+ 8 Be2 have become just as common as, say, the variations of the Orthodox or Cambridge-Springs Defences, it can be confidently verified that tactical sharpness is an integral feature of all modern closed openings.

The strategic device of the swift transference of action from the Q-side to the K-side is becoming more and more widespread, and occurs more and more frequently in the most quiet, 'non-tactical' opening systems.

Petrosian–Estrin
Moscow 1968

1 c4 e5 2 g3 Nc6 3 Bg2 d6 4 Nc3 Be6 5 d3 g6 6 b4! Qd7 7 b5 Nd8 8 Nf3 Bg7.

An interesting situation.

9 Ng5!

Having seized the initiative on the Q-side, White plans an attack on the K-side.

9...e4 10 Bb2 e×d3 11 Q×d3 a6 12 h4! a×b5 13 c×b5 Ne7 14 Qd2 0–0.

Black has a very difficult position. 14...h6 was unattractive in view of 15 N×e6 f×e6 h5! or 15...Q×e6 16 Nd5!

15 h5 g×h5 16 R×h5 Bf5 17 Be4 Bg6 18 R×h7!

With cinematographic rapidity White has switched the spearhead of his action to the K-side, and now he begins the concluding attack. This exchange sacrifice clears the way towards the hostile king.

18...B×h7 (18...B×e4 is very strongly met by 19 R×g7+ !) **19 B×h7+ Kh8 20 0-0-0! Ng8 21 Rh1 Nh6 22 Nd5 f6 23 Ne4 R×a2.**

Black allows a decisive combination, but his days have long since been numbered. Thus on 23...K×h7 there follows 24 N×f6+ !

24 R×h6! B×h6 25 Q×h6 Qg7 26 Qh4! Resigns.

The examples given show that players studying the opening are by no means bound to restrict their horizon to ancient systems which have been thoroughly studied. It is probably better to have in one's repertoire modern openings, seeking in them variations full of tactical complications.

We should, incidentally, remind the reader that, from the very start of his chess career, Botvinnik chose in the main closed openings.

What is important is not what you play, but how you play!

The strategic horizons of opening theory are constantly expanding. For this reason, many of the most natural plans and variations are undergoing a considerable reappraisal.

In his chess manual (1926) Lasker gives the following evaluation to one of the main variations of the Caro-Kann Defence: **1 e4 c6 2 d4 d5 3 Nc3 d×e4 4 N×e4 Nf6 5 N×f6+ e×f6 6 Bc4 Bd6 7 Qe2+ Be7 8 Nf3 0-0 9 0-0.**

"White's plan consists in exploiting his pawn majority on the Q-side, while remaining passive on the K-side. Black, on the other hand, attempts to force his opponent to advance one of his K-side pawns, so as to begin play against it with his own pawns."

The modern dynamic treatment of this position has resulted in a serious reappraisal of White's plan. A splendid example is provided by the game **Ragozin–Boleslavsky** (Sverdlovsk 1941): **9...Bd6 10 Re1 Bg4 11 Qe4 Bh5 12 Nh4 Nd7 13 Qf5!**

Having made a concrete evaluation of the position, White begins an unexpected attack on the K-side, exploiting both the tactically bad position of the bishop at h5, as well as the limited mobility of Black's pawn mass, defending his king (a factor which formerly had not been taken into account!). 13...Bg6 is bad in view of 14 N×g6 h×g6 15 Q×g6 Nb6 16 Bh6!

13...Nb6 14 Q×h5 N×c4 15 Bh6! Qd7 (15...g×h6 16 b3 Nb6 17 Nf5 Kh8 18 Q×h6 Rg8 19 Re8!) **16 B×g7 K×g7 17 Nf5+ Kh8 18 Re4 B×h2+ 19 Kh1 Resigns.**

The stage of transition into the endgame

Realizing an advantage

While the transition from opening to middlegame usually reveals the strength of activity of the pieces, the transition into the endgame leads in the first instance to a marked re-appraisal of middlegame values.

Thus the king, which until recently has been inaccessibly concealed, at last acquires real active strength, which is evaluated in many cases at the level of a rook. The pawns, which have until then been mere 'fledglings', or even 'cannon-fodder', become respected veterans. And each unit of material, even the weakest, begins to demand careful attention. In particular, passed pawns, which in the middlegame only in rare cases have real power, in the endgame become genuine heroes, for the 'heads' of which one has to pay a very high price. The rooks, which often find it awkward in the crowded space of the middlegame, are ready in the endgame, like cannon in good old battles, to 'reduce to dust' the opposing forces, which are now thinned out and lacking in reserves. But the leaps of the knights, and the long-range sweeps of the bishops, which until then have brought confusion to the strongest pieces on the board, in many cases now become restricted in their action, and their strength is often subject to a purely mathematical analysis.

A player must take serious account of these factors, each time that a game makes the transition into an endgame.

Almost everyone knows that, as a rule, simplification and the associated transition into an endgame favour the side which has a material advantage. After all, in this case the relative ratio of the forces diverges markedly (for example, when the queens are exchanged the ratio, instead of 41:40, may become 32:31, and so on), and the opponent's counter-play with his pieces may be 'extinguished'.

In other words, the transition into an endgame is closely linked with two other very important problems of chess—the realization of an advantage, and good technique, which frequently accompany this stage of the game. Of course, the very rich material of modern practice provides the most diverse examples of the opposite characteristic, when the realization of a material advantage is associated with an attack, and so on. But even so, the strategic device of simplification when realizing an advantage remains in force, and without mastering its technique it is impossible to achieve mastery.

Often the transition into an ending is favoured by weaknesses in the opponent's pawn formation, the possibility of the intrusion of a rook into his rear-guard, and other positional factors, which also presuppose the realization of an advantage. This is why, even in the heat of the fiercest middlegame battles, an experienced player endeavours not for one moment to forget about the most subtle features of a favourable endgame.

This position was reached after White's 18th move in the game **Alekhine–Znosko-Borovsky** (Birmingham 1926).

Black's position contains some marked 'rents' on the white squares. In this position, where there is an absence of tactical subtleties, White's plan in to take play into a favourable ending, with the subsequent exploitation of Black's pawn weaknesses.

18...a5 19 Ra3 Qd7.

Black has nothing better.

20 Q×d7 N×d7 21 b×a5 R×a5 22 R×a5 b×a5 23 Rb1 Rb8 24 R×b8+ N×b8.

Despite the great simplification, White has markedly increased his advantage. The a5 pawn is a good target for attack, while the threat of 25 g4 is unpleasant, when after 25... g6 26 g×f5 g×f5 27 f3 the f5 pawn is vulnerable. Incidentally, in his annotations to this game, Alekhine made an interesting comment: "Every chess master... is morally obliged to attempt to solve as well as possible the problem of a position without any 'fear' of simplification. Playing for complications is an extreme measure, to which a player should resort only when he cannot find a clear and logical plan".

25 Kf1 Nd7.

Better chances of saving the game were offered by 25...Kf7 26 Ke2 Ke7 27 Kd1 Kd7, although even here after 28 Nb3 or 28 f3 White has every chance of success.

26 Ke2 Nb6 27 Kd1 a4 28 d5 Nd7 29 Kc2 Ne5 30 Kc3 Ng4 31 Kb4 N×f2 32 K×a4 f4 33 e×f4 e3 34 Nf3 Nd3 35 Kb5 g5 36 f×g5 h×g5 37 a4 e2 38 h3! Nc5 39 a5 Nb3 40 Ne1 Nd4+ 41 Ka4 Resigns.

As we have already seen, many modern opening variations already in their 'embryo' contain favourable endgame motifs (cf., for example, p. 22). In other instances, such a transition from opening to a complicated ending is often motivated by the desire of one of the sides to avoid a sharp combinational struggle. Such a method of play is objectively, perhaps, not especially promising, but it is frequently employed in practice, if a player possesses good endgame technique.

An example is provided by a line from the Rauzer Variation of the Sicilian Defence: 1 e4 c5 2 Nf3 Nc6 3 d4 c×d4 4 N×d4 Nf6 5 Nc3 d6 6 Bg5 e6 7 Qd2 Be7 8 0-0-0 0-0 9 f4 N×d4 10 Q×d4 h6 11 Bh4 Qa5 12 e5!? d×e5 13 Q×e5 Q×e5 14 f×e5 Nd5 15 B×e7 N×e7 16 Bd3.

In this critical position White has allowed the creation of a pawn weakness (the isolated pawn at e5), which, of course, may prove to be unfavourable in the endgame! The motive behind the exchanging operation is White's desire to gain an advantage in space, which promises him an enduring initiative. In the given instance Black still has to overcome considerable difficulties, in order to untangle his forces successfully, i.e. solve the problem of completing his mobilization.

Thus, the straight-forward method of development, 16...Bd7?, creates great difficulties for Black, even though the game is still further simplified. After 17 Bh7+ K×h7 18 R×d7 Nc6 19 R×b7 N×e5 20 Re1 the ending is clearly favourable for White.

It should be mentioned that correct is 16 ...Nc6 17 Rhe1 Rd8! 18 b4 Bd7 19 b5 Na5 20 Ne4 Rac8 21 Nd6 Rc5! followed by ...Kf8-e7, aiming to become firmly established on the d-file, and gradually to create counter-play against White's e5. Black has good chances of equalizing.

It can be considered that in complex endgame positions, middlegame and endgame motifs are closely interwoven. The problem for each side is to exploit the advantages of his own position, while at the same time neutralizing the opponent's corresponding attempts.

Other key factors

We have examined two key stages of a game—the transition from opening to middlegame and from middlegame to endgame. But in practice, it is by no means in every game that these stages are important or even clearly defined. As regards the course and outcome of a game, other factors are often much more important, these normally being associated with an 'explosion' of tactical elements, or the organization of an uncompromising attack.

Very often one comes across games which

are full of adventures, although the actual stages of transition from opening to middlegame and from middlegame to endgame proceed relatively quietly.

Each time this is promoted by some individual reason, and in particular by a whole range of specific reasons, associated with the fact that a game of chess is set in motion not only by the principles of the game and the objective demands of the position, but in the first instance by people. The desires and wills of the players have a significant influence on the character of the game. Even in the outwardly most tedious situation, if there is a mutual desire a way can be found to produce fascinating and mind-boggling complications. Incidentally, this is a form of artificiality, a 'silent conversation', which deserves every encouragement. Moreover, in this lies the only sound way for the further development of the laws of strategy and tactics.

And are not the unforeseen turns in the following game attractive?

Capablanca–Alekhine
Match 1927

1 d4 d5 2 c4 e6 3 Nc3 Nf6 4 Bg5 Nbd7 5 e3 c6 6 Nf3 Qa5 7 Nd2 Bb4 8 Qc2 d×c4 9 B×f6 N×f6 10 N×c4 Qc7 11 a3 Be7 12 Be2 (at present the plan with 12 g3 is justifiably considered more dangerous for Black) 12...0–0 (and here 12...c5 is probably more energetic) 13 0–0 Bd7.

Again both sides play rather slowly. White could have played the blockading move 13 b4, while Black could have successfully freed his game by 13...c5.

14 b4 b6 15 Bf3 Rac8 16 Rfd1 Rfd8 17 Rac1 Be8 18 g3 Nd5 19 Nb2 Qb8 20 Nd3 Bg5.

The game has proceeded into a quiet, purely manoeuvring middlegame, where White maintains a certain pressure on Black's cramped position.

21 Rb1 Qb7 22 e4 N×c3 23 Q×c3 Qe7.

An imperceptible inaccuracy. After 23... Rc7, as Alekhine indicated, Black could have successfully fought for equality: 24 Bg2 Bf6 25 e5 Be7 26 Rbc1 Qc8 etc.

24 h4 Bh6 25 Ne5 g6 26 Ng4.

An error in return. Correct was 26 Nc4!, aiming after e4–e5 and Nd6 to occupy d6. In this case Black would probably have had to continue 26...Bg7 27 e5 h5! 28 Nd6 R×d6! 29 e×d6 Q×d6, with excellent drawing chances.

28...Bg7 29 e5 h5 30 Ne3 c5!

As often happens in practice, inaccuracies by both sides have merely led to a marked sharpening of the game. Fascinating tactical complications now begin.

29 b×c5 b×c5 30 d5?!

It was not yet too late once again to take the play along quiet lines: 30 Rb7 Rd7 31 R×d7 B×d7 32 d5 e×d5 33 N×d5 Qe6

34 Nf4 B×e5, leading to a simplified position with opposite-coloured bishops.

30...e×d5 31 N×d5 Qe6 32 Nf6+?

A serious error. Better chances of a draw were offered by 32 Rb7 B×e5 33 Qa5, although even here Black's position is preferable.

32...B×f6 33 e×f6 R×d1+ 34 R×d1 Bc6! 35 Re1 Qf5 36 Re3 c4 37 a4 a5.

After 37...B×a4? 38 Be4! White is no worse.

38 Bg2 B×g2 39 K×g2 Qd5+ 40 Kh2 Qf5 41 Rf3 Qc5 42 Rf4 Kh7.

Both here, and on the following move, Black had the possibility of the strong manoeuvre ...Qb6!, when White would have been in an unusual positional *zugzwang*.

43 Rd4 Qc6? 44 Q×a5 c3 45 Qa7 Kg8.

Thus the ending which came about on moves 38–39 appears to be of a purely technical and rather tedious nature. However the subsequent play, and the numerous analytical arguments around this ending, reveal its genuinely fantastic content.

46 Qe7 Qb6 47 Qd7?

This once again places White on the verge of catastrophe. Correct was 47 Rd7, for example: 47...Q×f2+ 48 Kh1! Qa2 49 Rd8+ R×d8 50 Q×d8+ Kh7 51 Qf8, and Black must give perpetual check.

47...Qc5 48 Re4 Q×f2+ 49 Kh3 Qf1+ 50 Kh2 Qf2+ 51 Kh3 Rf8 52 Qc6 Qf1+ 53 Kh2 Qf2+ 54 Kh3 Qf1+ 55 Kh2 Kh7 56 Qc4 Qf2+ 57 Kh3 Qg1!

This subtle move should have won. 57...

Q×f6 is insufficient, in view of 58 Rf4! followed by Rf3.

58 Re2.

After 58 g4 c2! 59 Q×c2 Re8!! Black wins! Isn't this a combinational masterpiece? And this in a 'purely technical ending'. Tedious positions really don't exist, only tedious styles of play.

58...Qf1+?

Black could have won by 58...Qh1+ 59 Rh2 Qf3!, when White has no satisfactory move, since on 60 Rc2 there follows 60... Qf5+, while 60 Re2 or 60 Ra2 is met by 60...Q×f6 61 Kg2 Rb8! etc.

59 Kh2 Q×f6 60 a5?

And once again the scales tip in favour of Black. After 60 Rc2 Re8 61 Kg2! a draw is inevitable.

60...Rd8 61 a6 (this leads rapidly to a crisis; 61 Kg2 would have held out longer) **61...Qf1!**

The deciding manoeuvre.

62 Qe4 Rd2 63 R×d2 c×d2 64 a7 d1=Q 65 a8=Q Qg1+ 66 Kh3 Qdf1+! White resigns.

In this exciting film the key shots were firstly around the 30th move, when at the height of a positional middlegame the game became markedly sharper, and then, secondly, deep into a technical ending (roughly on moves 46–47), when an even more significant change in the positional basis occurred.

It is not easy to find a new viewpoint onto this game, which has been thoroughly analyzed by top specialists. One could perhaps resort to a fashionable device of modern research—construct a graph of the strategic course of the game? Then the turning points indicated would be seen very clearly. Note that on each occasion this turning point was preceded by mistakes. But this merely shows that it is characteristic of man to err. In chess one can avoid mistakes only in simple, symmetric positions, where in addition one is not set the aim of defeating the opponent. But in complex, highly dynamic set-ups, mistakes are inevitable even for the strongest masters.

And this by no means spoils, but, on the contrary, enriches our ancient game. The philosophical understanding of mistakes is as yet very little studied. This complex question is still awaiting research.

Relative values of the pieces. Positional elements

The learning of a chess player begins with a scale of relative values of the pieces. From his very first lessons even the most unskilled beginner learns that in the relative scale of values the pawn is given the value of unity. A minor piece—bishop or knight—is roughly equal to three units, a rook to four and a half, and a queen—the most powerful attacking piece—to nine units. The king is of course in a special position. Its value in the opening or middlegame is difficult to give in numerical terms. But in the endgame, when it is rarely threatened by an attack, and it becomes an active piece, the numerical equivalent of a king is fairly large, and is roughly equal to five units.

In practice, a player very soon comes to the conclusion that this generally-accepted scale of values is a highly arbitrary and loose concept. But even so, one cannot get by without such a scale. It is the first, and virtually the most important guide for a chess player.

This is of course an enormous subject, and really requires a special section. Here we can only dwell briefly on certain methodological points, regarding both the relative values of the pieces, and some positional elements associated with them.

The relative values of the minor pieces

It is well known that the two minor pieces— bishop and knight—are 'equivalent'. Both the one and the other are worth three pawns. But this is only in the 'first approximation'.

A more careful examination of these pieces reveals a series of subtleties.

Even an inexperienced player knows that a bishop is very strong in its 'long-range' action.

At the same time there are many positions where a knight develops colossal energy, and this is especially apparent in battles at close quarters. The leaps of the knight are as dangerous as they are unexpected.

But which minor piece is the stronger? Of course, there can be no direct reply to this, since everything depends on the character of the position. The bishop is very strong in open positions, while the knight, with its 'jumping' ability, is stronger in closed positions. We can mention several further conditions, which are useful to bear in mind when assessing the relative values of these pieces.

1. The strength of a bishop is especially apparent in endings with play on both flanks. Here the knight, with its short jumps, is markedly inferior to the bishop. A good bishop is somewhat stronger than a knight.

2. In closed positions with blocked pawn chains, especially when the bishop is restricted by its own pawns, the role of the knight increases. A bad bishop is somewhat weaker than a knight, particularly if the knight occupies a centralized position (for example, blockading an isolated enemy pawn).

3. A centralized knight is equivalent to an active bishop.

And, finally, one cannot avoid mentioning the subjective side of this evaluation. A liking for bishop or knight is to a considerable extent a matter of style and taste. Thus, Steinitz and Tarrasch were fervent 'bishop worshippers', while Chigorin and Nimzo-witsch, in contrast, preferred knights, and even created entire opening systems based on this, such as, for instance, the Nimzo-Indian Defence, which is popular to this day, or the following: 1 d4 d5 2 c4 Nc6 3 Nf3 Bg4 4 c×d5 B×f3 5 g×f3 Q×d5 6 e3 e5 7 Nc3 Bb4 etc.

Among modern grandmasters too, such 'disagreements' have not diminished. Thus Spassky and Tal prefer bishops, while Petrosian's preference is for knights.

It is customary to regard the presence of opposite-coloured bishops as the herald of a draw. In the endgame this is indeed a serious ground for peace negotiations. But in the middlegame, in particular when there is an attack on the king, opposite-coloured bishops, on the contrary, as though completely 'forget' about their close relationship, and often perform like completely different pieces, either strengthening, or weakening the attack (or defence).

The open file for the rook. Penetration onto the seventh rank

The control of an open file by a rook is an important strategic success. Other things being equal, domination of the only open file in the majority of cases promises an enduring initiative, and at times even ensures a win.

In practice a particular role is played by the commonly-occurring stratagem of exploiting an open file for a rook, for its penetration into the enemy position, and in particular onto the seventh rank. Nimzowitsch, in his customarily categorical manner, once said:

"The aim of all manoeuvres on an open file is the ultimate intrusion along this file onto the seventh or eighth rank, i.e. into the enemy position".

Such a plan was energetically carried out by White in the game **Botvinnik-Boleslavsky** (13th USSR Championship, 1945).

White's secure occupation of the only open central file gives him a positional advantage. His plan is to intrude onto the 7th or 8th rank. This is preceded by a Q-side offensive, which has the aim of cramping still further the black pieces.

1 b4 Be6 2 Bb3 R×d2 3 Q×d2 B×b3 4 a×b3 Qe6 5 c4 Bf6 6 c5! Nc8 7 Qd7! The goal is achieved! The next phase is to realize the advantage attained, which involves organizing an attack on the king.

7...Q×b3 8 Q×b7 Bg5 9 N×g5 h×g5 10 Q×a6 Ne7 11 Qb7 Re8 12 Qd7 Kf8 13 Qd6 Q×b4 14 Ng4!, and White has a winning position.

Positions with unbalanced material

In modern strategy one frequently comes across situations where there is a positional battle with unbalanced material. As a rule, such a process is associated with a small sacrifice for the initiative (or, on the contrary, a gain of material, in return for which the opponent acquires the initiative). It is possible to give certain brief rules, by which one should be governed in a positional battle with unbalanced material:

1. A queen is slightly weaker than two rooks.

2. A queen is roughly equal to a rook, bishop and pawn, and very slightly stronger than a rook, knight and pawn.

3. A queen is weaker than three minor pieces by roughly one to one and a half material units.

4. A rook and two minor pieces are significantly stronger than a queen.

5. Three minor pieces are slightly stronger than two rooks.

6. Two minor pieces are normally stronger in the middlegame, and weaker in the endgame, than a rook and two pawns.

7. In the endgame a rook is roughly equal to a bishop and two pawns, and slightly stronger than a knight and two pawns. With rook and two bishops against two rooks and a knight, the chances of the two sides are roughly equal.

8. A protected and securely centralized knight or bishop, plus a pawn, are only slightly weaker than a rook.

9. In endgame positions a rook and an outside passed pawn are not inferior to two minor pieces.

Genuine positional flair consists to a great extent in the ability to determine correctly the relative strength of the pieces in the course of the game! The relative value of the pieces permits very fine and endless oscillations of 'short-wave' scale, and here at present there is an untouched field for research. Is it possible in every specific instance to create a dynamic scale of relative values of the pieces? This is a question for the future. At present one can only give starting points for the drawing up of a more or less accurate 'measurement by eye', which is essential for such a delicate weighing.

Dangerous consequences of pawn weaknesses

A large number of positional problems are associated with the basic fighting mass—the pawns. There is no need for us to show the important role played by a particular pawn formation in the centre. In modern strategy, a timely pawn sacrifice can give one the possibility of developing an initiative. A whole complex of complicated strategic problems—the advance of a pawn phalanx, a complex of weak squares etc.—are also very closely linked to the state of the pawns.

But in practice, perhaps most frequently one encounters elements associated with the formation of pawn weaknesses.

Many positions with organic defects in the pawn formation (isolated, doubled or backward pawns) are rightly considered unsatisfactory, and opening variations leading to them are rejected by theory.

Such pawns are not only weak in themselves, but the squares in front of them are serious weaknesses, providing convenient outposts for the intrusion of the opposing pieces.

At the same time, modern practice has shown that a pawn 'weakness' can become insignificant, if it is compensated for by the active and harmonious placing of the pieces. To strive in itself for a flexible pawn formation, to the detriment of other more important factors, is inadvisable, especially in the modern, highly dynamic, positional game.

Thus we can make the following generalization: if one does not succeed in creating sufficient compensation, for example, in the form of active play, even the most insignificant weakness in the pawn formation can contain a serious 'microbe' of overall defeat.

And, of course, one should always remember that every pawn advance is irreversible. And at times nothing can compromise a position more than a single superfluous change in the pawn formation.

2

IN THE PLAYER'S LABORATORY

How should a player arrange the work in his own laboratory? Much, although at times only in passing, has already been discussed by the author in the first part of his narrative. We have in mind a whole series of qualities, directly linked to the demands of practical play. Relating to this are problems associated with the rational choice of move, the technique of calculating variations, the development of positional flair, etc. Although they are developed in practice, their consolidation demands tireless polishing in the quiet of one's study.

But there are also many other 'concerns' which, although not so closely linked with direct practical necessity, are essentially no less important for improvement. I have in mind the perspective of a player's development, of his growth as a whole. Such 'long-range' study includes in particular the expansion of a player's chess outlook and culture (which, for example, is assisted by the study of chess literature), the analysis of his own games, the building and 'repairing' of his opening repertoire, the study of psychological factors and the tactics of tournament play, and so on.

There is no doubt that such work must in particular be serious and painstaking. And it must be work that is done regularly, if not every day.

The great grandmaster Akiba Rubinstein once said: "60 days a year I play in tourna-ments, 5 days I rest, and 300 days I work on my game". Of course, it is by no means to everyone that such a life style is admissible. But it is obvious that, even with a highly limited amount of free time, studies of this type must be systematic.

To put it in picturesque terms, the work of a chess player is similar to a blast furnace process: it is continuous and demands a heated... passion for chess.

This last question is highly important, and I will permit myself to dwell on it in more detail.

Frequently, for example, I have asked myself the question: why is it that from time to time a rather early exit is made from the chess arena by certain outstanding and un-doubtedly talented masters, still in the prime of life? (I am not talking, of course, of ill-nesses, or any other serious circumstances of life). On each occasion a closer acquaintance with the facts has convinced me that here it is a question mainly of rapid moral ageing. One player is lacking in flexibility and ca-pacity for work, while another is overambi-tious, and is unable staunchly to endure pe-riods of inevitable bad luck. But in all cases a common factor is a cooling towards chess itself, which then leads to creative stagnation.

It is also a noteworthy fact that, until very recently, 'stars of the first magnitude' have frequently 'begun to shine' in places which are by no means renowned for their chess traditions. Thus, for example, the sports traditions of Brazil have always revolved around football, and have had nothing to do with chess. And even so, this did not prevent the rapid flowering of the young Mecking's talent. Or take Denmark, where chess drags out a rather miserable existence. Nevertheless it was from there that, in 1956, that highly original player Larsen, who at that time had only just reached the age of twenty, emerged into big-time chess. And for similar examples in our own country we do not have to go far.

Life confirms that chess players of natural talent can carve their way to high standards of mastery, even in apparently highly unfavourable conditions.

And each time, along with talent, what is needed is an inexhaustible love for chess. It is no accident that chess fanaticism has become proverbial. Even with the most talented, chess will not 'forgive betrayal', or a cool, superficial attitude to it. It has long been known that you should not simply play each real game, but experience it! And in everyday lessons one requires not only great diligence and seriousness, but also constant activity of perception, and intensity of thinking and of the nervous system.

It is these qualities that an able teacher should foster in his pupils from the very start. While giving necessary theoretical information and all possible practical tasks, a genuine methodologist should not forget for one moment the overall scheme of development: to 'diagnose' and organize the individual work of young players, taking necessary account of their individual peculiarities.

Let us turn now to an examination of the basic features of the player's own laboratory, and attempt to look into the questions of the general improvement of a player.

Working on one's own games

The serious analysis of your own games is a very important method of improvement. Every game you play is keenly experienced by you, and for this reason its content is especially close to you, and hence, understandable. It is no accident that Ex-World Champion Botvinnik, when holding his consultations, in the first instance often asks young players: "How do you work on the study of your own games?"

Young players often endeavour to forget as quickly as possible about their failures and are much more ready to demonstrate their won games than their losses. This shows that they do not understand the aim of working on their games. But to improve, one must examine in the main one's mistakes. *However absurd a defeat may appear, it must be remembered that it is not accidental.* Even bad blunders almost always occur as a result of a deficiency in chess thinking, and to eliminate them what is required is a correct diagnosis, and, consequently, analysis.

Let us attempt to follow how such work should proceed, on the basis of the following example.

Suetin–Kuzmin
Sochi 1970

1 e4 c5 2 Nf3 Nc6 3 d4 c×d4 4 N×d4 e6 5 Nb5 d6 6 c4 Nf6 7 N1c3 a6 8 Na3 Be7 9 Be2 0–0 10 0–0 b6 11 Be3 Bb7 12 f3 Ne5 13 Qb3 Ned7 14 Rfd1 Qb8 15 Rd2 Re8 16 Kh1 Bd8 17 Rad1 Bc7 18 Bg1 Re7 19 Bf1 Qa7 20 Nc2 Rae8 21 R×d6 B×d6 22 R×d6 Qb8 23 Qb4 Rc8 24 B×b6 N×b6 25 R×b6 Rd7 26 e5 Q×e5 27 R×b7 Rd2 28 Qb3 h5 29 Ne4 N×e4 30 f×e4 Qf4 31 Ne3 Rcd8 32 Qc3 Qf2 33 h3 h4 34 Kh2 Qf4+ 35 Kg1 R8d3 36 Rb8+ Kh7 37 Qa5 f5 White resigns.

After a quiet opening in this game the play became markedly sharper. Let us attempt to determine the turning points of the battle, and, of course, to discover White's decisive mistake.

The result of the opening must be considered favourable for White. Black chose the rather elaborate plan of switching his knight from c6 to d7. Although the knight securely defended the b6 square, Black's possibilities of counter-play in the centre were sharply reduced, and he had to defend passively. The attempt by White to win the b6 square immediately would not have worked. After 14 Na4 Rb8 15 B×b6 N×b6 16 Q×b6 Q×b6 17 N×b6 B×e4, or 16...Qd7, the advantage would have clearly been with Black.

Up to the 21st move I played perfectly correctly, and gained a marked spatial advantage in the centre. In this respect White's moves 16 Kh1 and 18 Bg1 are instructive, neutralizing in good time the threat of ...d6–d5 (the hanging position of the bishop at e3 could have told).

Without a doubt, the decision to sacrifice the exchange on the 21st move was a debatable one. The simple 21 a4 Qb8 22 Qa3 followed by b2–b4 would have allowed White to strengthen his position unhindered, deferring radical measures until a better time. But the game was played in a training tournament...

I must frankly admit that my preliminary calculations did not show anything real. It was clear only that for the exchange White would gain two pawns, but that Black's pieces would be markedly activated.

Of course, White was not taking any great risk. Thus on the 25th move, by continuing 25 Q×b6, he could have retained the better chances, but avoided this because of the simplification after 25...Rd7 26 R×d7 N×d7.

It was an over-estimation of the position

that resulted in the decisive mistake on the 26th move: 26 e5? This was undoubtedly the culminating point in the game.

Much earlier, while considering his 21st move, White had pinned his hopes on this attack.

Practically every chess mistake has its emotional slant. For some reason I paid least attention to Black's main reply—the capture on e5: 26...Q×e5 27 R×b7 R×b7 (to 27...Rd2 there appeared to be a pretty convincing reply in *28 Nd5 R×c2 29 Ne7+ Kh8 30 N×c8*, with the threat of *31 Qf8+*) 28 Q×b7 Rb8 29 Q×a6 Nh5 30 Qa7 R×b2 31 Qe3!, and White retains a solid material advantage.

Black also has two possible retreats with his knight—to e8 and h5. After 26...Ne8 27 f4 his pieces are very cramped, while in the event of 26...Nh5 27 Rd6 Qc7 28 c5! White's advantage is undisputed.

After calculating all these variations, without much hesitation I advanced my e4 pawn. I must, however, admit that the more my opponent thought, the more I began to fear the capture on e5 (as yet merely intuitively).

And it was only when the move 27...Rd2 was made *a tempo* that I noticed to my horror that the continuation 28 Nd5 R×c2 29 Ne7+ Kh8 30 N×c8 fails to 30...Rc1! 31 Qf8+ Ng8, when White is the first to be mated. I was forced to 'beat a retreat', and seek salvation in passive defence. But, as often happens, the tactical oversight proved to be irreparable.

I should mention that, by playing 26 Ne2! (instead of the impetuous *26 e5?*) followed by 27 Ne3, White would have retained a minimal advantage: for example, 26...Rd1 is not good in view of 27 Ne3, when the bishop at b7 is hanging.

The finish of the game developed into a triumph for Black's heavy pieces. After 31... Rcd8 he was threatening 32...Rf2 33 Kg1 R8d2!, when the threat of 34...R×f1+ and 35...Qf2+ is irresistible.

By 33...h4!, securing for himself the square g3, Black essentially paralyzed all White's attempts to save the game.

Overall conclusion: the failure in this game was a consequence of inadequate penetration into the essence of the position.

Let us examine one further example. As an illustration, we will choose a game which is even richer in combinative complications.

Kupreichik–Suetin
Sochi 1970

1 e4 c5 2 Nf3 e6 3 d4 c×d4 4 N×d4 Nc6 5 Nc3 a6 6 Be2 Qc7 7 f4 b5 8 N×c6 Q×c6 9 Bf3 Bb7 10 e5 Qc7 11 0–0 Rd8 12 f5 Ne7 13 f6 Ng6 14 B×b7 Q×b7 15 Bg5 Rc8 16 Qe2 h6 17 f×g7 B×g7 18 Ne4 B×e5 19 Bf6 Rc4 20 Rae1 d5 21 Nd2 B×f6 22 N×c4 Bd4+ 23 Ne3 h5 24 Kh1 Be5 25 Qf3 Qe7 26 Rf2 Kf8 27 c3 Rh7 28 Nc2 Qh4 29 g3 Qg4 30 Nb4 Kg8 31 N×a6 Qc4 32 Nb4 h4 33 g4 Bg3 34 N×d5 e×d5 35 Re8+ Nf8 36 Rd2 Bc7 37 Rc8 d4 38 Re2 f6 39 g5 Q×a2 40 Qf5 Bd6 41 Rf2 d×c3 42 b×c3 Qa1+ 43 Rf1 Qa2 44 Rf2 Qa1+ 45 Rf1 Qa2 Drawn.

Complications began as early as the 12th move, when White, exploiting an inaccuracy by his opponent (*11...Nh6* or *11...Rc8* is correct), began a sharp offensive in the centre and on the K-side.

For ten moves (from the 12th to the 22nd) events developed practically by force. Against 16 Qe2 Black found the only reply: 16...h6!, parrying the highly dangerous threat of 17 Ne4, on which there would have followed 17...h×g5 18 f×g7 Qa7+! 19 Kh1 B×g7 20 Nd6+ Kd8 21 N×f7+ Ke7, when the chances are rather with Black. In such positions the calculation of combinative possibilities is essential, since positional considerations are clearly of secondary importance.

But even in very sharp games one must see not only tactical blows. Thus, instead of winning the exchange on his 22nd move, White had the strong move 22 R×f6, with pressure on g6 and e6. After 22...Rc6 23 Nf3 White's initiative more than compensates for the pawn.

At the same time, Black on his 23rd move was wrong to avoid the win of a pawn: 23... B×b2 24 c4 b×c4 25 N×d5 Bd4+ 26 Ne3 c3 or 26...Qe4, with roughly equal chances.

After this the situation turned out to be favourable for White, although Black had considerable resources. It only needed White to play 33 g4? (instead of *33 g×h4*), when there followed the strong counter-blow 33... Bg3!, when it was White who had to display maximum ingenuity in order to maintain the balance.

34 N×d5!, 37 Rc8!, 38 Re2!

After 40 moves a position of dynamic equilibrium was reached. 41 g6? is not good, in view of 41...Re7! 42 R×f8+ K×f8 43 Q×f6+ Ke8, when the chances are all with Black. In the event of 41 Qe6+ Q×e6 42 R×e6 Rd7 43 c×d4 f×g5 44 Rg6+ Kf7 45 R×g5 a drawn ending is reached.

Such is the purely chess part of the analysis of a game. But for a player wishing to improve, the cold analysis of mistakes is not enough. The problem is simultaneously to establish the psychological cause of these mistakes. Not sparing your pride, you should frankly re-establish the course of your thinking, endeavouring to give answers to approximately the following questions:

1. What specific variations did you calculate, when considering your moves, especially at the turning points of the game? It is very important to note what you missed in your calculations, and what your opponent showed you in your joint analysis after the game. To be honest, I overlooked that after 23...B×b2 24 c4 b×c4! the bishop at b2 was defended!

2. What considerations were you guided by in choosing your plan?

3. When evaluating your positional mistakes, endeavour to understand their cause. Were they the result of an insufficiently deep understanding of the position, or of tactical oversights? After all, oversights can often lead to positionally unfavourable situations.

It is essential that you be objective and self-critical, and that you do not embellish your ideas. You must be able to look honestly at your deficiencies and oversights, even if your opponent did not succeed in revealing them.

From the considerations given, some more general conclusions suggest themselves. A commentary on a game, irrespective of its character, should definitely:

a) show the turning points of the game;

b) disclose the course of the thinking of the two players, and, in particular, show specific calculations;

c) trace the strategic outline of the game;

d) convey the feelings of the players.

The art of analysis and of annotation does not by any means come immediately. It demands scrupulous study, and the mastery of special methods, of which more below. But for the moment here are a few simple but essential rules:

Do not be one-sided in your analysis, by examining only 'your' variations. Endeavour to look into the ideas of your opponent.

Each time that you point out a mistake, indicate the correct continuation.

Do not forget that analysis is not a practical game. It requires more specific proof than intuitive decisions.

In a game there can be fascinating, and, in contrast, 'boring' stages. But each time, by a thorough, serious analysis, even in the most uninteresting games you can find much that is useful and instructive.

The study of master games

A player wanting to improve has to work on chess literature. This is an axiom. An opening guide, or, say, a collection of master games, is just as necessary to a chess player as a stadium is to other sportsmen.

For this work, literature of various types is needed. This means text books on the various stages of the game, opening manuals and guides, tournament books, the best games of outstanding masters, and so on.

A special place is occupied by the study of games from major chess events. A harmony between evaluation and calculation in your play can be achieved only if you constantly practise analysis. Therefore it is essential to analyse master games, to be able to understand correctly their ideas and the reflection of these ideas in their annotations, and also to evaluate the quality of annotation.

Methods of annotation have long since

taken shape in chess literature, but they are undoubtedly continuing to develop. There are two main trends.

The first gives preference to evaluations of a general nature. Specific variations merely illustrate and confirm the general ideas.

This is how grandmaster Tarrasch used to annotate, and more than one generation of chess players learned from his notes. Here is a specimen of his annotation.

Schlechter–Em. Lasker
Match 1910

39 a4.

Regarding this committing move, Tarrasch wrote: "The opponent's steady strengthening of his position begins to frighten White, and he stakes everything on this move, sacrificing a pawn for an attack. But in fact, because of this advance he should have lost the game, even if it did give him certain chances. There was as yet no cause for desperation: his weaknesses (a3, e4 and h3) were sufficiently defended by his rook, and if he had avoided the exchange of queens, he could have readily continued play."

As you can see, without any variations at all the author gives a highly categorical evaluation of the position. This evaluation, constructed on a strictly logical basis, is correct.

The virtue of such a purely verbal method of annotation lies in the fact that it is easily understood, and corresponds most closely to normal everyday reasoning.

But let us follow further the course of the annotator's thinking.

39...Q×b4 40 a×b5 Q×b5 41 Rb3 Qa6 42 Qd4.

"At the present moment, of course, Black is not threatened by anything in particular. If he should succeed in opposing rooks, he will be able to repel the opponent's attack, and then win the game".

42...Re8 43 Rb1 Re5.

Parrying the threat of 44 Ra1.

44 Qb4 Qb5.

"44...Rb5 would have been bad in view of 45 Qc4. Black must in general beware of an intrusion into his territory by the enemy queen along the a2–g8 diagonal".

An interesting method of generalization, wouldn't you agree? In each comment the author in the first instance sheds light on the development of the main outline of the game. Not for one instant does Tarrasch forget about the logical, systematic course of the play.

45 Qe1 Qd3 46 Rb4.

The author of the comments attaches great significance to this point in the game: "In this position Black should have switched his rook to a5, so as to occupy with it one of the open files, and, in turn, to threaten the opponent with a devastating attack by 46...Ra3. In this case White would have had nothing better than to exchange rooks, by continuing 47 Rb3 Q×b3 48 Q×a5+.¦ In the resulting queen ending Black would, of course, have had excellent winning chances, thanks to his extra passed pawn. For example: 48...Kb7 49 Qd8 Qe6 50 f3 d5 51 e×d5 c×d5. Now Black (possibly after ...*Kc6* and ...*Qd7*) could have occupied a safe square with his king at h7, or could have even advanced his passed pawn, using his king for its defence, and in this case the white king would for a long time have been cut off from this pawn. As a result of the apparently very strong advance of the c-pawn chosen by Black, he wins the e-pawn, it is true, but this is not of decisive significance: on the contrary, with this move he would seem to let slip a deserved victory".

Note that Tarrasch was able to define very clearly the turning points of a game. Not without reason is it universally recognized that Tarrasch's comments can be read even without a board!

46...c5 47 Ra4 c4 48 Qa1 Q×e4+ 49 Kh2 Rb5.

Now Black's king comes under a dangerous attack.

50 Qa2 Qe5+ 51.Kg1 Qe1+ 52 Kh2 d5 53 Ra8 Qb4 54 Kg2.

With the aim of gaining the possibility of playing Qa6, which at present would be a mistake in view of the reply ...Qd6+. For this reason White on his 52nd move would have done better to move his king to g2 immediately.

54...Qc5?

A new turning point, and the final one in this dramatic encounter. Tarrasch's comment on it is extremely apt: "Lasker fails to see the danger threatening him, and as a result loses the game. But could he in general have won it? On 54...Rb8 there would have followed 55 Ra7+ Rb7 56 Ra8. What could Black have done in this case to strengthen his position? In addition, neither of the passed

pawns would have been able to advance, without immediately being lost. This is why it was a mistake to advance the pawn on the 46th and 47th moves".

55 Qa6!

Now the black king, deprived of the defence of his pawns, is bound to succumb to the attack by the heavy pieces.

55...Rb8.

After 55...Rb7 White would have won by 56 Qe6.

56 Ra7+ Kd8 57 R×g7 Qb6 58 Qa3 Kc8, and Black resigned.

Thus Tarrasch in his annotations proceeded from the general to the particular.

The opposite method was used by the great Russian grandmaster Chigorin. Out of variations he deduced an evaluation of the position, i.e. he proceeded from the particular to the general. Chigorin comparatively rarely gave broad generalizations, but gave obvious preference to the detailing of analysis, and to the study of latent combinational resources. Here is an example of his comments.

Chigorin–Tarrasch
Match 1893

After lengthy consideration Tarrasch played **20...g×h6,** declining the win of a second pawn by 20...R×g4+. Chigorin writes: "It would be risky to surmise as to why Dr. Tarrasch did not capture the g4 pawn. *Deutsche Schachzeitung* makes the following comment on Black's 20th move: 'An incomprehensible oversight. By 20...R×g4+ Black could have won a second pawn, and with it, in all probability, the game; then Dr. Tarrasch would have emerged the winner from this great battle'. *Deutsche Schachzeitung* is mistaken. On the conclusion of the game, Dr. Tarrasch himself stated to the spectators that it would have been extremely dangerous for him to take the pawn. It seems to us that Tarrasch's first impression is much more valid, as the reader will now see from the variations given... Just how diverse and dangerous White's attack could have been if Black, while defending, had attempted to retain the two pawns won by him, is shown by the following variations.

20...R×g4+ 21 Kh1 g×h6 22 Bc4! Bd7 23 b4 Rf8 24 a4.

A. 24...N×b4 25 Ne5 Rg7 26 N×d7 N×d7 27 B×e6+ Kh8 28 d5 a6 29 Ne4 (threatening *Nc5*) 29...b6 30 Ng3 R×f1+ 31 R×f1 Re7 32 Nh5, and White, who threatens B×d7, wins.

B. 24...Rg7 25 d5 e×d5 26 N×d5 N×d5 27 B×d5+ Kh8 28 Ne5 R×f1+ 29 R×f1 Re7 30 Rg1, and White wins a piece.

C. 24...Rg7 25 d5 Nd8 26 Ne5 Bc8 27 d×e6 N×e6 (*27...B×e6 28 R×d8* etc.) 28 R×f6 R×f6 29 Rd8+ Rf8 30 R×c8 R×c8 31 B×e6+ etc.".

Later Chigorin wrote: "In variation **A** after 28 d5 Black would have probably found the best defence, which is to give up the c7 pawn and play 28...Nc2 29 Nb5 Ne3 30 R×f8+ N×f8 31 Rd3. But in this case the game would have become level, and its result problematic".

And only after all this very detailed analysis does Chigorin permit himself to make the following brief, but highly interesting generalization: "I have given these interesting variations merely with the aim of showing that, in the given position, Black's two extra pawns do not constitute a clear advantage, such as would have assured him of winning the game".

Thus there are two methods of annotation, and both are perfectly lawful. Each reflects chess reality: deductive (from the general to the particular)—the strategic content of a game, and inductive (from the particular to the general)—the tactical content.

Let us now examine some comments made in our own time. They belong to grandmaster Tal (*The Botvinnik–Tal Match, 1960*).

Tal–Botvinnik
Match 1960

White has three pawns for a piece, which indicates approximately equal chances. Nevertheless the position is still full of life, and contains numerous tactical and strategic subtleties.

The following comment by Tal is highly interesting. In it are reflected two diametrically opposite approaches to the position: the strategic approach of Botvinnik and the tactical approach of Tal.

"As soon as the black rook has neutralized White's pressure on the e-file, it can be assumed that Black's main difficulties are behind him. This circumstance was sensed by Botvinnik, and I too should have agreed to it.

Here I should like to digress somewhat. During the course of a game, the thinking of the two players can develop in completely different ways. Many players (especially of the younger generation) throughout the whole five hours of play occupy themselves in the main with calculations, and their work during a game reduces approximately to the following: if I go here, he goes there, and so on, as much as strength will permit. More experienced players, who have deeply studied the secrets of their art, frequently do not tire themselves with such a lengthy process, and, being guided, in the main, by unshakeable (in many, but not all cases) principles, they plan their subsequent play. To illustrate this, I should like to present the dialogue which took place after the conclusion of the ninth game between Botvinnik and myself. When I began firing out, with machine-gun like rapidity, the variations I had calculated during the game, which demonstrated how comfortable Black's position was, Botvinnik said: 'At first I thought that this position was more favourable for White, but then I found the correct plan: I had to exchange rooks, but retain the queens'.

At first such an evaluation of the position seemed to me to be amazingly abstract, but when I began working through those same numerous variations, I could only conclude that Botvinnik was absolutely right: in an ending without queens White's flexible pawn chain, supported by his active bishop, gave him a definite advantage. But with the queens on the board Black could hope for a strong attack, in view of the weakening of the g4 square.

White's next move is perfectly correct—he associated it with the idea of fighting for the e-file, but at the decisive moment I wrongly did not believe myself".

All this is interesting and convincing. And one is forced to the conclusion that, proceeding along completely different, even opposite, ways, it is possible to come to one and the same result!

Returning to the further course of the game, we should mention that after **20 Qd3 Kg7 21 Qg3?** (correct is 21 f4 Rae8 22 Re5!, retaining equal chances) **21...R×e1+ 22 R×e1 Q×g3 23 f×g3 Rf8! 24 c4 Ng4 25 d5 c×d5 26 c×d5 Ndf6 27 d6 Rf7 28 Rc1 Rd7 29 Rc7 Kf7 30 B×f6 N×f6 31 Kf2 Ke6 32 R×d7 K×d7 33 Kf3 K×d6 34 Kf4 Ke6 35 g4 Nd5+ 36 Ke4 Nf6+ 37 Kf4 Nd5+ 38 Ke4 Nb4 39 a3?** (39 a4 is better) **39...Nc6 40 h5 g5 41 h6 Kf6 42 Kd5 Kg6 43 Ke6 Na5 44 a4 Nb3!** Black gained a winning position, and confidently realized his advantage on the 58th move.

The modern way of annotating a game aims as though to synthesize both methods, harmoniously combining specific analysis with generalizing evaluations.

One of the most striking annotators of this 'synthesizing' tendency was undoubtedly Alekhine.

His comments in the books *My Best Games, The International Tournament in New York, 1924,* and *The International Tournament in New York, 1927,* to this day remain unsurpassed models.

Here is one such example.

Capablanca–Em. Lasker
New York 1924

Here Black played **23...Ne4+?**, about which Alekhine, giving a general assessment of the game, wrote the following:

"Black has attained a perfectly sound position, and, as is apparent from the previous note, he had nothing to fear even if it were now White to move. But Black should have remembered that the move ...Ne4 was possible only after White has played g3–g4, and in order to provoke this advance it was perfectly sufficient to play 23...Qd7 or 23...Rc7, since it is unlikely that White had at his disposal any active preparatory moves.

After this the result of the game would have been highly unclear. The premature move played allows White the possibility of making a correct sacrifice, after which he gains an enduring initiative and is assured of at least a draw".

Thus we have here an example of a generalizing evaluation, picking out with amazing accuracy the essential feature of the position.

Up till this point the battle has been mainly of a positional nature. But now the play becomes sharper, and White begins a determined attack on the king:

24 B×e4 f×e4 25 Qg4! f5 26 N×f5 e×f5 27 Q×f5 h5 28 g4 Rc6 29 g5.

Here Alekhine makes a comment of a quite different type, bringing to the fore specific combinational analysis. "Better winning chances were offered by the immediate 29 N×d5,

in view of the fact that White did not have to fear the check at h4, for example: 29...Bh4+ 30 g3 (but not *30 Kg1 Bg3*) 30...Rc2+ (or A) 31 Kg1 Rc1+ 32 Kg2 Rc2+ 33 Kh3 h×g4+ 34 K×g4! Bd7 35 R×h4+ Q×h4+ (if *35...Kg8*, then *36 Nf6+* followed by *Q×d7*, while if *35...Kg7*, then *36 Rh7+* etc.) 36 g×h4 B×f5+ 37 K×f5, and the ending is won for White, for example: 37...R×b2 38 Ke6! Kg7 39 f5 Kf8 40 h5 Ra2 (or *40...Rh2 41 Nf4*) 41 f6 R×a3 42 h6 Ra6+ 43 Kf5 Kg8 44 Ne7+ etc.

A. 30...Bg6 31 Qe5+ Bf6 32 N×f6 Q×f6 33 Q×f6+ R×f6 34 g×h5 Bf5 35 Rh4 followed by g2–g4!"

Note the timely moment chosen for giving a detailed analysis.

29...Kg8 (29...Rd6! is more accurate) **30 N×d5 Bf7 31 N×e7+ Q×e7 32 g4 h×g4.**

We will study one further comment by Alekhine, which on this occasion combines both specific analysis, and a general evaluation.

"Here Lasker again chooses a rather difficult path. It is true that after 32...Bg6 33 Qd5+ Bf7 34 Qe5 Q×e5 35 d×e5 h×g4 36 f5 Rc5 37 Kg3! R×e5 38 K×g4 etc. it is doubtful whether Black could have gained a draw more easily than after the continuation chosen. Although White has only two pawns for the piece, the weakness of the e-pawn and the threatened intrusion of the white rook onto the 7th tank would have caused Black considerable trouble. But the simplest way to draw was by 32...Rc2+ 33 Kg3 (after *33 Kf1 Qc7!* Black obtains a mating attack) 33...Re2 34 g6 h4+ 35 R×h4 R×e3+ 36 Kg2 Re2+ 37 Kf1 Re1+, when White would be unable to escape from perpetual check".

A splendid example of the harmonious combination of specific and abstract factors in the study of a position!

The subsequent course of the game was a sharp tactical battle, in which Black did not exploit all his defensive resources.

33 Qh7+ Kf8 34 Rh6 Bg8 35 Qf5+ Kg7 36 R×c6 b×c6 37 Kg3 Qe6?

The decisive mistake. By continuing 37... Bf7! Black would have retained every chance of a draw.

38 K×g4 Q×f5+ 39 K×f5 Bd5 40 b4 a6 41 Kg4! Bc4 42 f5 Bb3 43 Kf4 Bc2 44 Ke5 Kf7 45 a4 Kg7 46 d5 B×a4 47 d6 c5 48 b×c5 Bc6 49 Ke6 a5 50 f6+ Resigns.

Up till now we have been talking about the correct methods of annotating a game. But although these methods have long been known, annotations are, alas, not always good. One comes across both contradictions in the evaluation of the turning points of a game, and mistakes in specific analysis. Often the commentary is 'fitted' to the result of the game, according to the principle that 'the winner is not criticized'.

At any event, the ability to make a critical evaluation of a commentary being studied, the ability to think independently, are essential qualities for an analyst. Even authoritative annotations should not be believed blindly.

In many instances it is undoubtedly very difficult to penetrate deeply into the content of a game. But perhaps it is here that genuine mastery can be tested?

It is not our task at all to disclose typical mistakes in game annotations. This is a special, and undoubtedly topical theme, but not for this book. We will merely follow how the essence of the struggle in a complicated game is normally revealed as a result of successive analyses and a business-like dispute in the press, which in the end creates excellent material for study.

Petrosian–Spassky
Match 1969

Here Petrosian played **32 b4?**, and after **32...Rac8** came under a crushing attack. Numerous critics in chess periodicals promptly condemned White's reckless advance, but avoided giving any specific analysis. The majority of the commentators recommended that for the moment White should adopt waiting tactics.

But then grandmaster O'Kelly subjected the position to a more specific analysis. On the basis of the variation 32 f3 Ng3 33 b3 he put forward a radically different evaluation of the position as perfectly satisfactory for White. For example: 33...R×d4 34 e×d4 Q×d4+ 35 Kh2, or 34...Ne2+ 35 Kh1 Nc3 36 Rc1 etc. White also has good chances of saving the game in the event of 32...Nd6 33 Nf2 h5 34 Ne2.

The following, and very important, word was stated by Geller. He cast doubts on the evaluation given by O'Kelly.

Here is his analysis: 32 f3 Ng3! 33 b3 Rc3! 34 Qb2 Rac8! 35 b×a4.

White is defenceless after 35 Nb5 R×d3! 36 Q×f6 R×d1+ 37 Kf2 Nf5!

35...h5! 36 Nf4 Qe5 37 Qf2? Rc1; or 36 Qf2 R×d3 37 R×d3 Rc1+ 38 Kh2 h4, and Black wins. White also stands badly after 36 a5 Qg5!, or 36 Qb7 Kg7 37 a5 R×d3! etc.

Does this analysis exhaust the possibilities in the critical position? Geller himself merely states that it is sufficient to confirm the evaluation of the position as won for Black. At the same time the grandmaster considers that the position after 35...h5! demands the study of a much larger number of variations.

But this is already for the lovers of analysis. I think that the essence of the position is clear.

The adoption of an evaluative or calculative method of analysis depends in the main on the character of the position. If the play is taking a positional course, it is perfectly appropriate to give general evaluations, on the basis of which the individual peculiarities of the position are studied. In positions full of combinative possibilities, specific analysis must undoubtedly come to the fore.

And one should always remember about the flexibility and mutual connection of these methods, which reflect the two most important aspects of chess thinking.

In conclusion, some methodological advice, which may be useful in choosing material for analysis. This question was studied very seriously by the Soviet methodologist Romanovsky in one of his books. Since the points raised by him have not lost their topicality even today, the author can recommend them to the reader.

Games selected for analysis should satisfy the following criteria:

1. They should be between players of high standard.

2. The games should be accompanied by detailed, good-quality annotations.

3. They should contain those themes in which the student is currently interested.

Romanovsky correctly recommended that each game should be played through not once, but twice, three times, or even more, if there was anything of importance that still remained unclear. Such a useful repetition guards against superficiality, and develops one's thinking.

Work with literature

From the examples examined above, it will already be clear just how important for improvement is the ability genuinely to use chess literature. "Study feeds the young, and gives joy to the old". The words of Lomonosov* are particularly applicable to the chess text book—that invisible partner of a player in his everyday studies, irrespective of his age and playing strength.

A disdain for the reading of methodological works and especially the study of information is fraught with unpleasant consequences. The 'natural player' will never attain any great heights. On the other hand, the reading of chess books is by no means a simple matter. It should not be forgotten that chess material, in whatever form it is taken, always demands active perception. But this presupposes in particular a business-like, critical study of literature, which is not at all easy to attain. It should be mentioned that an over-scrupulous tracing through 'from cover to cover' of even the most authoritative books can lead to a loss of lively individual thinking, to a loss of 'taste' for chess. How can a sense of proportion be achieved here? I think that this depends on setting yourself a correct goal of improvement. And this is closely

* The great Russian scholar and poet, after whom Moscow University is named (translator's note).

linked with the development of your analytical ability.

Before turning to a broader examination of this latter problem, we will dwell on certain examples, illustrating the importance of active independent perception in the study of source material.

Let us turn to the classic methodologists. The following extract from Nimzowitsch's book *How I became a grandmaster* cannot fail to enrich the laboratory of any chess player. The author wrote: "I took the book of the 1906 Nuremberg tournament with notes by Tarrasch, and gave it to a bookbinder, and asked him to sew into the book blank pages between each two pages of text. Then I began working through the games... Any results found were immediately noted down on the intermediate pages. I always 'played' for one of the two sides—either for White, or for Black. I first endeavoured to find the best move, and then looked at the move made in the game. In this way each 'game' lasted at least six hours. I consolidated my learning roughly as follows. In one of Salwe's games, a typical isolated queen's pawn position was reached: white knight at f3 and pawn at d4, black knight at d7 and pawn at e6 (in addition, each side had a mass of pieces). It turned out that White had no reason at all to hurry over the occupation of e5 with his knight, since within a few moves the black knight itself set off to attempt to reach d5, and thus, without any effort on the part of White, the square e5 nevertheless fell into his hands. Such a state of affairs was immediately recorded by me on the blank page, and, what's more, the point of it was not the purely chess content of the manoeuvre, but, so to speak, its psychological peculiarities. Frequently squares are vacated automatically. The result of my efforts was as follows:

1. I had a prepared opening repertoire.

2. I became proficient at playing in a slow, waiting style, and I found it quite incomprehensible that formerly I could have sacrificed without an exact calculation...

3. An important achievement was also the fact that, thanks to a careful study of certain games, I began to understand the strategy of closed positions, and, in particular, grasped the principles of the pawn chain, and also partly of centralization".

Of course, different types of chess literature have their specific peculiarities for studying. But even so, I think that there are a number of uniting factors. Whatever chess book we study, we should always be able to separate the important from the second-rate, and disclose the essence of the problems raised, etc. And in studying chess, the art of critical analysis is always especially important.

The test of mastery

It is difficult to overestimate the role of analysis. In connection with this, it will not be out of place to recall the following point, raised by Botvinnik in his introductory article to the book of the 11th USSR Championship, 1939: "What does the art of a chess master consist of? Basically—in the ability to analyse chess positions"... And later: "The conclusion is self-evident. Anyone wishing to become an outstanding player must strive for perfection in the field of analysis".

The question arises: how, by what means, does one learn to analyse correctly? From the elucidation of the aim of this work to its realization is 'a distance of enormous dimension'.

It would be incorrect to picture analysis as being something ceremonial. Yes, it is fascinating, but mainly for players who are already masters of chess thinking. But it can be cultivated by no means straight away. A player must first master various principles, schemes, and characteristic tactical and strategic devices. At the same time the development of one's thinking is preceded by the acquisition of combinative vision. This is also a complicated process. At first a player notices only simple threats, then he begins to see all sorts of double attacks, and, finally, that harmonic interaction which leads to combinations. Only after going through such a schooling does a player obtain the necessary basis, which allows him to use flexibly his knowledge and skill. The analysis of complex positions, where strategic and tactical factors are closely interlaced, is first and foremost very hard work. For the unprepared it may even be beyond their strength. Therefore, don't try to take too many steps at once. Get to know your true capabilities, each time, of course, setting yourself new problems. Along this path there is much disillusionment, causing annoyance and dissatisfaction. Without these bitter feelings you cannot get by. But remember that if you are dissatisfied, it means that you are searching. This is one of the fascinations of the art of chess.

I cannot avoid recalling an unsuccessful, but by no means useless attempt by me at analysis. In 1948, when I was still a candidate master, I became interested in the following position from the 'Meran' after the moves: 1 d4 d5 2 c4 c6 3 Nf3 Nf6 4 e3 e6 5 Nc3 Nbd7 6 Bd3 d×c4 7 B×c4 b5 8 Bd3 a6 9 e4 c5 10 e5 c×d4 11 N×b5 a×b5 12 e×f6 Qb6 13 f×g7 B×g7 14 0–0 Nc5 15 Bf4 Bb7 16 Re1 Rd8 17 Rc1 Rd5 18 Be5.

Certain experts suggested 18...0–0 here, evaluating the resulting position as perfectly sound for Black.

I, for perhaps the first time in my life, became literally obsessed with the analysis of a position. The result of this was the variations: 19 B×h7+ K×h7 20 R×c5! R×c5 21 Qd3+ f5 22 Ng5+ Kg6 23 B×g7 K×g7 24 Qg3 Rg8 25 Qh4 Rh8 26 Q×d4+ e5 27 Q×c5! Q×c5 28 Ne6+ etc., or 20... Q×c5 21 Qd3+ f5 22 Ng5+ Kg6 23 B×g7

Qb4 24 R×e6+ K×g7 25 Qg3! and so on.

I sent my analysis to *Shakhmaty v SSSR*, and soon afterwards it was published. Six months later—on the pages of the magazine—there appeared a highly weighty retort, belonging to grandmasters Keres and Bondarevsky. In the first variation they had found an excellent reply: instead of 24...Rg8?—24...e5!, after which Black's chances are better.

Thus it turned out that my analysis had a 'hole' in it, by which at the time I was rather badly upset (the bitter feeling did not disappear, even after I had found an improvement for White: instead of 20 R×c5?!—20 b4!).

But some two years later I regarded my not altogether successful experience in a different light. Firstly, I had begun in general to analyse better, and had rid myself to a certain extent of superficiality. Secondly, this analysis had brought me into the complicated sphere of modern theory. Finally, a 'bitter' feeling is by no means such a bad thing. Self-satisfaction is a sign of stagnation and narrow-mindedness. And in the overcoming of these banal qualities lies one of the fascinations of chess.

This is an appropriate moment to recall one of Tartakover's aphorisms: "Chess ennobles man, since it is full of disappointments".

I think that young players should fear least of all such disappointment.

The analysis of adjourned games

The best teacher in mastering the art of analysis is practice: learning comes both during play, and in the subsequent study of a completed game. For the development of analytical skill, very much can be given, for example, by work on adjourned positions. I should mention that certain young players at the moment have a formal approach to such work, regarding adjourned positions as some kind of useless burden. Such players avoid sitting long over the analysis of their adjourned games. It is no wonder that on resumption they are very often caught by unexpected surprises. But also, the analysis of adjourned positions should be regarded not only from the practical point of view. Each well analyzed position increases the ability of a player.

Ragozin–Botvinnik
Leningrad 1930

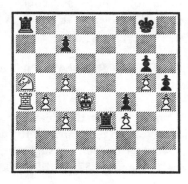

Here we have a very sharp and instructive ending. White's position looks the more promising, since he has the dangerous threat of advancing his b-pawn. Such positions, full of specific points, are sometimes called analytical (i.e. they lend themselves to specific calculation).

For the next 12 moves Botvinnik plays in accordance with his adjournment analysis:

38 b5 R×f3 39 b6 c×b6 40 c×b6 Rd8+!

The only way. 40...Re3 is wrong in view of 41 b7 Rd8+ 42 Kc5 f3 43 Nc4, when Black stands badly.

41 Kc4 Re3 42 Nc6.

An imperceptible inaccuracy. White over-estimates his chances. Correct is 42 Ra2! Rc8+ 43 Kb4 Re6 44 Kb5 Re5+ 45 Kb4 Re6, agreeing to a repetition of moves.

42...Re4+ 43 Nd4.

43 Kb3 fails to 43...R×a4 44 K×a4 f3! 45 N×d8 f2 46 b7 f1 = Q 47 b8 = Q Qa1+, and Black wins.

43...f3 44 Ra2 Rc8+ 45 Kb4!

Other moves lose. On 45 Kd3 or 45 Kb3 there follows 45...Re7 and ...Rb7, while after 45 Kd5 Re7 46 N×f3, 46...Rd7+! and again ...Rb7 is decisive. Also, 45 Kb5 is bad in view of 45...Re5+ 46 Kb4 Rb8!

45...Re1 46 c4 Re4 47 Kc3 Re3+ 48 Kb4 Re4 49 Kc3 Rd8! 50 Nc6?

The decisive mistake. He had to play 50 Nb3 Re2 51 Ra1 f2 52 Rf1 Rf8 53 b7 Rb8 54 Na5, when a draw is probable.

50...Re3+ 51 Kb4 Re2 52 Ra1 f2! 53 N×d8 (53 Rf1 Rf8 54 b7 similarly fails to 54...Rb2+! etc.) **53...Re1 54 Ra8 f1 = Q 55 Nc6+ Kg7,** and Black soon won.

In his book of selected games, published in 1938, Botvinnik wrote that he was very proud of this analysis, since up till then he had been much weaker in this field.

Of course, the 'extent' of the analysis must be chosen rationally. In many cases the content of the adjourned position cannot be exhausted by specific analysis. Then the main thing is to gain a feeling for the basic ideas of the position, and for the various tactical and strategic subtleties—in other words, to penetrate into the spirit of the position.

This relates in particular to complicated middlegame positions, as, for example, in the following case.

Suetin–Solntsev
Minsk 1952

It is difficult to make an analysis of this tactically quiet position. The chances can only be with White, since Black's pawn formation is seriously weakened (in particular, of course, on the Q-side). But for the moment Black's pieces are actively placed, and prevent not only any intrusion by White, but also the opening up of the game. But without opening up the game in the centre and on the K-side, White cannot even think of realizing his advantage. Of course, here there are no forcing paths, although one still cannot get by without lengthy analytical assessments.

Black's very first move showed that in his analysis he had by no means taken account of all the strategic subtleties of the position...

41...Nd4.

This move allows White to make a favourable exchange of knights. And after all, the knight at a3 was without prospects, whereas the knight at e6 was the pride of Black's position.

42 Nc2 N×c2 43 Q×c2 Be6 44 Rcd1 Rb5 45 Qc3 Re8 46 h3 Ra8.

It is easy to see that White's advantage has increased. Black must passively await the opening of the game, whereas White is pre-

pared for the long-planned break-through—f3–f4! It is true that, for the moment, the knight is stuck on the edge of the board, but it too is performing an important task, by eliminating counter-play by Black on the Q-side.

47 Qe3 Kg7 48 f4! Re8 49 f×e5 f×e5 50 Qc3 Bc8 51 Rf1 Rf8 52 R×f8 K×f8.

The further simplification is also in White's favour, although he is certainly not aiming for an ending. He now has an excellent 'duo' of heavy pieces, whereas for the moment the black rook is out of play. Attack on the king is the motto of White's subsequent action. His immediate problem is to bring his knight into play.

53 Qf3+ Ke8 54 Rf2 Rb4 55 Nb2! Ba6 56 Qc3 R×e4.

Black cracks under the defensive strain, and allows White to build up a swiftly decisive attack. But it is difficult to suggest a satisfactory defence against 57 a3 Rb5 58 Nd3! etc.

57 Q×a5 Bc8 58 Nc4 Rf4 59 Qa8! Qe6 60 Re2 e4 61 Qb8 Rf7 62 R×e4!

A simple blow, crowning White's plan.

62...Q×e4 63 Q×c8+ Ke7 64 Q×c7+ Resigns.

In such a 'non-variational' analysis one must learn to think in schemes, rather than in moves: which pieces to exchange, which to preserve, how to deploy the forces, what type of ending to aim for, and so on.

One further important feature of adjourned positions is the fact that the majority of them are of an endgame nature. The endgame is not our theme, but we will take the opportunity to emphasize the importance of studying it. Experience has shown that it is precisely in the endgame that the largest number of mistakes is made by inexperienced players.

Perhaps the small number of pieces on the board makes the study of the endgame a boring task for young players. But we have already seen what interesting, tactical variations can arise in endgame positions.

Tactics are just as inseparable from the endgame, as from the other stages of the game.

Zinn–Bronstein
Berlin 1968

Does White have a draw? He does, but by no means 'just as he pleases'. The only way to achieve it is by 75 Rf8+ Kg4 76 Rg8!, when Black is in an unusual form of *zugzwang*, since 76...K×g3? fails to 77 R×g5+ R×g5 78 h×g5, when White even wins.

In the game, White was evidently relying on Tartakover's aphorism 'all rook endings are drawn', and he continued 75 h×g5? There followed 75...K×g5 76 Rg8+ Kf5 77 Rf8+ Kg4 78 Rg8+ Rg5 79 Ra8 K×g3 80 K×e4 h4 81 Ra3+ Kg4 82 Ra1 h3 83 Ke3 h2 84 Kf2.

This is the position White had aimed for, mechanically assuming that after 84...Kh3 he had the saving check 85 Ra3+, when the white king apparently reaches g2. But, like lightning from a clear sky, there followed **84...Ra5!** Now 85 Rb1 is bad because of

85...Ra2+, and after **85 R×a5 h1 = Q** Black easily realized his advantage.

Suetin–Mnatsakanian
Kiev 1965

White stands badly, and it hardly seems worth wasting time on analysis. But his defensive resources turn out to be very considerable.

Note that if White should succeed in winning one of the K-side pawns, and then in sacrificing a rook for the a- and b-pawns, he may be able to reach a theoretically drawn ending. But this is the question: has White sufficient time to carry out this plan? At any event, the first task is clear: to activate the rooks, by combining threats on both wings.

When preparing for the resumption, I recalled a similar ending.

Portisch–Smyslov
Havana 1964

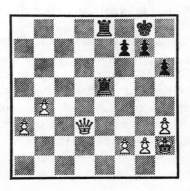

This game continued as follows: **43...Re2 44 a4?** (better is 44 f4 Ra2 45 Qf3!) **44... R×f2 45 a5 Rb2!** 46 Qb5 (46 b5 fails to 46...Re5 47 a6 Rb×b5 48 a7 Ra5 49 Qd8+ Kh7 50 a8 = Q R×a8 51 Q×a8 Re6, when Black has created a fortress) **46...Re4 47 Qb8+ Kh7 48 b5 Reb4 49 b6 Rb5 50 Qa7 f5,** and a draw is inevitable.

The resumption of my game with Mnatsakanian for a long time followed adjournment analysis: **42 Rg3+!** (42 Re6? is bad on account of 42...Qc4 or 42...g6, when White does not succeed in co-ordinating the action of his rooks) **42...Kh6 43 Re8 Kh7** (in the event of 43...g6 44 Rh8+ Kg7 45 R×h5 Black again loses a pawn) **44 Re7 Qb2 45 Rg5 a4 46 R×h5+ Kg6 47 Ra5 a3 48 Rea7.**

Here my adjournment analysis came to an end. White has fulfilled the first part of his plan—he has won the h-pawn, and deployed his rooks so as to threaten the possible sacrifice on a3.

48...Qd4 49 R7a6+ Kh7 50 Rh5+ Kg8 51 Rha5 Kf7 52 Ra7+ Ke6 53 Kh1 g6 54 R7a6+ Kf7 55 Ra7+ Kf6 56 R7a6+ Kg7 57 Kh2 Kh6.

Now 58 Ra4! would have led to a draw, but White made a careless move, which could have cost him dearly.

58 Ra7? b3 59 R×a3 b2? (correct is 59... Qd6+, so as on 60 Kh1 to reply 60...b2!, and if 61 Ra1, then 61...Qd4) **60 Rb7 Qd6+ 61 Rg3!,** and the result was after all a draw.

To conclude this section—a few pieces of advice.

1. When analyzing positions which are objectively lost, try to find a concealed trap. Analyze very carefully those few continuations where you have some practical chances. In practice, all kinds of 'miracles' occur, when the unsuspecting opponent makes a fool of himself.

2. On the other hand, if you have a winning position, don't lose your grip, otherwise the miracles mentioned may turn against you!

3. When analyzing complicated positions (if they are not of a forcing nature) do not become carried away by endless variations. Restrict yourself to a general assessment of the possible course of the game and to an optimum 'supply' of specific tactical ideas, while conserving your energy.

If a player tries to remember every possible and impossible variation, it means that on resumption he deprives himself of the ability to think independently, and instead of searching, thinking and studying, he endeavours only to remember.

4. When analyzing endgame positions, remember that work on literature can help you: it will enable you to link your analysis with theoretical positions.

The awakening of the artist in a chess player

Even the most unskilled players value the artistic elements in their favourite game. But the very concept of art presupposes a study of the methods of the attendant Muse. After all, every great player is first and foremost an artist—this is noticeable in his analytical work. Therefore, when the opportunity presents itself, try to watch a master analyzing. This will enrich your analytical ability, and such a lesson can be more useful than any theoretical lecture. For example, anyone who has observed how two masters 'look at' a game just played between them cannot fail to be impressed by the rapidity and accuracy of their analysis.

In my youth (and even now!) I always admired in such analysis an attribute which was uncommon even among great masters: to see, behind the at times strictly mathematical, almost dead abstract schemes, a lively spirit, the inexhaustible flame of creativity, the soul of a particular set-up.

I will dwell on this question in more detail, and will give a few examples.

My first encounter with a grandmaster occurred in the USSR Trades Union Team Championship in 1949, when, while still a candidate master, I appeared on top board for the Sports Society 'Trud'. In only the second round my opponent was Boleslavsky, then a contender for the World Championship. When preparing for the game (with Black), I decided to place my choice on a little-studied variation of the Ruy Lopez: 1 e4 e5 2 Nf3 Nc6 3 Bb5 a6 4 Ba4 Nf6 5 0–0 Be7 6 Re1 b5 7 Bb3 d6 8 c3 0–0 9 h3 Na5 10 Bc2 c5 11 d4 Qc7 12 Nbd2 g6 13 Nf1 Re8 14 Ne3 Kg7.

I proceeded from the fact that, in the recently-concluded 17th USSR Championship, this continuation had been successfully employed against Boleslavsky by Furman, where there had followed 15 d×e5 d×e5, when Black was well prepared for White's K-side offensive.

Of course, I realized that it was unlikely that I would have here such a 'quiet life'. But there was no one with whom to consult, and my curiosity outweighed caution.

But I had hardly pressed the clock after moving my king, when there followed the quite unforeseen flank blow 15 b4!, and after 15...c×b4 16 c×b4 Nc4 17 N×c4 b×c4 18 Bb2 it became clear that my position was unsatisfactory. By some miracle I managed to save the endgame. I cannot avoid mentioning that Boleslavsky, who was noted for his exceptional modesty and kindness, did not express even a hint of disappointment. On the contrary, he sincerely congratulated me on a difficult defence.

Soon we became great friends, and spent many hours in analysis together. I always admired not only his splendid analytical skill, but also his exceptionally demanding attitude

to himself, especially in the study of his lost games. Boleslavsky was first and foremost a chess artist. At times he was not too concerned about the result itself of a game, but in subsequent analysis he was always obliged to dig down to the true sources of its development, and always his searchings were of a specific, dynamic nature.

Even before my personal acquaintance with grandmaster Ragozin, I knew that he was a player of highly original thinking, although in practice his play was by no means always noted for its evenness. In 1955 I happened to work with him on a certain manuscript, which, unfortunately, was not published. The work demanded the rapid analysis of many games, with subsequent efficient comments on them. With a few rare exceptions, all these games were of a genuinely master-like, complicated nature. Frequently, because of working necessity, it became necessary to avoid deep, specific searchings, and stick in our annotations to the well-trodden path of evaluations from general considerations. And on each such occasion I noticed how in Ragozin a protest was involuntarily raised. At times the tempo of our work was sharply reduced. But what was there to do?! The genuine artist had been awakened, who forgot about everything except the richness and beauty of intrinsic chess ideas. And, in his analysis, with what wonderful tints were revealed the secret harmonious connections of the chess pieces!

This position was reached in the game **Geller–Kotov** (22nd USSR Championship, 1955).

White's subsequent idea, **16 b3!**, fascinated Ragozin for a long time. Indeed, from this point onwards a dynamic struggle develops, where, for the sake of gaining the initiative on the K-side, White sacrifices his central e4 pawn.

In the game there followed: **16...Nb4 17 Bb1 N×e4 18 Bb2 Bb7 19 d5 c4 20 b×c4 b×c4 21 B×e4 R×e4 22 Ng5.**

The critical position for assessing the strength of White's attack. On 22...Ree8 there can follow 23 Qg4, with the dangerous threat of Nf5–h6. Kotov played **22...Re7**, but after **23 Qh5 h6 24 Nf5! R×e1+ 25 R×e1 h×g5 26 Re3!! Bc8 27 B×g7!** he came under a crushing attack. After **27...B×g7 28 Re8+ Bf8 29 R×f8+ Black resigned.** Thus everything seemed to proceed smoothly for White. But at the start of our analysis, Ragozin's combinational flair prompted him to think that everything was by no means so simple in this position. He perceived that, in reply to 22 Ng5, Black had a promising counter-sacrifice of the exchange: **22...R×e3! 23 R×e3 N×d5**, which was undoubtedly the correct counteraction. Black has every justification not only for parrying White's attack, but also for equalizing. Thus, for example, 24 Qc2 g6 25 N×h7 Bg7 does not work for White, while 24 Qh5 can be met by 24...h6. It is no accident that, since the time of the 2nd Moscow International Tournament, Ragozin was regarded as an acknowledged specialist on such sacrifices.

Grandmaster Keres was a 'magical' analyst. On several occasions I was able to 'look into' the internal laboratory of this great player. But probably what remains most clearly in my memory is our joint analysis, immediately after the game, of our first meeting in the 18th USSR Championship in 1950. During the course of the game I gained a big advantage. As White, I employed an innovation in Keres' favourite variation of the Two Knights Defence, and step by step, to my great astonishment, without particular difficulty increased my advantage. But when the win required just one more slight effort, I 'remembered' that I was playing a great player, and, not believing my good fortune, made several incomprehensibly weak moves, after which I had to be content with a draw. My astonishment increased still further when, in our analysis, Keres began demonstrating a series of variations, many of which were incomparably better than those chosen. Here, for the first time, I sensed what a hindrance it could be in certain games to have an excessively deep understanding and insight into the inner process of the chess struggle.

Later I became acquainted with several of the training methods employed by Keres. Thus, for example, he liked to study one and the same position from opposite points of view. If, say, a pawn was sacrificed for the initiative, with inexhaustible ingenuity he would seek resources for the attack. But then came the 'dead point'. Keres would turn the board through 180°, and with equal ingenuity and energy would begin searching for resources of defence and counter-play.

And again that wonderful zest, giving genuine life to the pieces. As a result he as though 'soaked in' the internal spirit of the position.

For a number of years (roughly from 1963 to 1971) my chess life was in many respects linked with Petrosian. Many are the intensive analytical hours searching for unexplored paths that I have spent in a 'trio' with the wonderful company of Petrosian and Boleslavsky.

It is interesting that, cautious and accurate though Petrosian was in his play, he could be just as impetuous and risky in his home analysis. Sacrifices and searches for head-spinning complications always occupied a considerable part of his preparations. He as though 'pumped' himself full of all possible tactical stratagems, so as to be prepared for any form of struggle at the board.

I recall such an episode from the period of his preparation for the World Championship match of 1966. Petrosian suddenly became totally fascinated by the position arising after: 1 d4 Nf6 2 c4 g6 3 Nc3 Bg7 4 e4 d6 5 f3 0–0 6 Be3 Nbd7 7 Nh3 c5 8 d5 a6 9 a4 Qb6?!

He was fascinated in particular from the point of view of the head-spinning complications and the queen sacrifice in a number of variations, resulting after 10 a5 Q×b2 11 Na4 Qe5, or even 11...Q×a1?! 12 Q×a1 N×d5 etc.

And although Petrosian's preparation time was very limited, and it was obvious that the analysis of this position was of precisely zero practical significance, it was very difficult to tear him away from his searchings. Who knows, perhaps such a deviation from rationalism is a vital necessity for a genuine artist.

Anyone who remembers with what strength and ingenuity Petrosian played in that 1966 match (especially in the first half) can draw the corresponding conclusions from this example.

I cannot avoid mentioning one further association. In the autumn of 1955 they phoned from Riga, and invited me for 2–3 weeks

to help train the young master Tal before the Semi-Final of the 23rd USSR Championship. By that time I had met Tal several times in USSR Team Championships, and in general terms knew of his great ingenuity and tenacity. But then the lessons began. Tal, who was then a very shy youth, was hardly able to 'guess' at his potential, and was absorbed in problems of a purely chess nature. In one of our first lessons he began showing me, as I now recall, his game with Gurgenidze from the 1955 USSR Team Championship. After a very sharp struggle, it ended in a draw. In demonstrating the game, Tal began lamenting the fact that he had avoided a direct attack on the king. In corroboration of his words, he began literally 'firing out' such a fantastic volley of variations, which he had seen at the board, of roughly 20 moves in depth with a large diversity of 'range', that, without exaggeration, it became clear to me that the player sitting opposite me was no young master, but an exceptional grandmaster... It is a great pity that I have forgotten this wonderful improvisation. I was overwhelmed by something else. It was obvious that a brilliant future in chess awaited Tal, and the swift realization of this did not greatly surprise me.

Don't be afraid to take risks

From my own methodological experience, I can conclude that the most promising young players are those who, from their very first steps, display analytical inquisitiveness. While their first attempts may not always be successful, what is important here is initiative!

I recall a conversation with Yefim Geller in 1947, who was then a very young and little known player. He is now the greatest expert on the King's Indian Defence, but was then merely beginning to 'get his teeth' into its depths. At that time opening theory was on a much lower level than it is today, and for many variations what was characteristic was a 'fixing' of categorical labels on the basis of only one or two games.

Geller became seriously carried away by the analysis of the game Alatortsev–Kashlyaev (Moscow 1945), where a line of the Sämisch Variation, topical at that time, occurred: 1 d4 Nf6 2 c4 g6 3 Nc3 Bg7 4 e4 0-0 5 f3 d6 6 Be3 e5 7 Nge2 e×d4 8 N×d4 c6. The game continued: 9 Nc2 Re8 10 Qd2 d5 11 0-0-0 Qa5 12 c×d5 c×d5 13 e×d5 b5!? 14 B×b5 Bd7 15 Bc4 Rc8 16 Bb3 Na6 17 Ne4.

17...Nb4 18 Nc5 Nf×d5 19 a3! Rab8 20 a×b4 N×b4 21 Q×d7, and White remained with a decisive material advantage.

Geller related how for a long time he had literally lived this game, which had pursued him even during the night. And, after untangling a most complicated mass of specific possibilities, Geller, in his own words, had not only found a series of improvements for Black, but had also begun genuinely to perceive the essence of many ideas in the King's Indian Defence. I was not familiar with the subtleties of his analysis, but after our conversation I became interested in this game, and gave my attention to the position shown in the diagram. Instead of 17...Nb4, the sacrifice 17...R×c2+ suggests itself, with the possible variation 18 K×c2 Nb4+ 19 Kb1 Bf5!, when Black's attack is very dangerous. I think that there is also much to think

about at other points of this tense tactical battle.

I should also mention that, apart from the gambit idea 13...b5, Black can also continue 13...Na6 14 g4 Bd7 15 Kb1 Rac8 16 Bd4 Nb4 17 N×b4 Q×b4 18 Bg2 Rc4, with good counter-play (Sajtar–Eliskases, 10th Olympiad, 1952).

Where the necessary is combined with the useful

For a young player, wishing to raise the standard of his play, it is important, even essential, to make analysis an integral part of his home training. The starting positions for this can (and should!) be most varied (after all, in practice one has to deal with all kinds of situations). But nevertheless, the emphasis should undoubtedly be on complicated middlegame set-ups, full of tactical content... For the most part, such a criterion is well satisfied by positions arising at the transition from opening to middlegame in present-day openings. It is no accident that it is on such problem set-ups that the strongest players sharpen their analytical mastery. In this way a dual aim is achieved: the development of analytical skill, and a penetration into the jungle of a particular opening system, which one can add to one's 'armoury'.

For those who like head-spinning attacks, what a wealth of possibilities is opened, for example, by the following line of the Sozin Variation of the Sicilian Defence: 1 e4 c5 2 Nf3 Nc6 3 d4 c×d4 4 N×d4 Nf6 5 Nc3 d6 6 Bc4 e6 7 Be3 Be7 8 Qe2 a6 9 0-0-0 Qc7 10 Bb3 Na5 11 g4 b5 12 g5 N×b3+ 13 a×b3 Nd7.

Here White has to choose between the positional way of conducting the storm: 14 h4 b4 15 Na4 Nc5 16 Kb1 Bb7 17 h5, and the sharp gambit continuation 14 Nf5!? e×f5 15 Nd5 Qd8 16 e×f5 Bb7 17 f6 g×f6 18 Rhe1, with unfathomable complications.

In both cases there is as yet no definite evaluation.

What generally happens is that, the deeper you go into the jungle of such positions, not only does the evaluation not become clearer, but often the player is faced with an even more confused picture.

But this should not dismay the analyst.

A knowledge of highly complicated, practically inexhaustible positions opens up enormous scope for the development of the most varied aspects of chess thinking. The result is that, along with the development of analytical potentialities, the player's genuine understanding of chess grows, without being confined within some formal framework. Also, the deeper your analysis of positions in the transition from opening to middlegame, the greater the advantage you gain over your future opponents. And in opening preparation, virtually the most important thing for the practical player is to be constantly ahead in your 'production secrets'.

Thus, you should attempt to be a Sherlock Holmes of chess. And remember that each time you can get down to the essence of the problem by a combination of painstaking and inventive work, worthy of a clever detective.

It is not all positions, arising on the transition from opening to middlegame, that are full of specific content. But always, after the completion of mobilization, there arise a certain complex of strategic and tactical problems (provided, of course, that in the opening neither side has made some bad mistake, allowing the opponent quickly to gain a serious advantage).

Therefore, when studying variations, you should attempt in particular to see the 'physical meaning'—the intrinsic strategic and tactical ideas. In short, when studying an opening (i.e., in essence, a specific middlegame) you should not so much aim to remember the variations, but rather to study the most important critical positions that arise

here. Otherwise, for the trees you may not be able to see the wood!

Consider the following example. In the exchange variation of the Slav Defence after 1 d4 d5 2 c4 c6 3 Nf3 Nf6 4 c×d5 c×d5 5 Nc3 Nc6 6 Bf4 there has long been the problem of which defence is the more rational—6...Bf5 7 e3 e6, or 6...e6. Of course, on each of these themes a multitude of games has been played. Putting aside the various tactical details, we can come to the following strategic conclusion. In the first method Black successfully solves the problem of the development of his white-squared bishop, but, strangely enough, the fact that it is cut off from the Q-side is noticeable. From a comparison of various games, one general feature is apparent: in this case White usually aims for active play on the Q-side.

The development of the game Botvinnik–Tal (match, 1961), for example, was instructive: 8 Bb5 Bb4 9 Ne5 Qa5 10 B×c6+ b×c6 11 0–0 B×c3.

Black also has a difficult game in the event of 11...Rc8 12 Na4 0–0 13 a3 Be7 14 b4, or 11...c5 12 Nc6 Qa6 13 Qa4 Q×a4 14 N×a4 Rc8 15 N×b4 c×b4 16 Rfc1, when White has strong pressure on the Q-side.

12 b×c3 Q×c3 13 Qc1! Q×c1 14 Rf×c1 0–0 15 f3 h6 16 N×c6 Rfe8 17 a4 Nd7 18 Bd6 Nb6 19 Bc5 Bd3 20 N×a7!, and White achieved his aim.

After 6...e6, in contrast, practice has shown that Black normally has to fear an attack on the K-side.

We give here two games for individual study.

Lipnitsky–Smyslov. 7 e3 Be7 8 Bd3 Nb4? 9 Bb1 0–0 10 a3 Nc6 11 Qd3 Bd7 12 h4 Qb6 13 Ne5! Rfd8 14 Ra2 Kf8 15 g4 N×e5 16 d×e5 Ne4 17 f3 N×c3 18 Q×h7 Ke8 19 b×c3 Rdc8 20 Kf2 Bf8 21 g5! Rc4 22 Kg3 Kd8 23 Qg8 Kc7 24 Q×f7 Bc5 25 Bd3 R×c3 26 Rb1 Rb3 27 Rc1 Qa5 28 Rac2 b6 29 Qe7! R×d3 30 R×c5+ b×c5 31 R×c5+ Q×c5

32 Q×c5+ Bc6 33 Qd6+ Kb6 34 a4 Re8 35 g6 a5 36 Bg5 Rc8 37 Bd8+ Kb7 38 Qe7+ Kb8 39 B×a5 Rb3 40 Bb4 d4 41 Bd6+ Ka8 42 Q×e6 Resigns.

Portisch–Petrosian. 7 e3 Bd6 8 Bg3! 0–0 9 Bd3 Re8 10 Ne5 B×e5 11 d×e5 Nd7 12 f4 Qb6? 13 0–0! Q×e3+ 14 Kh1 Qb6 15 Qh5 Nf8 16 Rf3 Ng6 17 Bf2 Qd8 18 Nb5 Nce7 19 Nd6 Bd7 20 Bh4 Qb6 21 Rh3 h6 22 Bf6 Q×b2 23 Rf1 Nf5 24 B×f5 Resigns.

Thus the present-day opening is indissolubly linked with the subsequent middlegame. So that, to a great extent, work on the opening simultaneously gives knowledge of the middlegame. It is very important each time to discover the strategic content of the opening variation in question.

The technique of opening preparation

When working on opening analysis, a player involuntarily encounters a very important problem—the correct organization of this work. Whatever one says, without the necessary order one cannot hope for success in chess.

In work on one's opening repertoire, this is reflected in the correct selection of information for analysis. Indeed, without the necessary material on which to make a judgement, it is difficult to imagine any subsequent serious analysis. No less important is the habit of being systematic and orderly in the complex of specific and general chess knowledge.

To be fair, it should be mentioned that my experience with many as yet inexperienced young players shows that the card index has now become a highly fashionable and widespread phenomenon.

But in this collecting of information it is important to have a sense of measure. It must be borne in mind that, in practice, the selection of material for an opening repertoire must be restricted only to games which are the most important in the theoretical sense (this is what grandmasters and masters do). Otherwise there is a risk of 'drowning' in the abundance of material (in general, the creation of an encyclopaedic card index is a matter for chess clubs, and only those of high standard).

Therefore initially it is probably expedient to copy out in full games which interest you, with the most important specific comments on the opening and middlegame. Such a way of collecting material is highly laborious, but it will undoubtedly facilitate subsequent analysis, and make it more productive.

Of course, learning to choose the most important games, i.e. the information which deserves complete trust, is not an easy matter. It is here that the help of a trainer is extremely useful, or that of a stronger and more experienced player. However, the difficulty of taking independent decisions should not be exaggerated. For help, for example, one can always call on a topical theoretical magazine.

Suppose that you are interested in the following sharp variation of the Sicilian Defence: **1 e4 c5 2 Nf3 Nc6 3 d4 c×d4 4 N×d4 Nf6 5 Nc3 e5 6 Ndb5 d6 7 Bg5 a6 8 B×f6 g×f6 9 Na3 f5**. Here one can hardly pass by the subsequent combinational struggle of ideas, as occurred, for example, in the game **Kuzmin–Kupreichik** (Minsk 1971), and was published in its time in *Shakhmaty v SSSR*, as well as in a series of other periodicals.

In this game there followed **10 Qh5 d5!**.

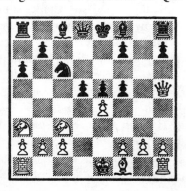

Exceptionally sharp play results, full of rich combinational possibilities. Using the following analysis as an example, we will attempt to give an illustration of the arguments just given, regarding working on information while at the same time following the development of opening ideas in the middlegame.

11 N×d5(?)

A comparison with other games given below shows that this natural move is not the best, and that it gives Black a dangerous initiative. Black also has an excellent game after 11 Nc4 Bb4! 12 0–0–0 B×c3 13 R×d5 Qf6 14 b×c3 Be6 15 Nd6+ Kf8 16 Rc5 f×e4 17 N×b7 Bc8 18 R×c6 Q×c6 19 Q×e5 f6 20 Qc5+ Q×c5 21 N×c5 f5, and the ending is favourable for Black; or 11 0–0–0 B×a3 (*11...Nd4!? deserves consideration*) 12 b×a3 f×e4! (better than *12...Nd4 13 e×f5! Qa5 14 R×d4 e×d4 15 Bb5+ a×b5 16 Re1+*, with a dangerous attack) 13 R×d5 Qe7 14 N×e4 Q×a3+ 15 Kd1 Be6 16 Nd6+ Ke7 17 Qg5+ Kf8 18 Qh6+, with a draw (Fischer–Seidler, simultaneous display, Buenos Aires 1971).

Probably White does best to continue here 11 e×d5 B×a3 12 b×a3 Qa5 13 Kd2 Ne7 14 Qe2 (*14 Bc4 is parried by 14...Be6!*) 14...e4 15 Qc4 Bd7 16 Qb4 Qc7 17 Rd1 Qe5, with roughly equal chances (Zhelyandinov–Kupreichik, USSR Championship Semi-Final 1970).

This point is undoubtedly the most important in the strategic development of the given game. It is also here that as much exact theoretical information as possible is required.

But no less instructive for a young player is the subsequent development of the middlegame, which we give with necessarily brief comments.

11...B×a3 12 b×a3 Qa5+ 13 c3.

The game Buza–Ungureanu (Rumanian Championship 1973) went instead 13 Kd1?! Be6 14 Nf6+ Ke7 15 e×f5 Rad8+ 16 Bd3 Qc3 17 Rc1 Bc4 18 Ne4 R×d3 19 c×d3 Q×d3+ 20 Nd2 Rd8 21 Qg5+ f6 22 Qg7+ Bf7 23 Qh6 Nd4! 24 Rc7+ Rd7 25 R×d7+ K×d7, and Black soon won.

13,..Be6 14 0–0–0 f×e4 (14...0–0–0 is also very good) **15 Nf6+ Ke7 16 N×e4 Q×a3+ 17 Kd2.**

In the event of 17 Kc2 Black wins by force, continuing 17...Qa4+ 18 Kd3 Rad8+ 19 Ke3 Q×d1 20 Qh4+ Kd7.

17...Rad8+ 18 Bd3 f5!

Both kings are 'wandering' about the centre. But whereas Black's king finds a secure shelter at c8, the white king has no good refuge. White's position is lost.

19 Qh4+ Kd7 20 Ng5 e4 21 N×e6 K×e6 22 Qh6+ Kd7 23 Bc4 Qb2+ 24 Ke3+ Kc8 25 Qg7 f4+ 26 K×f4 Q×f2+ 27 Kg5 Q×g2+ White resigns.

Thus sensible economy in choice of information, and an ability to determine the value of opening ideas, create the basic preconditions for independent analysis.

Practical advice

The mastery of general principles undoubtedly assists the conscious perception of opening variations, and makes a player's thinking more economical and effective. But even so, a genuine knowledge of opening theory is impossible without the development of a special memory. This memory should be exercised by regular and sensible training.

From your first steps you should beware of 'swotting up' multitome encyclopaedias. It can only kill your lively interest in chess, and hence your ability as a player.

You can work correctly on the opening only while improving your overall standard of play. You should study the opening together with the ideas inherent in the subsequent middlegame.

What should you be guided by in your choice of opening? This is a problem which every player has to face. You should not aim to remember as many variations as possible, but equally it is not good to overdo one and the same set-up. For tournament play you should build up a definite opening repertoire, consisting of a limited number of carefully worked out systems.

Ways of working on opening theory depend to a great extent on the character of the player. Whether it should be a greater or lesser diversity of schemes, a deep analysis of a narrow range of variations, or play in a variety of strategic systems—this is a matter of taste. There are no general prescriptions.

But to make it a rule to learn from your own games and from others', and not to repeat mistakes made earlier—this is an already patent prescription for everyone. And here is an illustration of the point.

Since the time of the game **Levenfish–I. Rabinovich** (11th USSR Championship, 1939) it has been known that after **1 e4 c5 2 Nf3 d6 3 d4 c×d4 4 N×d4 Nf6 5 Nc3 g6 6 f4** the continuation **6...Bg7?** is unsatisfactory (6...Nc6 or 6...Nbd7 is correct), since White can make a very strong central breakthrough—**7 e5! d×e5 8 f×e5**, and both after **8...Nfd7**

9 e6!, and after 8...Nd5 9 Bb5+ Kf8 10 0–0! White wins virtually by force.

Although since the time of this game more than 30 years has passed, the number of people who fall into this trap, which is meticulously recorded in literally all opening guides, does not decrease.

Not long ago, in the USSR Team Championship in Riga (1968), in the game **Shiyanovsky–Rumyantsev**, Black, not suspecting any danger, played **6...Bg7?**, and after **7 e5 d×e5 8 f×e5 Nd5 9 Bb5+ Kf8 10 0–0 B×e5 11 Bh6+ Kg8 12 N×d5 Q×d5 13 Nf5 Qc5+ 14 Be3** resigned. This game had a number of predecessors, two of which were **Olifer–Levitan** (1959) and **Schwartz–Markwardt** (Berlin, 1950). In the first of these the moves **14...Qc7 15 Nh6+** were made, while in the second Black struggled on until mate: **15...Kg7 16 R×f7 mate!**

Of course, few players are able to avoid traps in the opening. But if such misfortunes are consigned to oblivion, there is a great danger of repeating the course of bitter experience. In order to avoid such unpleasantnesses, you should make it a habit to investigate your opening mistakes, consistently accumulating and supplementing valuable experience.

And we should once again point out that, in building up his opening repertoire, it is expedient for a young player to adopt systems rich in sharp play.

PART II

Work on the Elimination of One's Shortcomings, and Other Problems of Self-Improvement

3

CERTAIN TENDENCIES IN A CHESS PLAYER'S THINKING

Impulsive thinking

Impulsive thinking is characterized by the absence of a single strategic line, by play 'from move to move'. At times this affects highly talented players, who do not, however, have a proper positional training. The course of their thinking is roughly as follows: some outwardly striking move or variation appeals to them, and the immediate reaction follows. Then they are attracted by something else, markedly different in content and direction, which leads to a similar impulse. The result is normally that, without investigating the true possibilities of the position (in this way one can calculate fairly correctly, although not deeply, the immediate variations), the player takes a premature decision.

Such a 'coffee-house' style of play, as it was called in olden times, is quite unpromising. Such a 'bustle' through the variations in search of an easy chance success is in principle doomed to failure.

We will begin with one simple example.

In the game **Gasanov–Arakelov** (Baku 1960) after **1 e4 d6 2 d4 Nf6 3 Nc3 g6 4 Bg5 Bg7 5 Qd2 0–0 6 0–0–0 a6 7 f3 b5 8 g4 Nbd7**, instead of the logical continuation of his K-side offensive by 9 h4, White was tempted into a pseudo-active thrust in the centre: **9 e5?**, which, however, ran into the strong counter **9...b4!** It turns out that after 10 e×f6 b×c3 11 Q×c3 N×f6 Black gains the better chances, since his bishop at g7 is markedly activated, and an important line for counter-play has been opened—the b-file.

White preferred **10 Ne4**, when there followed **10...N×e4 11 f×e4 Bb7 12 e×d6 c×d6 13 Bg2 a5 14 h4 Qc7! 15 Bh6?**

Once again White plays impulsively. Meanwhile he should have been thinking in the first instance of the defence of his king, and should have played 15 Kb1. Now Black's combinational attack develops very efficiently.

15...b3! 16 a×b3.

Forced, since in the event of 16 B×g7 b×a2! or 16 a3 B×h6! Black wins immediately.

16...a4! 17 Kb1 a×b3 18 c×b3 B×h6 19 Q×h6 Ra1+! White resigns. After 20 K×a1 Qc2! he is mated.

It would be incorrect to think that only weak, inexperienced players are susceptible to impulsive play; it is widespread even among masters. Practice has shown that at times the vice of impulsive thinking is highly 'corrosive' even with highly experienced players. We are not thinking of play in time trouble, where such thinking is inevitable for even the strongest masters, but first and foremost of an organic defect of thinking under normal conditions. There are a number of specific causes of such 'misfires'. Thus, for example, impulsive fits can result from nervousness, inevitably arising during the course of a game, especially if the play is of a highly tactical nature. And what about competitive aims? After all, they frequently run contrary to the purely chess development of events on the board, and at times it is not common sense and logic that predominates here, but an 'off-chance' hope. The result is impulsive decisions, which can have sad consequences if the opponent plays correctly. But most often the causes of impulsive play are a superficial evaluation of the position and carelessness in calculation, an inability or unwillingness to investigate deeply into the essence of the position.

We will follow the course of events in the game **Matanovic–Polugayevsky** (European Team Championship, Moscow 1977), where after Black's 19th move the following position was reached.

An objective evaluation of the position insistently demands cautious action by White. Thus, in the spirit of the position was 20 Nd4, with the possible follow-up 20...Bg7 21 Bd3 Nc5 22 Nce2, maintaining the balance.

White, however, was tempted into making an active knight move on the K-side, since he was under the impression that his basic plan in such a situation involved an attack on the black king.

There followed **20 Nh6(?) Bg7 21 Bd4 Qd8 22 g3(?).**

And now White makes an unjustified weakening of his K-side, and soon ends up in a hopeless position. It is instructive to follow how Black develops his initiative over the whole front, combining growing positional pressure with sharp tactical threats.

22...Nf6! (with the unequivocal threat of 23...R×c3) **23 Qe3 Nc6! 24 Bb6 Qe7 25 Kh2 Nd7 26 Qd2 N×b6 27 a×b6 Ne5 28 Raf1 Qd8 29 Bg4 Q×b6 30 B×e6 f×e6 31 Nd1 Qc6 32 Qf4 Rf8.**

Black is a pawn up with the better game, making his position easily won. He concludes the game confidently.

33 Qh4 R×f2+ 34 R×f2 Qb6 35 Kg2 Qd4 36 Nc3 b5 37 Ne2? Qe3! 38 Nf4 Q×e4+ White resigns.

Here we must mention one important point: under no circumstances should impulsive thinking be confused with the necessity of flexibly changing plan in the course of a game.

Very often in practical play one has to adapt to new conditions, and correct the 'course' of the plan. But each time what is regarded as of paramount importance is the conscious necessity for a new plan, based on an objective evaluation of the position. This is no longer blind impulsiveness, but a rapid and necessary reaction to the overall strategic line.

Consider the following example, which contains many typical features of a flexibly carried out plan.

This position arose in the game **Karpov–Hort** (Alekhine Memorial Tournament, Moscow 1971).

Here Black continued **21...Be5**. He appears to have in prospect an excellent regrouping of his forces. He threatens 22...Qh4, and after 22 Bg5 Qb6 23 Be3 Qc7 followed by ...0-0-0 or ...R×h2 Black has no difficulties. But it is White to move, and, exploiting his latent dynamic resources, he begins an interesting and highly flexible plan of active play, which in the end is directed against the opposing king. But first he attempts to prevent the planned deployment of Black's forces.

22 Rg4! Qf6.

22...B×h2 was rather better. But Black fails to sense the danger, and, guided only by his own 'interests', aims to develop his forces as quickly as possible.

23 h4!

The first surprise. It turns out that the apparently doomed white h-pawn is very much alive. 23...N×h4? fails to 24 Bg7!

23...Qf5 24 Rb4!!

The most difficult move for White in the game. Incidentally, directly after the game Hort told me that this rook manoeuvre had come as a complete surprise to him. Now 24...0-0-0 fails to 25 Bg4, and at the same time the b7 pawn is attacked.

24...Bf6 25 h5 Ne7.

Forced. The natural 25...Ne5 can be met by 26 Rf4!, winning a piece.

26 Rf4! Qe5 27 Rf3!

The rook, which in the middlegame is usually an unwieldy piece, displays amazing mobility. It not only assists in the attack, but also splendidly fulfils its defensive obligations. Thus Black gets nowhere by 27... Q×h5 28 R×f6 Qh1+ 29 Bf1 Ng8 30 Qe1+, when White wins. Black's position is already very difficult. White's outwardly impulsive, but in reality deep and subtle play has imperceptibly shattered his opponent's defences.

27...N×d5 28 Rd3 R×h6 29 R×d5.

But not 29 Q×h6, in view of 29...Bg5 and 30...Ne3+.

29...Qe4 30 Rd3!

Another amazingly subtle manoeuvre, which begins a decisive attack by White on the opposing king.

30...Qh1+ 31 Kc2 Q×a1 32 Q×h6 Be5 33 Qg5. Here Black overstepped the time limit, but it is easy to see that his position is hopeless.

Of course, in practice, highly 'delicate' situations sometimes arise, when, especially in a sharp tournament battle, it is very difficult to distinguish that border, beyond which there follows no longer logical, but impulsive thinking. This explains the mistakes of this type, inexplicable on first acquaintance, which occur even with strong players.

But the causes are already known to us. A far from minor role among them is played by the attempt to change forcibly the logical course of the game in one's favour. Consider the following examples.

In the game **Makarichev–Suetin** (Daugavpils 1978), where the Ponziani Opening was played, after the well-known initial moves **1 e4 e5 2 Nf3 Nc6 3 c3 Nf6 4 d4**, Black, instead of the exhaustively studied 4...N×e4, chose a continuation which occurs rarely in practice,

4...d5!?. The game continued **5 Bb5! e×d4 6 e5 Ne4 7 N×d4 Bd7.**

A familiar position from the Two Knights' Defence has been reached, with an extra tempo (c2–c3) for White.

It was this factor which White attempted to exploit, by playing **8 Qb3?!**

What is this, a tactical refutation, or an impulsive experiment? At first sight Black's position appears critical. Bad is 8...N×d4 9 B×d7+ Q×d7 10 c×d4, when loss of material is inevitable.

But nevertheless Black discovers some excellent resources (a fact which is embodied in the very nature of the position, since he has not made any serious mistake): **8...a6! 9 Q×d5** (on 9 Be2 Black can play 9...Be6!) **9...a×b5 10 Q×e4 N×d4 11 Q×d4** (11 c×d4 Bc6! favours Black) **11...Ra4!**

For the pawn Black has a strong initiative, which is at least enough to equalize. After **12 b4 c5 13 Qe3 c×b4 14 c×b4 B×b4+ 15 Bd2,** by 15...Qe7! he could have set his opponent a number of difficult problems.

Thus the cause of White's troubles evidently lay in the move 8 Qb3. In view of this, the recommendation made by Khristov deserves consideration: 8 0-0, and if 8...Be7, then 9 Qb3!.

But Black can play 8...Bc5, and here too it is not easy for White to utilize his extra tempo.

The following position is one from the middlegame.

Romanishin–Savon
Yerevan 1976

A complicated strategic situation has arisen. White has sacrificed a pawn, but has built up a strong pawn centre, and now threatens the unpleasant pin 13 Bg5!, which may lead to an attack on the black king. The threat of Bg5 is highly unpleasant, and probably Black's most important task was to parry it by 12...h6, although even then the initiative remains with White after 13 Ne5!

But Black impulsively concluded his development by **12...Bb7,** after which White's onslaught began to grow inexorably: **13 Bg5! h6 14 Bh4 Qe8** (14...g5 would have been met by 15 N×g5!) **15 B×f6 g×f6 16 Nd2 Kh7 17 Bf1 b5?**

Another impulsive, superficial decision, which leads to a hopeless position for Black. He could still have resisted after 17...Ba6 18 Qf3 Qe7.

18 Qf3! f5 19 Qf4 Nb3.

19...Qc6 is very strongly met by 20 d5! (*20 Bg2* is also good) 20...Qc5 21 e×f5 Q×d5 22 Ne4 Q×f5 23 Q×f5 e×f5 24 Nf6+! etc.

20 N×b3 c×b3 21 Bd3 f×e4 22 B×e4+ B×e4 23 R×e4.

Black suffers a decisive loss of material.

23...Qe7 24 Re5 Rg8 25 Rc5 c6 26 R×b3 Rac8 27 Qe4+ Rg6 28 R×c6 R×c6, and **Black resigned.**

Thus, impulsive thinking is highly 'diverse', which merely demonstrates the difficulties one faces in trying to eradicate this vice. I should also remark that this defect is best tackled in a player's early years. Later on it can become a harmful habit, especially in difficult and unusual practical conditions. For this reason, experienced trainers do everything possible to warn young players against hastiness, and train them to take a conscious decision when choosing a move.

Now let us turn to one of the thinking tendencies which is most common in practice, and endeavour to disclose its good and bad sides.

Play on general positional grounds

This is a definite method of thinking, which arose from the fairly high level of chess theory development during the second half of the 19th century. Its founder was Wilhelm Steinitz, but a whole series of principles assisting the origination of this method were established somewhat earlier in the games of Paul Morphy. The methods of the positional school struck a strong blow in particular against the type of play which predominated at that time, which was for tempting complications, suspect from the positional point of view, and resulting in all sorts of impulsive decisions.

The basis of a player's thinking now became a plan, which was built on a realistic evaluation of the position and on accurately formulated principles of positional play.

From that time chess became elevated to the level of a science, and ceased to be a game of chance and inspiration. The struggle should develop first and foremost on the basis of certain laws! Such was one of the postulates of the Steinitz theory.

We will examine some examples which illustrate the positive aspect of play on general positional grounds.

Steinitz–Sellman
Baltimore 1885

With his next move Steinitz begins an accurate and deeply conceived plan of a Q-side offensive, utilizing his spatial advantage and the strong square d4 for his pieces.

13 b4! Be7 14 a3 f5?

A characteristic mistake. By blocking the position in the centre, Black merely makes it easier for the opponent to achieve his goal. 14...f6 was better.

15 Rc1 Bb7 16 Be3 Qd8 17 Nd4 Nf8 18 0–0 h5 19 Nc3 Kf7 20 Nb1!

White's knight heads for a5, which will increase still further his pressure on the Q-side.

20...g6 21 Nd2 Nd7 22 N2b3 Rc8 23 Na5.

White has gained an overwhelming position.

After **23...Ba8 24 R×c8 Q×c8 25 Rc1 Qb8 26 Qc2! Bd8 27 Nac6 Qb7 28 N×d8+ R×d8 29 Qc7** a picturesque position was reached, where Black's pieces were almost in *zugzwang.* **29...Qb8 30 Bf2! Qb6 31 Nf3 Q×c7 32 R×c7 Ke8 33 Ng5 Nf8 34 Bc5 Nd7 35 Bd6 Resigns.**

And now here is an example of a plan where a complex of black squares is occupied. The player with White was one of the brightest and most talented representatives of the positional school.

Schlechter–John
Barmen 1905

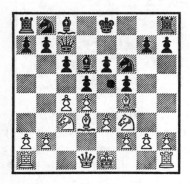

A strategic battle is in progress in the centre around the square e5. White's next move is highly instructive: **8 g3!**

From this point White begins to carry out an exact plan of play on the black squares, with the aim of achieving domination over them, which, in turn, will lead to the 'suffocation' of the black bishop at c8. White's subsequent play develops not only very logically, but also easily, as if by clockwork: **8...0–0 9 0–0 Ne4 10 Qb3 Kh8 11 Rac1 B×f4** (the threat was 12 c×d5 e×d5 13 N×d5) **12 e×f4 Qf7 13 Ne5 Qe7 14 B×e4!**

An instructive point. White appears to be making something of a concession in exchanging his strong bishop. But in the given position, where he is playing for a 'bad' black bishop, White's knights are very strong. And, in connection with the following pawn break, this exchange merely assists the strengthening of White's position in the centre, and his domination over the black squares.

14...f×e4 15 f3 e×f3 16 Rce1 Qc7 17 Qa3!

Now 17...Nd7 fails to 18 Qe7!

17...Kg8 18 R×f3 Na6 19 b3 Qd8 20 c5 Nc7 21 Qb2 Bd7 22 Qc2 Qe7 23 Ref1 Rae8 24 g4 Bc8 25 Rh3!

An instructive detail. White forces 25...g6, which leaves the black squares in the opponent's position completely weakened.

25...g6 26 b4!

After depriving his opponent of all hopes of active counter-play, White commences a broad offensive over the entire front, preparing a decisive break-through on one of the flanks, according to circumstances.

26...Qf6 27 Rhf3 Re7 28 a4 a6 59 Nd1 Rg7 30 Ne3 Qe7 31 g5 Bd7 32 N3g4 Be8 36 Nh6+ Kh8 34 Qe2 Qd8 35 Neg4 Bd7 36 Qe5 Ne8 37 Rh3 Qc7 38 Nf6! Q×e5.

Forced, since 38...Qd8 is decisively met by 39 N×h7!

39 f×e5 Re7 40 Rhf3 N×f6 41 R×f6 R×f6 42 e×f6

Now the e5 square becomes an excellent 'transit point', first for White's knight, and then for his king, whose advance decides the game.

42...Re8 43 Nf7+ Kg8 44 Ne5 Rd8 45 Kg2 Kf8 46 h4 Be8.

Black is forced to defend against the threat of opening the K-side by h4–h5. But now the space gained by White on the Q-side becomes important. It is here that Schlechter makes the decisive break-through:

47 Kf3 Bf7 48 Kf4 Ke8 49 Rb1 Kf8 50 b5! Resigns.

Indeed, after 51...a×b5 52 a×b5 Be8 53 b×c6 B×c6 54 N×c6 b×c6 55 Ke5 White wins easily.

And now a further example, from the play of another leader of the positional school, grandmaster Siegbert Tarrasch.

We have here a position from the game **Tarrasch–Noa** (Hamburg 1883).

A purely positional battle is in progress, in which White's chances are clearly preferable, in view of the weakness of the black squares in his opponent's position.

29 g4.

A characteristic ploy. Having achieved a strong position on the Q-side, White begins to break up the opponent's K-side fortifications.

28...Be8 29 Nd2 Nd7 30 Nb3 Nb6 31 Nc5!

The first part of the plan is completed. The white knight has been established on a strong square, tying down Black's forces.

31...Nc4+?

This attempt by Black to make a similar intrusion merely increases his difficulties. White is not concerned by the fact that now Black gains a protected passed pawn on the Q-side, since at the same time the important open file is blocked, which deprives Black of counter-play. White's rooks are freed for the decisive attack on the K-side.

32 B×c4 d×c4 33 N5e4 b5 34 Nd6 Rb8 35 f5! Bd7 36 Rf2 Nd5+ 37 N×d5 e×d5 38 g5 h5 39 Rcf1 Kg8 40 g6 f6 41 Re2 Bc6 42 Rfe1 Rd8 43 Kf4 f×e5+ 44 R×e5 Kf8 45 Nf7 Re8 46 Ng5 Rce7.

This loses immediately, but Black's position could no longer be defended. For example: 46...R×e5 47 d×e5! Re7 48 f6! g×f6 49 e×f6 R×e1 50 Nh7+ Ke8 51 f7+ Kd7 52 f8 = Q Rf1+ 53 Kg5 R×f8 54 N×f8+ Ke7 55 g7!, and White wins.

47 Nh7+ Resigns.

In all the examples quoted we see first and foremost a logical chain of reasoning. Specific variations appear to stem from it, and to support the ideas of the master. It is not at all unwieldy, and enables the player to play easily and economically. A promising and at the same time very pleasant mode of thinking, wouldn't you agree? But how wide are its boundaries? And just how straightforwardly does the thinking process develop here? We should straight away remark that this easiness is purely apparent. It should not be forgotten that, in the play of such great masters as Steinitz, Tarrasch and Schlechter, the simplicity of their decisions bears the stamp of genius! And, while playing on general grounds, they undoubtedly were masters of all the necessary calculating skills. Otherwise they would not have been great masters and artists of the chess board.

In our time the positional school has by no means lost its value. Today the teaching of general principles is approached from the viewpoint of their real strength in this or that specific situation. A mastery of all the various methods of the positional school characterizes in particular the standard of education and culture of a player, without which the attainment of genuine mastery is impossible. A whole series of such methods have become a necessary standard, which go to make up the technical arsenal of a player.

Consider the following instructive example from the game **Karpov–Bagirov** (38th USSR Championship, 1970).

There followed **23 Be5!**

A strong manoeuvre, which restricts still further the black knight at d6. As Karpov mentions in his notes to this game, playing for the restriction of one of the opponent's minor pieces is one of the most effective devices of modern strategy. In view of the threat of 24 B×f6 Q×f6 25 Nd7 Black is forced to exchange on e5, but this gives White a strong outpost at d4, and thus creates the pre-conditions for his subsequent Q-side offensive.

23...B×e5 24 d×e5 Nb7.

After 24...Ne4 25 Nb3 the position of the black knight at e4 would have been very shaky. White also gains the advantage after 24...Nb5 25 B×b5 R×b5 26 Qa4 Rb8 27 Nd7 Qe8 28 Q×a7 Ra8 29 Qb7 Qe7 30 Rc7! (pointed out by Karpov).

25 Nb3 Qb6 26 Bd3 Ne7.

In Karpov's opinion, Black's only chance was the audacious attempt to break out of the vice by 26...a5!? 27 B×f5 (after *27 b5 a4 28 Rc6 Qd8 29 Nc1 Ne7* Black has some counter-play) 27...e×f5 28 Qd4 Q×d4 29 N×d4 a×b4 30 a×b4 Nd8, with hopes of saving the game.

27 Qg4!

Particular attention should be paid to this move. Its positional aim is the seizure of the key central square d4. But this is not simply a technical manoeuvre, but at the same time a clever trick, with a considerable 'seasoning' of tactics. There is the incidental threat of 28 B×h7+ K×h7 29 Qh4+ and 30 Q×e7, while 27...a5 is unfavourable because of 28 b5, when ...a5–a4 is not possible.

27...f5 28 Qd4 Nd8.

When Karpov played this game he was still quite young. On the background of his strictly specific comments on this game, this makes the following short reasoning even more interesting: "Essentially, the position is already *technically* [my italics–A. S.] won for White. Utilizing the good co-ordination of his pieces, it merely remains for him to set in motion his Q-side pawns and create a passed pawn". A typical evaluation on general grounds, wouldn't you agree? But in the given instance it is in full accordance with the specific development of the game. In such situations it is very important to determine the direction for the main strategical blow, whereupon the subsequent play will develop without a hitch.

29 b5! g5 30 a4 Ng6 31 Qa1 Qb7 32 Rfe1 Qg7 33 Nc5 Rf7 34 a5 Re7 35 Na6 Ra8 36 Bf1 Nf7 37 Nc7 Rd8 38 Rc6 Nf8 39 b6! a×b6 40 a6 Nh6 41 Rec1 Ng4 42 a7 N×e5.

Also bad is 42...Q×e5 43 Q×e5 N×e5 44 R×b6.

43 R6c2 Nc4 44 a8=Q R×a8 45 N×a8 b5 46 Ra2 Resigns.

Such are the good points. Now let us talk about the drawbacks to playing on general positional grounds. There can be no doubt that Steinitz's theory greatly facilitated the practical thinking of a chess player. Moreover, it began to seem to many of his followers that playing chess was a very simple matter. Stick to certain rules, make natural moves on 'general grounds' (occupy open files, weak squares etc.), and the results will follow of their own accord! Such a routine approach is no less dangerous than impulsive play without the observance of principles (incidentally, in a number of cases impulsive play is closely adjacent to routine play). Of course, a talented player, naturally endowed with positional flair, can achieve satisfactory results even with such an approach. But they will always be lower than his optimum level. If he is guided only by play on general grounds, without the necessary attention to specific calculation, a player will never reveal his full capabilities. Perhaps common sense and natural 'flair' will not let you down even in nine cases out of ten, but with such a way of thinking, regular 'flops' are nevertheless inevitable. After all, irrespective of its course, practically every chess game is full of individual and latent resources, where no general considerations can be of any help. Only the calculation of variations, delving into the combinational essence of the game, its dynamic state (of course, along with general positional principles!) will enable the correct path to be found.

Players who play on general grounds are always particularly unsuccessful against their antipodes—combinational players, if the latter are no weaker in playing strength.

Here is a typical example of a debacle resulting from play on general grounds.

Alatortsev–Levenfish
Match 1939

Black has harmoniously deployed his forces, and the somewhat unfortunate position of the white queen promises him excellent counterplay. White should probably have thought in terms of equalizing and of completing his development as quickly as possible. But, on general grounds he does not wish to reconcile himself to the true state of affairs, and contends for the advantage of the first move, which no longer is there.

11 Rd1 c5!

It was precisely against this freeing advance that the rook manoeuvre was directed, and even so black plays it! Who is right?

12 d×c5 B×c5 13 Ne5?

The logical consequence of 11 Rd1. After the natural 13...Qc8 14 B×b7 Q×b7 15 N×d7 N×d7 16 Bf4 followed by Bd6 White apparently gains a 'small plus'. But, like lightning from a clear sky, there follows:

13...Qb6!!

A brilliant combination, which refutes White's strategy. In the event of 14 B×b7 there follows 14...B×f2+! 15 Kf1 Q×b7 16 N×d7 Qh1+ 17 K×f2 Ng4 mate! Slightly better is 16 R×d7, although even then after 16...Qh1+ 17 K×f2 Q×h2+ 18 Kf1 Q×g3! White's position is barely defensible.

14 N×d7 N×d7 15 B×b7.

On 15 R×d7 there follows 15...B×g2 16 K×g2 Qc6+. White's only chance was to return his rook to f1, but even then after 15...B×g2 16 K×g2 b4 Black has a marked advantage.

15...B×f2+ 16 Kf1 Nc5!

The point of Black's combination. He now regains his piece, and retains a decisive material advantage.

17 Qb4 N×b7 18 Ne4 Bg1! 19 Kg2 a5 20 Nf6+ g×f6 21 Qg4+ Kh8 22 R×g1 Qc6+ 23 Kh3 Rg8 24 Qh4 Rg6 25 Rf1 Nd6! 26 Bf4.

Alas, 26 R×f6 Nf5 27 Qf4 R×f6 28 Qe5 does not work, since on 27 Qf4 there follows 27...R×g3+! 28 h×g3 Qh1+ 29 Kg4 Rg8+! etc.

26...Ne4 27 Qh5 e5 28 Be3 Rag8 29 Rac1 Qe6+ 30 Qf5 N×g3!, and Black won easily.

Now here is an example of a correct specific solution, where at the same time one continually senses the purposeful development of the main strategic blow.

Karpov–Uhlmann
Madrid 1973

22 g4!!

Anticipating simplification and an endgame, White significantly restricts the mobility of the black bishop, cutting off its return to the c8-h3 diagonal, and planning, after the retreat of the bishop to g6, the advance f2-f4-f5. The plan is first and foremost a strategic one, but at the same time specific.

22...N×d4 (22...Rac8 is slightly better) **23 Q×d4 Q×d4 24 c×d4 Rac8 25 f3 Bg6 26 Re7 b6.**

This delay is equivalent to suicide. Black should have tried 26...Rc2.

27 Rae1 h6 28 Rb7 Rd6.

Now 28...Rc2 is not good, in view of 29 Re2 R×e2 30 B×e2 Rd6 31 Bb5, when the white king heads for the centre.

29 Ree7 h5 30 g×h5 B×h5 31 g4 Bg6 32 f4.

Again an interesting positional idea, based on specific calculation. The position of the white king appears to be considerably exposed, but Karpov has calculated accurately that the black rook at d6 will not succeed in coming into the game, whereas White's pair of rooks will develop a very strong attack along the seventh rank.

32...Rc1+ 33 Kf2 Rc2+ 34 Ke3 Be4 35 R×f7 Rg6 36 g5 Kh7 37 Rfe7 R×b2 38 Be8 Rb3+ 39 Ke2 Rb2+ 40 Ke1 Rd6 41 R×g7+ Kh8 42 Rge7 Resigns.

At the present time, when chess has become extremely dynamic, thinking on general grounds has become an archaic and manifestly inadequate method. But I consider that, as a subsidiary means, especially as regards evaluation of a position, it is perfectly admissible. Besides, in a whole series of so-called typical positions, where strategic motifs predominate (without a knowledge of them, mastery cannot be attained), such a method of thinking is essential to the play, and is undoubtedly logical. Here play on general grounds becomes another name for middle-game technique. I should remark that nowadays technique is a highly important factor, which is of primary practical importance.

Play by analogy

This thinking tendency, which is closely dependent on the previous method, is also one of the most typical.

In our time, when chess theory in all stages of the game has reached an exceptionally high level, it is practically impossible to attain mastery without a stock of definite chess analogies.

During the tournament at Sarajevo in 1965 I was tremendously impressed by the purely positional game **Polugayevsky–Trifunovic.**

1 c4 c6 2 Nf3 Nf6 3 b3 g6 4 Bb2 Bg7 5 g3 0–0 6 Bg2 d5 7 0–0 Bf5 8 d3 Qc8 9 Re1 Bh3 10 Bh1 Rd8 11 Nbd2 Na6 12 Rc1 Qf5 13 a3 Bh6 14 b4 Ng4 15 c×d5 Q×d5 16 Qc2 Qf5 17 e4 Qh5 18 Red1 Bg7 19 B×g7 K×g7 20
d4 Nf6 21 Nc4 Nc7 22 Nfe5 Nb5 23 Qb2 Kg8 24 Na5! Rab8 25 a4 Nc7 26 Qc3 Ne6 27 Rd2 Rdc8 28 f4 Qh6 29 Qe3 a6 30 Bf3 Nf8 31 g4 N8d7 32 N×d7 N×d7 33 Bd1 Qh4 34 Qf2 Q×f2+ 35 K×f2 h5 36 g×h5 g×h5 37 B×h5 Nf6 38 Bf3 Kh7 39 Re1 Bd7 40 Rd3 b6 41 Nc4 c5 42 d×c5 b×c5 43 Ne5 c4 44 N×d7 c×d3 45 N×b8 R×b8 46 e5 Nd7 47 Bc6 Nb6 48 Rc1 N×a4 49 B×a4 R×b4 50 Be8 R×f4+ 51 Ke3 Rh4 52 B×f7 R×h2 53 K×d3 Kg7 54 Be6 Rh6 55 Rg1+ Kh8 56 Bc4 Rh3+ 57 Kd4 Rh4+ 58 Kc5 Rh5 59 Kd5 Resigns.

Somewhat to my surprise, after the game Polugayevsky said to me: "You know, it was very easy for me today. I essentially did not make a single move 'of my own'. Before the tournament I carefully studied a number of games by the great Rubinstein, and his brilliant strategic ideas have stuck in my memory. And by analogy, one of them was literally reproduced by me in the game with Trifunovic".

It remains for me to add that the idea was creatively reproduced. And, of course, the merit in the creation of this 'canvas' belongs first and foremost to the author. But, since there is no reason for not believing Polugayevsky, one is led to the conclusion that associative thinking plays a certain role in his success. It should be remarked that the analogy here is by no means a simple one. It is the reproduction not of some variation or specific idea, but an aggregate of subtle strategic ideas typical of the structure in question (cramping of the black forces, favourable and unfavourable exchanges, a large-scale pawn offensive over the whole front, etc.). Here one sees the reflection, as if in a mirror, of the grandmaster's great chess culture, and his mastery of the arsenal of classical methods.

One further important point: there can be no doubt that the ability to utilize one's own practical experience is a very important and valuable means of improving. And here (both in practical play, and in 'laboratory' work) one must be able to find successful analogies, as it were to set in motion one's previous store of knowledge and experience, and on the basis of this to make necessary generalizations.

This process is in the main a creative one. In connection with this we will examine some interesting examples from the practice of Karpov. In 1966 **Karpov**, who was then 15 years old, played an interesting game in Leningrad against **G. Ravinsky** (White). Incidentally, in this tournament Anatoly became a master.

This position arose after White's 26th move. Despite the considerable simplification, the battle is by no means over. Slowly, and by no means forcingly, it develops on the flanks. 'From inertia' White endeavours to mount an offensive on the K-side, while Black conducts his counter-play on the Q-side. But while, in view of the simplification, White's offensive is ineffective, Black's counter-offensive, by contrast, soon becomes the basic strategic factor of the game.

26...b4 27 h5 Kg7 28 Bd1 Nf7 29 h×g6 h×g6 30 Nd2 Nc5 31 b3.

This active attempt to hinder the offensive is merely playing into Black's hands, since it creates further weaknesses in White's position.

31...c×b3 32 a×b3 Qb6 33 Ngf1 Nd6 34 c4 Qc6 35 Bc2 a4!

And now comes this decisive break-through, by which Black creates a strong passed b-pawn.

36 b×a4 B×c4 37 Ng3 Bf7 38 a5 Qb5 39 f4 Q×a5 40 f×e5 Qa1+ 41 Kf2 Q×e5 42 Nf3 Qb2 43 Q×c5 b3 44 Nd4 b×c2 White resigns.

Subsequently Karpov has frequently utilized the idea, acquired in this game, of a pawn offensive. On each occasion, depending on the specific situation, he has creatively found the necessary way to embody a similar plan. One such analogy is pointed out by Mikhail Tal in his introductory article to the book of Karpov's selected games.

We have here an episode from the game **Barcza–Karpov** (Caracas 1970). In this tournament the 19-year-old Karpov first reached the International Grandmaster norm.

The position on the board appears not only simplified, but also symmetrical. Nevertheless, a clear plan for Black begins to take shape.

19...b5 20 a3 Qd6 21 Bf3 Be6 22 c×b5 a×b5 23 Be3 Rfc8 24 Qd2 b4!

Step by step Black develops his Q-side offensive, inexorably increasing his positional advantage. Soon the 'mercurial' b-pawn becomes a decisive force.

25 a×b4 c×b4 26 Ba7 Rb5 27 Rec1 R×c1 28 Q×c1 b3 29 Qc6 Q×c6 30 B×c6 **Ra5 31 Be3 Ra2 32 Bg5 b2 33 Kg2 e4 34 d4 Bb3 White resigns.**

Thus, play by analogy occupies an important place in the thinking of a player. The forms of it are quite diverse, and sometimes require considerable creative zest. But, to perhaps an even greater extent than play on general grounds, play by analogy can only be a subsidiary means in the creative thinking process.

We should warn the reader that there are good and bad analogies. Just as play on general grounds can turn into superficial 'groping', so play by analogy sometimes becomes the blind copying of some fairly specific strategic scheme. However attractive the original may appear, its unthinking reproduction, lacking in creativity, is fraught with the most ruinous consequences.

After all, every reasonably complicated chess position has its own peculiarities, and in the overwhelming majority of cases, however much the worthy analogies suggest themselves, specific analysis must be regarded as of paramount importance.

We will consider some examples, taken in the main from the analysis of opening problems. One of the currently topical opening variations arises in the King's Indian Defence after 1 d4 Nf6 2 c4 g6 3 Nc3 Bg7 4 e4 d6 5 Nf3 0–0 6 Be2 e5 7 0–0 Nc6 8 d5 Ne7. It is known that here White normally aims for active play on the Q-side, and Black on the K-side. But to do this Black must first of all move his knight from f6, to clear the way for his f-pawn. The square for the knight should be chosen in accordance with the

specific action taken by White. Thus after 9 b4 it is most expedient to move the knight to h5, for example: 10 g3 (*10 Nd2 Nf4!*) 10...f5 11 Ng5 Nf6 12 f3 h6 13 Ne6 B×e6 14 d×e6 c6 15 b5 Qc7 Rb1 Rfd8 17 Qa4 Qc8 18 b×c6 b×c6 19 Be3 Q×e6 20 Rb7 f4! etc., with good counterplay for Black (Taimanov–Simagin, Moscow 1961).

In the event of 9 Bd2, along with other moves 9...Ne8 is perfectly good.

But after 9 Ne1, only 9...Nd7 is correct. It would be a considerable mistake here to follow the analogy with the previous variation, 9...Ne8?, since White then has an effective way of beginning play in the centre, namely by 10 Nd3 f5 11 f4!, with a strong initiative. If Black's knight were at d7, such a plan would be considerably less strong, since his knight would take up an excellent post at e5. But with the knight at e8 the opening of the centre is clearly to White's advantage. Thus the two moves by the knight from f6 are by no means equivalent!

Playing by analogy is especially often harmful during the transition from opening to middlegame, where complex situations normally result, and the successful realization of a plan is assisted by the apparently most insignificant factors. This is why it is so harmful mechanically to play by rote certain opening variations, without a fundamental study of them and a mastery of the opening system as a whole.

Negative thinking. Certain problems relating to positional feeling

This method of thinking is also a fairly complex process. We are talking here of the search for the correct or best play by the method of excluding incorrect decisions. Let us suppose that a casual glance by a player enables him to determine that, in a fairly complicated position which is generally favourable for him, there are two or three continuations which are apparently equally good. It is by no means always that, on the basis of a general assessment, he can quickly determine the best or even the optimal specific path to take. One of the criteria for searching may be the following. Let us first try variation 'A'. If it is no good, let's try 'B', and if 'B' does not work, there remains 'C'. If all three variations fail to satisfy the specified goal, make an additional comparison of them, and choose the optimum one.

Consider the position arising after the opening moves 1 e4 e5 2 Nf3 Nc6 3 d4 e×d4 4 N×d4 N×d4? 5 Q×d4.

In practice this variation occurs very rarely. And no wonder. After the premature exchange of knights, White's queen has occupied a strong position in the centre. It is readily apparent that now Black has considerable difficulties over the development of his K-side. Let us begin with the most natural tries. It turns out that 5...Be7? fails to 6 Q×g7, while 5...Nf6? is strongly met by 6 e5!, when the knight must return with loss of time to its initial position.

Continuing our analysis of variations, we involuntarily reach the relatively best move: 5...Qf6. This is Black's most purposeful attempt to neutralize the action of the white queen, which is his immediate task. And although after 6 e5! Qb6! 7 Qe4 White retains a persistent advantage, even so Black can relatively successfully solve his difficult development problems.

Here we have seen a short, but graphic path of negative thinking: an ascent from the worst to the best.

In practice even experienced masters resort to negative thinking, when they are convinced that their 'diagnosis' of a position is correct, but cannot find specific paths to confirm this evaluation. It is at this point that the process of elimination commences.

Here is an example from my own experi-

ence. This game was played on the threshold of my chess youth, in 1945. My opponent was the Moscow player **M. Zlotnik,** who had White.

After **1 e4 c5 2 Nf3 d6 3 d4 c×d4 4 N×d4 Nf6 5 Nc3 g6 6 Be2 Bg7 7 Be3 Nc6 8 Nb3 0-0 9 f4 Be6 10 0-0 Na5 11 g4 Nc4 12 Bd4 Rc8 13 g5 Ne8** a sharp position arose. By **14 f5!?** (instead of the more cautious 14 Rb1) White provoked great complications. The subsequent stage of the game can be subject to exact, specific analysis right up to Black's 21st move. But I must confess that, when embarking here upon the path of complications, practically right up to the critical moment I was guided more by intuitive considerations, and each time chose (by 'negative selection') what was in my opinion the best move. At the basis of such a way of calculating was the firm belief that the initial position was in favour of Black. But nearer and nearer came the moment when this had to be exactly demonstrated.

14...N×b2!

Only in this way can a path be sought to demonstrate the general assessment, since after 14...Bd7 15 B×g7 N×g7 16 f6! Black's position is simply bad.

15 Qc1 B×d4+ 16 N×d4 Qb6 17 Qe3 Nc4 18 Qf2 Ne5! 19 Na4 Qb4.

It is easy to see that Black's last few moves have been forced, and have not even caused him any problem as regards choice.

20 f×e6 Q×a4 21 Bb5.

The critical moment has been reached. If the queen moves there follows 22 Bd7! Rd8 23 e×f7+ N×f7 24 Be6, and White wins. Can it be that Black's entire preceding conception was erroneous, and that at the very outset his position was lost? But in the opening I did not make any mistake; on the contrary, it was White whose play was eccentric!

After reasoning thus, I threw a further, 'fresh' glance at the position, and found the answer:

21...Nf3+!!

Here it is, the combinational counter-blow, which cuts the Gordian knot.

22 Kh1 (22 N×f3 Q×b5, or 22 Q×f3 Q×d4+ 23 Kh1 f5!) **22...Q×d4 23 Bd7 Q×f2 24 R×f2 Rc3 25 e×f7+ K×f7 26 Raf1 Kg7 27 Bg4 N×h2,** and **White resigned.**

Does this mean that this method of thinking is correct? Much depends here on the art of evaluating the initial position. What can result from an incorrect evaluation is shown by the game **Suetin–Zhidkov** (Kaliningrad, 1972). Here an interesting situation arose after **1 e4 d6 2 d4 Nf6 3 Nc3 g6 4 f4 Bg7 5 Nf3 0–0 6 Bd3 Nc6 7 e5 d×e5 8 f×e5 Nd5 9 N×d5 Q×d5 10 c3 Be6 11 Qe2 Rad8.**

At this point it appeared to me that White had a slight advantage. I must admit that this was promoted by factors of a purely subjective nature, which insidiously suggested that, due to my position in the tournament, I had to think only in terms of winning. Perhaps, therefore, taking the desirable state of affairs to be the actual, White rejected the normal continuation, 12 0–0 f6, which, incidentally, would have promised him slightly the better game. And, without delving too deeply into specific calculation, I played **12 Ng5.**

While my opponent sank into a prolonged period of thought, it became more and more apparent to me that I had chosen a highly committing continuation. How should Black reply? The threat of 13 N×e6 is very strong, and on 13...Bc8 there follows 14 Bc4 followed by e5–e6, after which Black's position quickly collapses. (Note, that the thinking is

again negative, although from the opposite 'side'). My suspicions grew. Surely Black's position couldn't be so difficult? After all, he had not made any fundamental mistake. In view of this, doesn't the move Ng5 break the laws of chess, and shouldn't it meet with a decisive refutation? After all, White is behind in development, and his king is still in the centre. And here is the confirmation of White's unpleasant conjecturing: Black has the very dangerous counter-blow 12... N×d4!. Logically, my experienced opponent was bound to find it. And how thoughtless I had been in taking my previous decision! Moves such as 12 Ng5, which essentially force the opponent to seek a refutation, should be made only after they have been weighed up most carefully.

The subsequent course of the game confirmed my worst fears. There followed **12... N×d4! 13 c×d4 Q×d4 14 N×e6 f×e6 15 Bc4 B×e5! 16 g3** (16 Be3 Qh4+ 17 Bf2 R×f2 18 Q×f2 Q×c4 is also bad for White) **16...Rf2!,** and Black won quickly.

As we see, at times negative thinking is closely associated with the 'mysteries' of positional feeling. In general, questions of positional feeling are of wide importance, and at the same time are very deep. We will frequently return to this problem, freely or unwittingly. But for the moment we will dwell only on one highly significant problem: how an incorrect approach to the evaluation of a position can distort the creative thinking process of a player, with unfortunate consequences.

Observe how the following game developed.

Kan–Boleslavsky
20th USSR Championship 1952

1 d4 Nf6 2 c4 g6 3 Nf3 Bg7 4 g3 0–0 5 Bg2 d6 6 0–0 Nbd7 7 Qc2 e5 8 Rd1 Re8 9 Nc3 c6 10 e4.

We have reached the critical position of a topical variation in the King's Indian Defence. Black is faced with a choice: he can either maintain the tension in the centre (for example, by 10...a5 or 10...Qe7), or he can immediately open up the game by 10...e×d4. Boleslavsky selects the second, sharper path.

10...e×d4!? 11 N×d4 (after 11 R×d4 Qc7 12 Bf4 Ne5 13 Rad1 Bg4! Black has an excellent game) **11...Qe7 12 h3?**

This natural move is a mistake. The position demanded of White energetic measures, which would have been met by 12 Bf4, preventing 12...Nc5 because of 13 N×c6! b×c6 14 B×d6. In this way White could have gained a slight spatial advantage, whereas now Black firmly seizes the initiative.

12...Nc5 13 f3.

In combination with the move h2–h3, this is obviously a poor arrangement for the pawns, which enables Black to build up threats on the K-side.

13...a5 14 g4?! Nfd7 15 Rb1 Ne5 16 b3 f5!

17 e×f5?

An accurate description of the underlying cause of this mistake was given by Boleslavsky

in his notes to the game: "White evidently considered his preceding play to be correct, and Black's 16th move to be an audacious one, for which he should be punished".

White should have done everything possible to avoid opening the game on the K-side and in the centre, and continued 16 Be3. Although even here Black's advantage would have been obvious, White could still have held the position.

Let us digress temporarily from the analysis of the specific course of play, and attempt to establish the reason for White's defeat in this game. There can be no doubt that it lies in an incorrect evaluation both of the position in the diagram, and of the entire course of events. The entire plan chosen by Kan proved to be unsuccessful, although he completely failed to sense this. And, on encountering Black's vigorous reply, from inertia and reasoning 'in reverse', rather than proceeding from the actual situation on the board, he still assumed that White could not stand worse. Yes, such difficulties of thinking occur even in the games of strong masters.

17...g×f5 18 g×f5 (similarly after 18 N×f5 B×f5 19 Q×f5 Rf8 20 Qg5 Q×g5 21 B×g5 N×f3+ 22 B×f3 R×f3 23 Ne2 Ne4 Black has a completely won position) **18...Ned3! 19 R×d3 N×d3 20 Q×d3 Qe1+ 21 Bf1 Qg3+ 22 Kh1 Re1! 23 Be3 Q×h3+ 24 Kg1 Qg3+ 25 Kh1 Qh4+ 26 Kg2 R×e3 27 Q×e3 B×d4 28 Qe8+ Kg7 29 f6+ B×f6 30 Qe4 Qg5+ White resigns.**

In the following example of Boleslavsky's play, his deep penetration into the dynamics of the position, in combination with an original plan, again helped him to reveal the negative side of his opponent's thinking. On encountering a new system, White failed to see his way through the subtleties of the position.

Shaposhnikov–Boleslavsky
Semi-Final 19th USSR
Championship, Sverdlovsk 1951

1 e4 e6 2 d4 d5 3 Nc3 Bb4 4 e5 c5 5 a3 B×c3+ 6 b×c3 Ne7 7 Qg4 0-0.

At that time this was an innovation, and for White it no doubt came as a surprise.

8 Nf3 Nbc6 9 Bd3 f5 10 e×f6.

It was possibly better to retain the wedge at e5, and retreat the queen. For example: 10 Qg3 Qa5 11 Bd2 Qa4 12 d×c5 Ng6 13 0-0, with the initiative for White.

10...R×f6 11 Qh5?

Proceeding from a subjective desire to 'punish' Black for the liberty taken in the opening, Shaposhnikov essentially approaches the solution of the problem from 'the back door'. He should have continued 11 Bg5, with a double-edged game.

11...h6 12 Ne5(?) N×e5 13 d×e5 Rf8 14 g4 c4 15 Bg6.

15 Be2 was the lesser evil, although even here after 15...Bd7 Black has a clear advantage. Now Black switches to a decisive counter-attack.

15...N×g6 16 Q×g6 Qh4! 17 Be3 Bd7 18 0-0-0 Qe7! 19 Qh5 Be8 20 Qh3 Bg6 21 f3 Q×a3+ 22 Kd2 d4! 23 B×d4 Rad8 24 Rhf1 Qb2 25 Ke3 B×c2 26 Rde1 R×d4 27 c×d4 Rd8 28 Kf4 Bd3 29 Rg1 Qf2 White resigns.

As we see, the causes of negative thinking, and the forms it takes, are highly diverse. One is led to conclude that in the majority of cases it is associated with the subjective problems to which the player restricts himself, without investigating the objective reality of the position in the game.

Traits of negative thinking, on the basis of a correct evaluation of the position, are contained in the historic game Capablanca–Marshall, played in 1918 in New York. In it Black employed a sharp variation against the Ruy Lopez, which became known as the Marshall Attack: 1 e4 e5 2 Nf3 Nc6 3 Bb5 a6 4 Ba4 Nf6 5 0-0 Be7 6 Re1 b5 7 Bb3 0-0 8 c3 d5!?. Capablanca, who was faced with the solving of a completely unfamiliar problem, accepted the challenge practically without hesitation, and took the sacrificed pawn. As he wrote in his notes to the game, he believed in his positional feeling, and was convinced of his ability to parry the opponent's piece attack.

The text of this famous game is given in many chess publications, and appears in the first part of this book (p. 24). Capablanca succeeded in winning, and many of the decisions taken by him had to be intuitive, since it was impossible to calculate all the variations at the board. Later, analysts found an even stronger plan for White, and also showed that at a certain point Marshall could have gained a draw. But this does not belittle the importance of the game. To this day one can only marvel at it, while recognizing Capablanca's amazing feeling and the courage he displayed in a very sharp situation. After all, in contrast to his thoroughly prepared opponent, he had to find each move at the board. This game is in the nature of a standard of the practical thinking of that time. And if, under the 'X-ray' of analysis, certain errors have come to light, this merely signifies the general progress and strength of modern specific chess thinking.

To conclude the chapter, let us sum up.

The negative way of thinking, which is perfectly possible in a number of instances, although it is by no means the most economical, has its limits. It is useful in particular for the control of specific plans. But, undoubtedly, in many instances it is not merely unproductive, but also simply erroneous to follow the path 'in reverse'. The persistent adoption of negative thinking signifies essentially a 'half-blind' choice, made only on the principle that the rest is 'even worse'. But in practice it is often the opposite that happens: while rejecting relatively playable continuations, a player chooses an erroneous one, as in some of the examples given.

Let us turn now to an examination of characteristic thinking defects. Of course, the aim here is not to embrace all such defects—there are a vast number of them. My task is first and foremost, on the basis of the examples given, to direct the reader towards independent thinking. Expecially since, up till now, such problems have been little studied in chess literature.

4

A CHESS PLAYER'S CHARACTERISTIC THINKING DEFECTS

Sense of proportion

Correct thinking presupposes a sense of proportion. It comprises in particular an objective evaluation of the situation on the board, and the taking into account of certain factors of a psychological nature. A sense of proportion displays itself in everything, including the constant maintenance of the necessary belief in one's powers, and at the same time of necessary modesty. Necessary, because conceit in general closes the road to improvement.

Grandmaster Tartakover once said: "Chess ennobles man, because it is full of disappointments". He had in mind the excruciating creative searching, which invariably accompanies the work of a player. But it is this factor which raises chess to the level of an art form.

Objectivity in the evaluation of a position is lost both with excessive self-confidence, as well as with paralyzed uncertainty. The course of a game is inevitably accompanied by human feelings, since without them there is no creativity, and no real upsurge of strength. Irrespective of his individual qualities, during a game a player can experience the most varied emotions. Rapidly changing waves of fortune can raise a player up to heights of confidence, and sometimes even pride, and then drag him down, where he now has to retain an essential reserve of optimism, to avoid falling into the quagmire of uncertainty.

This can happen in an individual game, or in a single tournament; this is essentially what a player's career as a whole comprises. It is rightly said that all these experiences are the corner-stones of the testing of a player's character and intellect.

But now let us consider in more detail certain typical mistakes which are made, irrespective of the individuality of the player. We will see that the over-evaluation of one's possibilities, and striving for the initiative at all costs, can lead to defeat.

The following position arose in the game **Tal–Balashov** (45th USSR Championship, Premier League, 1977).

Here Black gained full equality by the queen manoeuvre 17...Qc5! There followed **18 Qd2 Bc6 19 Rfb1 a5 20 Qe2 Bd8 21 Rd1 Kf8 22 Rd3 h4 23 Bg4 Bb6.** Now it would have been most sensible for White to play 24 Rad1, maintaining the balance. But instead he plays for a win, and provokes dubious complications, failing to reckon with his opponent's counter-play.

24 Nd5?! e×d5! 25 Rc3 Q×c3!

A brilliant counter-blow, which enables Black firmly to seize the initiative.

26 b×c3 Re8 27 Qd2 d×e4 28 Bd7 Bc5!

Now after 29 B×e8 K×e8 30 h3 Rg8! Black wins quickly. The game went **29 B×c6 b×c6 30 Qe2 f5 31 Rb1 Kg7 32 h3 Rb8 33 Rd1 Rb2 34 Kh2 Rh6 35 g4 h×g3+ 36 Kg2 Rh4 37 K×g3 Rh6 38 h4 Rg6+ 39 Kh3 Rg4!**, and the white king was caught in a mating net.

It often happens that one of the players has a minimal superiority, but is unable to find a practicable way to increase his advantage. He starts being stubborn, deviates from the correct course, and step by step approaches his downfall. There are a multitude of such examples, and to whom hasn't this happened!

Such a sin is sometimes committed even by players noted for their objectivity in positional evaluation. Observe what happened in the game **Smyslov–Dorfman**, played in the same tournament.

As a result of lengthy manoeuvring, White has gained a minimal advantage, in the form

of a slightly freer position. But there are no vulnerable points in the black position, and soon White finds himself running into a brick wall. There followed **58 Ne6!? Qb7 59 Nf4 f5 60 Qd4 f×e4 61 Nf2 Bf5 62 N×e4 B×e4+ 63 Q×e4 Ne8 64 Bg4 Nf6 65 Be6+ Kg7 66 Qe2 Qb6.**

Black defends very carefully, and White is quite unable to develop an initiative. But Smyslov, urged on by competitive considerations, stubbornly continues to seek chances, even to the extent of taking risks.

67 Bh3 Qb7 68 Kh1 Nc4 69 g4!?

A bold, if rather risky decision. White threatens g4–g5, and his pawns are invulnerable, since 69...N×a3 is decisively met by 70 g5 and 71 Qb2+!, while after 69...N×d5 70 Qe4 White wins a piece.

69...Qf7 70 Bg2?

Correct is 70 Qf2 or 70 Qd3, maintaining the balance. Now the situation on the board changes with cinematographic rapidity.

70...h5 71 Ne6+ Kg8 72 Ng5?

And this is the reverse psychological reaction. Under the influence of his mistake on the 70th move, Smyslov loses the thread of the game and makes an impulsive move, which immediately leads to disaster. 72 g×h5 was the lesser evil.

72...Qe8!

It was this move that White failed to foresee. Now he is faced with a melancholy dilemma: either to suffer serious loss of material, or to play an ending where Black wins the a3 pawn.

One curious feature is that psychological errors of this type are normally in the end associated with tactical oversights. And one tactical oversight can have much more serious consequences than several positional mistakes!

73 Q×e8+ N×e8 74 Be4 N×a3 75 B×g6 Nc4! 76 g×h5 a3 77 Bb1 Nd2 78 Ba2 Nf6 79 h6 Nfe4 80 Kg2 N×g5 81 h×g5 Ne4 82 Kf3 Nc3 83 Bb3 a2 84 B×a2 N×a2 85 g6 N×b4 86 Ke4 Na6 87 Kf5 Nc7 White resigns.

Although excessive self-confidence and uncertainty would appear to stand poles apart, in fact they often turn up side by side. Judge for yourself. Self-confidence sooner or later leads to a mistake, which leads to a sharp and unfavourable change of events. But this entails an unpleasant 'stress', from which follows a decline in strength and uncertainty.

However, there are many possible causes of uncertainty: fear of one's opponent, the 'awkward' opponent (even if objectively he is not stronger), an unfamiliar position, the prolonged overcoming of objective difficulties in defence, shortage of time, etc. But the main trouble is an under-estimation of one's own strengths and possibilities. For further improvement it is essential to battle against these, and considerable assistance can be rendered by self-analysis and psychotherapy.

Some young players, who are naturally very talented, suffer from lack of confidence. And this defect, if it is not tackled with great determination, can become an unpleasant complex. Remember La Rochefoucauld's splendid aphorism: "Cowardice does not realize the strength of its own fear!" The 'energy' of fear must be turned into effective playing energy.

Here is an example of uncertain play in the face of an unexpected and audacious opening innovation, which, incidentally, is also a typical instance.

In the game **Zilberstein–Kim** (Daugavpils,

1978) after the opening moves **1 d4 Nf6 2 c4 c5 3 Nf3 c×d4 4 N×d4 b6 5 Nc3 Bb7 6 Bg5!?** a6 White offered a pawn sacrifice which was unusual in such set-ups: **7 e4!?** Possibly it would have been better to decline the gift, and play 7...Nc6 8 B×f6 g×f6 9 Nf5 e6 10 Nd6+ B×d6 11 Q×d6 Qb8, with a slightly inferior, but fairly sound position for Black, as in the game Rashkovsky–Suetin (RSFSR Championship, 1974), but Black accepted the challenge: **7...N×e4 8 N×e4 B×e4 9 Qe2!**

At this point Black already began to feel uncomfortable. His next move **9...Bg6** was essential, since bad is 9...Bb7 10 Nf5! d5 11 0-0-0!, when he has great difficulties over his development, while things are no better after 9...d5 10 f3 Bg6 11 Rd1!

10 g4!?

An interesting reply. White boldly advances his g-pawn two squares, intending in some cases to play f2–f4–f5.

10...f6 11 Bg2 Ra7 12 Bd2 e6 13 Rd1 Qc7 14 0-0 h5?

Up to this point Black has held White's onslaught, but psychologically, no doubt, he was put out of his stride back on the 7th and 9th moves. At the same time, objectively Black's position, although not easy, was nevertheless perfectly tenable, and by playing 14...Bd6 or 14...Bf7 he could have set up very secure defensive lines. But now comes an immediate rout:

15 N×e6! d×e6 16 Q×e6+ Qe7 (after 16...Be7 17 Bf4! Q×f4 18 Qc8+ Kf7 there follows mate by 19 Bd5!) **17 Q×b6! Qc7 18 Rfe1+ Be7 19 R×e7+! K×e7 20 Bb4+ Kf7 21 Bd5+ Ke8 22 Qe6+ Kd8 23 Bb7+ Qd7 24 Ba5 mate!**

The young player clearly failed to cope with, in particular, the psychological demands, and quickly collapsed in the face of a dangerous, although far from clear innovation.

In a number of the examples we have considered, the cause of failure has been the loss of a sense of danger. This occurred in the games Tal–Balashov and Smyslov–Dorman. The ability to sense danger beforehand and to avert it is not possessed by everyone, not even by many strong masters. Incidentally, players who have been distinguished to a high degree by this quality are Botvinnik and Petrosian, while Karpov is also fully endowed with it.

Sense of proportion is graphically reflected in the ability to foresee danger, but it is very easy to lose this quality in the heat of the battle. Strictly speaking, a player encounters such a problem literally at every step.

The following subtle example is highly instructive.

This position arose in the 6th game of the **Spassky–Karpov** Candidates' Match (Leningrad 1974).

Spassky, playing White, has the freer position. But can this factor be exploited immediately? White experienced little doubt in playing **22 d5?!**, which was incorrect, since it soon turns out that this loses him his small advantage. 22 Rd3 was more circumspect.

22...c×d5 23 c×d5 e5!

This reply was evidently overlooked by White. In the event of 24 N×e5 Q×e2 25 R×e2 Bd6 26 Rde1 N×e5 27 B×e5 B×a3 Black has the advantage in the ending.

24 d6.

Consistent, but again not the best decision Preferable was Botvinnik's recommendation of 24 Qb5 Bc5 25 N×e5 N×e5 26 B×e5 B×f2+ 27 K×f2 R×e5 28 R×e5 Qf4+ 29 Kg1 Q×e5, with a roughly equal game.

24...Bf6 25 Nd2?

A further error. The resulting ending is clearly favourable for Black, who gains an excellent post for his king at e6. 25 Qb5 was now essential.

25...Q×e2 26 R×e2 Rc8!

The start of an important regrouping, the ultimate aim of which is to surround the d6 pawn.

27 Ne4 Bd8 28 g4 f6 29 Kg2 Kf7 30 Rc1! Bb6 31 Rec2 R×c2 32 R×c2 Ke6 33 a4 a5.

Otherwise b3–b4 is unpleasant.

34 Ba3 Rb8!

Planning a possible ...b7–b5. 35 Nc3 is strongly met by 35...Rc8!

35 Rc4! Bd4 36 f4!

Finding himself in a difficult position, White makes a desperate attempt to equalize. The result is a genuinely grandmaster struggle, in which White nevertheless fails to escape from his opponent's clutches.

36...g6 37 Ng3 e×f4! 38 R×d4 f×g3 39 K×g3 Rc8 40 Rd3 g5!

There are three pawn weaknesses in White's position, but for the moment his pieces are highly mobile.

41 Bb2 b6 42 Bd4.

To be considered was 42 Rc3 R×c3 43 B×c3 Nc5 44 Kf3 N×b3 45 d7 K×d7 46 B×f6, with fair drawing chances (pointed out by Botvinnik).

In reply to 42 Rc3 Karpov recommends 42...Rh8!, maintaining the tension.

42...Rc6 43 Bc3 Rc5! 44 Kg2 Rc8 45 Kg3 Ne5 46 B×e5 f×e5 47 b4?

White nevertheless fails to cope with the difficulties of conducting a gruelling and prolonged defence. He could have retained drawing chances by 47 Kf3 Rd8 48 b4 R×d6 49 Rb3, although even here, as shown by Karpov, after 49...Rd4! 50 b×a5 Rf4+ 51 Kg3 b×a5 52 Rb6+ Kd5 63 Rb5+ Ke4 54 R×a5 Rf3+ 55 Kg2 Ra3 56 Ra8 Kf4, or 51 Ke3 R×g4 52 R×b6+ Kf5 53 Rb8 R×a4 54 Rf8+ Kg4 White would still have had serious difficulties.

47...e4! 48 Rd4.

Things are also bad for White after 48 Rb3 K×d6 49 b×a5 b×a5 50 Kf2 Kd5 51 Ke3 Rc5 52 Ra3 Ke5 53 Rb3 Rd5 54 Rc3 Rd3+ etc.

48...Ke5 49 Rd1 a×b4 50 Rb1 Rc3+ 51 Kf2 Rd3 52 d7 R×d7 53 R×b4 Rd6 54 Ke3 Rd3+ 55 Ke2 Ra3 White resigns.

Here we have encountered another important feature: the psychological difficulty of defending outwardly simple, but inferior positions, where there is no counter-play. Mistakes in such situations are practically inevitable.

As we see, a sense of proportion is closely linked with psychology, from which also originate many other important features of a chess player's thinking.

Flexibility of thinking

Even very strong and experienced players sometimes suffer from a lack of necessary flexibility in their thinking. This manifests itself in, for example, excessively fervent adherence to some objectively unclear, or simply dubious, opening system, in an unwillingness to take timely prophylactic measures and make necessary concessions in the event of a dangerous attack by the opponent, and so on.

Modern practice demonstrates the ever greater importance of flexible, elastic thinking, and an ability to adjust to swift changes of scene during a game.

We will examine several examples of a successful defence in difficult positions. It is interesting to follow how the player who finds himself in a critical situation does not restrict himself to passive defence, but finds resources of active counter-play. In such situations flexibility of thinking plays a highly important role.

This position occurred in the 8th game of the **Spassky–Karpov** match (1974). Karpov was playing Black, and his position looks very difficult—his king is under a dangerous attack. On 25...Kg7 White had prepared 26 f4!, with numerous threats. So much the more instructive is Karpov's decision.

25...Nf6!

A splendid idea. Black does not intend to cling to his h6 pawn, but aims first and foremost to strengthen his defensive lines, by bringing up his knight. The tempo is more important than the pawn.

26 R×h6.

The preliminary 26 d6! was stronger.

26...Kg7 27 Rhh1 Rad8 28 d×e6 f×e6 29 Nc2 Qf4!

Another important move. Black prevents 30 Nd4, while after 30 Q×e6 R×d1+ 31 R×d1 Q×g4 he has everything in order.

30 f3 Kf7 31 a3 e5 32 Nb4 e4! 33 f×e4 R×d1+ 34 R×d1 Re8!

The final subtlety, which enables Black to equalize fully. In contrast, it would have been a mistake to play 34...Q×g4 35 Q×g4 N×g4 36 Rf1+! Ke7(g7) 37 Rg1.

35 N×a6 Q×e4+ 36 Q×e4 R×e4 37 Nc7 b4 38 a×b4 R×b4 39 Rf1 Rf4!

Here the players agreed to a draw.

Kuzmin–Kochiev
Baku 1977

An evaluation of the position shows that White has a clear spatial advantage, and threatens a decisive Q-side offensive with b3–b4! etc. If the rook moves, 24...Re8 (*24...Rd8?* fails to *25 Nd5 Qd7 26 b4*, and wins), there follows 25 Nd5 Qd8 26 b4 Nd7 27 b5 Rc8 28 Rdb1, with very strong Q-side pressure. But at this point Black resorts to a device typical of active defence: a positional exchange sacrifice for the sake of activating his forces.

24...R×b6! 25 a×b6 Q×b6 26 Rdb1 Qc6 27 b4 Nd7 28 Rc1 Qc7.

At the cost of a slight material concession, Black has eliminated White's menacing Q-side build-up. In the subsequent lively play he succeeds in maintaining the balance.

29 f4 Nf6 30 f5 Bd7 31 g4 Bc6 32 Bf2 b6 33 h4 a5 34 g5 h×g5 35 h×g5 Nh7 36 g6 Nf6 37 g×f7+ K×f7 38 b×a5 b×a5 39 c5!? d×c5 40 Qc4+ Kf8 41 B×c5 Bb7! 42 Bf2 Qd7 43 Bf3 Qd2 44 Bc5. In this position a draw was agreed.

In the modern game one frequently comes across games which are full of strategic metamorphoses. It only requires one of the players to sacrifice a pawn with the aim of seizing the initiative, when his opponent, who up till then was considering an attack, is for a long time forced into the role of defender. It is then that flexibility of thinking is tested.

Kapengut–Kasparov
Daugavpils 1978

The pawn structure is characteristic of one of the topical variations of the Caro-Kann Defence. White commands more space, and holds the initiative on the Q-side. Here Kasparov makes an interesting decision: he sacrifices a pawn, with the aim of upsetting his opponent's plans: **16...b5!? 17 c×b5 c×b5 18 Q×b5 Nd5.**

The initiative on the Q-side has now passed to Black, and for the player with White it is psychologically not easy to find himself in the role of defender. Now exceptionally accurate and careful play is demanded of him.

There followed **19 Ne5 N×e5 20 d×e5 N×c3 21 b×c3 Qc7 22 Rh3 Rfd8 23 Qe2 Rd5 24 f4!**

This accurate move is essential. In the game Belyavsky–Bagirov (Baku 1977) White incautiously played 24 Re3? in this position, and after 24...R×e5! (Belyavsky overlooked this tactical blow) 25 Kf1 R×e3 26 Q×e3 Rd8 27 Kg1 Rd5 28 Qf3 Rf5 29 Qa8+ Kh7 30 Qe4 Q×c3 he ended up in a lost position.

24...Rad8 25 Re3 Qb6 26 Rc1 Rb5 27 Kf2 Rb2 28 Rc2 Rb1 29 Kg3!

White has completely regrouped for defence. After sensibly weighing up the situation, he has rejected any ambitious ideas. Within a few moves the game ended in a draw.

Flexibility of thinking is a quality which has developed together with the development of chess theory and practice. Formerly, no great importance was attached to it. For example, many of the top masters of the 19th and early 20th centuries did not strive to attain it. At times they suffered from a dogmatic adherence to a definite set of ideas. As a rule, it was this quality which distinguished the fervent upholders of the strict positional, and the purely combinational trends. They considered it a matter of honour to try to vindicate to the last their creative credo. Regardless of the great practical risk, the founder of the positional school, Wilhelm Steinitz, played with amazing persistence eccentric variations such as 1 e4 e5 2 f4 e×f4 3 Nc3?! Qh4+ 4 Ke2, or 1 e4 e5 2 Nf3 Nc6 3 Bc4 Nf6 4 Ng5 d5 5 e×d5 Na5 6 Bb5+ c6 7 d×c6 b×c6 8 Be2 h6 9 Nh3?!

Even in the middlegame he frequently kept his king in the centre, endeavouring to demonstrate the correctness of his conception regarding the centralization of the king at all stages of the game.

Or take Chigorin, that wonderful chess innovator and, at the same time, striking representative of the combinational style. On the general background of his splendid creative ideas there were some rather fanciful schemes, which, however, he would uphold, disregarding his lack of practical success with them. How much trouble was he caused in his match with Steinitz by his favourite system, which was soon given his name: 1 d4 d5 2 c4 Nc6!? But with genuinely chivalrous courage, regardless of everything, he continued to employ this opening.

For all its creative inventiveness, this system did not gain any great popularity. But the idea of it, the creation of piece pressure on the opponent's centre, proved to be exceptionally valuable and far-sighted. In our time it is strongly reflected in such topical openings as the Nimzo-Indian and Grünfeld Defences.

In these historical examples, the deficiencies are a kind of continuation of virtues. Firm convictions, and persistence in upholding them, are necessary for the true artist. Such 'fervour' in the defence of their views was displayed by Tarrasch, Rubinstein, Nimzowitsch, Réti, Spielmann, and many other chess knights of the past. Faith in their principles and their subsequent carrying out in practice also characterize the play of the leading players of recent times, such as Botvinnik, Keres, Smyslov and Portisch.

Thus in the broad sense of the word, the concept of dogmatism does not just have one meaning. Flexibility is more highly valued if it occurs in a firm material.

Underestimation of the opponent's threats

Very often we hear or read of how a player fell into a difficult position, as a result of underestimating his opponent's threats, or of overrating his own chances, In each case we are dealing with a one-sided, subjective evaluation of the position.

Once, in conversation about a mature master, who for a long time had suffered poor results, although he was noted for his diligence, I offered the opinion that the cause of his depression lay in combinational weakness. The person I was talking to, who knew the master much better than I did, retorted: "No, that isn't quite the point. He is fine when it comes to seeing his own tactical threats, but bad with his opponents'". After thinking about it, I had to agree with this opinion.

Indeed, in practice one frequently encounters such a thinking deficiency, and moreover, it applies not only to tactics, but also to strategy. Of course, one's own ideas, be they tactical or strategic, are closer, and, so to speak, more dear. But the logic of chess insistently demands that one should equally keenly see the opponent's threats.

Here is an interesting example from the game **Lisitsyn–Tolush** (Leningrad 1938).

As he awaited his opponent's move, Lisitsyn was very optimistically inclined: it appeared to him that the loss of the c7 pawn was inevitable. Against attempts to defend if (by ...c6 or ...b6) he was threatening the unpleasant 19 Qg5! But meanwhile Black had some hidden resources, and very serious ones at that.

The subsequent course of the game is an eloquent confirmation of this: **18...h6! 19 Q×c7 Nf5!** This is the point of Black's counter–play: his 'cavalry' develops a very dangerous offensive on the K-side. Thus after 20 Re2 Ng4 21 g3 Qh3 22 Rfe1 N×g3 (22... h5, with the threat of ...h5–h4!, is also good) 23 h×g3 Q×g3+ 24 Kf1 Nh2+ White's defeat is inevitable.

The game went **20 h3 Ng3,** and White, after losing the exchange, incurred a lost position.

Apparent from this are the consequences which can follow from a one-sided understanding of the play, and the underestimation of the opponent's threats.

And now an example of a similar type, where in addition, psychological factors have a marked effect. Here we recall another game from the **Alatortsev–Levenfish** match (1939).

White played **15 Rfd1 (?)**.

Carried away by his own plans, involving the development of pressure in the centre, Alatortsev incautiously weakens his K-side. This gives Black an excellent opportunity for a sharp counter-attack on the square f2.

15...Rc8 16 Qb3 (16 Qe2 was more cautious, but White sees only his own threats, and concentrates his attention on the square d5) **16...B×f3 17 g×f3 N×f2!**

A splendid combinational blow. Even if objectively it is not good enough to win, psychologically it proves to be highly effective.

18 K×f2 Ng4+! 19 Kg3?

Shocked by the sudden turn of events, White immediately makes a serious error. He had to play 19 f×g4 Qh4+ 20 Kg2! Q×g4+ 21 Kf2, after which Black has a choice between a draw, and the interesting although risky winning attempt 21... B×e3+?! 22 K×e3 Qg2.

19...N×e3 20 f4 Rc6 21 Rg1 Qd7! 22 h3 Rh6 23 Rh1 R×h3+! 24 R×h3 Qg4+ 25 Kf2 Qg2+ 26 Ke1 Q×h3. It is readily apparent that Black has a won position (although it is never too late to go wrong: Levenfish was unable to win this game!).

Loss of consistency

We have already given a number of 'warnings': on keeping a sense of proportion, displaying flexibility, and paying due attention to the opponent's threats. Among these qualities, a far from minor place is occupied by the ability consistently to put one's ideas and plans into action. We will dwell on this in more detail.

The fulfilment of a plan, just like an individual tactical idea, can in practice be a highly difficult matter. And this refers not just to those instances when the fulfilment of the plan proves to be unattainable due to purely objective hindrances, i.e. when the projected idea proves to be simply unreal. Even there, where, in principle, there are sufficient preconditions for the achievement of the aim, it is by no means simple to put one's plan into practice. What is required here is considerable patience and the utmost attention, to say nothing of such important qualities as tactical ingenuity and subtle positional flair. The following grandmaster example shows how difficult it can be to achieve one's desired goal.

Kuzmin–Petrosian
45th USSR Championship,
Premier League 1977

White has a Q-side pawn majority. Black's immediate task it to block the advance of these white pawns.

25...Be4!

An elegant move to start with, provoking an exchange of minor pieces favourable to Black.

26 Nd7.

26 B×e4 Q×e5 27 B×b7 Q×e3 28 f×e3 Rb8 29 Bf3 R×b2 is unfavourable for White.

26...N×d7 27 B×e4 Nf6 28 Bf3 b6 29 Qd4 Kg7 30 c4 Rc8 31 b3 Qe7 32 Qc3 a5 33 Qe5 Qb4 34 Rd4 Rc5 35 Qe3 Rc8.

Black has not only set up a complete blockade on the Q-side, but has also gained firm control of the black squares, and with great precision has carried out two important steps of his defensive plan.

36 Rh4?!

An unexpected turn in White's strategic course. Having lost faith in his active possibilities in the centre and on the Q-side, White attempts to mount a rather eccentric attack on the K-side.

36...Qc5 37 Qh6+ Kg8 38 g4 g5! 39 Rh3 Qe5 40 Be2 Rd8?

Up to this point Black has played excellently, but this natural move, made on general grounds (aiming to bring the rook into play as quickly as possible, and covering the important square d3), suddenly cancels out all his preceding painstaking work. And meanwhile, by continuing 40...Kh8! followed by ...Rg8 (White achieves nothing by *41 Bd3 Qa1+!*), ...Rg7 and ...Ng8, Black would have had at least equal chances.

Now the 'Ariadne thread' is hopelessly broken.

41 Re3! Qf4 42 g3!

The conclusion of the game is forcing in nature, and is highly instructive.

42...N×g4 43 B×g4 Q×g4 44 Re5 Qd4 45 R×g5+ Kh8 46 Rh5 Qg7 47 Qe3!

It is here that Black's Q-side weaknesses tell, and, by the irony of fate, the game is nevertheless decided by a Q-side pawn advance by White.

47...Qd4 48 Q×d4 R×d4 49 Rb5 Rd6 50 Kf1 Kg7 51 Ke2 Rc6 52 c5! R×c5 53 R×c5 b×c5 54 Kd3 e5 55 Kc4 f5 56 K×c5 h5 57 b4! a×b4 58 K×b4 f4 59 a5 e4 60 Kc3 e3 61 Kd3 Resigns.

The success of a strategic plan depends on every detail being correct. One must therefore check carefully even the most obvious and natural moves. And it must not be forgotten that, while carrying out your own plan, you must also reckon with your opponent's counter-plan. Essentially, you must constantly solve a minimum of two strategic problems: a positive one (your own plan) and a negative one (neutralization of the opponent's plan). And to this must sometimes be added a highly complex set of purely tactical problems.

In the Kuzmin–Petrosian game the fulfilment of the plan was suddenly cut short for tactical reasons. Another typical instance is the loss of 'positional feeling', which leads to the correct line of play being missed, and sometimes leads imperceptibly to catastrophe. There are many factors which can effect the loss of this 'feeling'. Of these, a far from minor one is, for example, the factor of competitive agitation, which can express itself in a desire to change favourably the course of the game by forceful methods. Loss of the correct plan and loss of sense of proportion, about which we have already spoken, are related factors.

An instructive example is provided by the

development of the game **Romanishin–Tal** (Tallinn 1977).

Black has quite happily overcome his opening difficulties, and now, by playing simply 16...Nc6, could have completely consolidated his position. But Tal had more ambitious ideas. Wishing to obtain counterplay as soon as possible, he continued here **16...Qb4,** on which White coolly replied **17 b3**. It should be mentioned that after 17 N×d4 B×c4 18 Qe3 c×d4 19 Q×d4 Qc5 20 Q×c5 d×c5 21 Rfc1 B×e2 22 R×c5 White's position would also have been slightly better.

17...f5!?

Here 17...Nc6? 18 Q×d6 was unfavourable, but the lesser evil was 17...N×f3+ 18 B×f3 Rfd8, with an acceptable game.

18 N×d4! f×e4 19 Q×e4 Bh3 20 Qd5+ Kh8 21 Nb5!

When he went in for this position, Black probably only took account of the fact that he was winning the exchange, and forgot to evaluate more carefully the resulting unusual position. This knight move emphasizes the groundless nature of Black's strategy. In return for the exchange White gains an adequate material equivalent, and, what is more important, his pieces, supported by his powerful pawn centre, now play the dominating role in the position.

21...B×f1 22 R×f1 Rf6 23 e4! Rf3 (23... Raf8 24 f4!) **24 N×d6 Raf8 25 Nf5! Kh7 26 Qd6 Rf7 27 Qe6 Rf8 28 Qe7 Rg8 29 N×h6! Rb8 30 Nf5.**

The outcome is a decisive attack on the black king.

30...Qc3 31 Qh4+ Kg8 32 Qh5 Rd8 33 Ne7+ Resigns.

One often hears the following from insufficiently experienced young players: "I can't understand how I ended up in a lost position. I seemed to put the pieces on the right squares, and didn't make any oversights, but it still turned out badly".

Yes, this can quickly happen, if you play passively and without a plan. Even without any direct mistakes, such play can quickly spoil a position.

Something of this sort occurred in the game **Shereshevsky–Gufeld** (Daugavpils 1978): **1 d4 Nf6 2 Bg5 Ne4 3 Bh4 c5 4 f3 Nf6.**

Following Boleslavsky's example, for a long time the sharp plan with 4...g5 was predominant. But, as the course of the present game shows, the quiet retreat of the knight to f6 is also perfectly playable.

5 d×c5.

This would appear to be the initial cause of White's subsequent difficulties. The critical continuation is 5 d5! Now Black develops unhindered.

5...e6 6 Bf2 Qc7 7 Nc3 B×c5 8 B×c5 Q×c5 9 Qd2? (9 e4 is better) **9...d5 10 0–0–0 Nc6 11 e4 d×e4 12 N×e4 N×e4 13 f×e4 0–0 14 Nf3 e5.**

It is readily apparent that Black already has the better chances. A Sicilian-type structure has arisen, in a form clearly advantageous for Black. It is extremely difficult for White to create any threats on the K-side, whereas on the Q-side he must constantly reckon with a possible Black offensive. And in the coming endgame White's prospects are by no means bright, since his e4 pawn is very weak. Subsequently it is this pawn that becomes the chief target of Black's attack. Shereshevsky ends up in a difficult, and then even hopeless position mainly because he plays without a definite strategic aim.

15 Qd6(?) Qe3+ 16 Kb1 Be6 17 Bd3 h6 18 Qa3 Rac8 19 Rhe1 Qb6 20 b3 Rfd8 21 Qb2 Qc5 22 Be2 a6 23 R×d8+ R×d8 24 Rd1 R×d1+ 25 B×d1 Qe3! 26 Qa3 Q×e4.

Black's goal is achieved. He is a healthy pawn to the good, and now confidently realizes his advantage.

27 Qd6 Qe3 28 Kb2 g6 29 Qd2 Q×d2 30 N×d2 f5 31 c4 Kf7 32 Kc3 Kf6 33 b4 e4 34 Kb3 Ke5 35 Kc3 Bc8 36 b5 a×b5 37 c×b5 Nd4 38 b6 Kd5 39 Nb3 N×b3 40 B×b3+ Kc5 41 Bf7 g5 42 Bg6 e3 White resigns.

Chess culture

The great French philosopher Voltaire once said that falsehoods have many advantages over the truth. If this witty saying is applied to chess, we can say that in the majority of cases there is but one correct path, whereas the reasons for deviating from the correct strategic course are numerous.

Our age is the age of exact knowledge. To a great extent this also applies to chess. It can hardly be an accident that tens of thousands of pages have been devoted to chess theory, which is a living reflection of concentrated and generalized practical material.

In our time it is difficult to imagine a player perfecting himself, without continual work on the opening and the endgame. The role of exact knowledge is especially marked here. But it sometimes happens that players who are already experienced do not know, say, the most elementary basics of the endgame. About such players it is said that they are lacking in chess literacy or culture!

Take for instance the fairly simple matter of mating a lone king with bishop and knight. Such endings occur rarely in practice, and it can happen that a player will encounter this when he has already reached the master level. And here it is possible to be confused, if you are not familiar with the winning method. As is well known, the enemy king must be driven into a corner corresponding to the colour of the bishop. This is achieved by the combined action of the king and the two minor pieces, the knight's manoeuvres following a definite pattern, which it is useful to memorize.

In connection with this, I cannot help recalling an amusing episode which occurred with a certain master. He was a fairly talented player—in the main a dangerous tactician—but was not noted for his industry. And while his opening knowledge was tolerable, the endgame he had simply never studied, and he did not know the most simple things, but assumed that in case of necessity he would work things out for himself at the board. And when he was already of a mature age, for the first time he had occasion to play the ending with knight and bishop against king. Time passed, and he just couldn't find a mate. Seizing the opportunity, he stood up from the board, went up to one of his colleagues, and asked him: "How do you give mate?". "Drive him into the bishop's corner", the latter quickly replied. "That's what I'm trying to do, but his king won't go!" Alas, there was no time for him to receive any more detailed instructions, and the outcome was that the master was unable to give mate in the stipulated 50 moves.

Of course, such examples of illiteracy are rare. But one should not only study the basic rules and principles of the endgame, but should even reduce this knowledge to automation. After all, in a practical game one sometimes does not have long to think, and to work out all the variations. It should be mentioned that, if there is no definite guideline, endgame variations can be very laborious to work out.

The following rook ending occurred in the game **Geller–Fischer** (Palma de Mallorca, 1970).

Black played **65...Rf1**.

Objectively the position on the board is a draw, which would have been most simply achieved by 66 Kg3!. In a calm situation it is easy to see this. But it so happened that, affected by time shortage and fatigue, Geller, who had been expecting 65...Rg2, to which he had intended 66 Rd2 Kh4 67 K×f5 with a draw, here too automatically played **66 Rd2?**.

Although this move does not lose, it has unpleasant consequences for White: **66...Kh4 67 K×f5** (bad is 67 Rb2 g3 68 Kf3 Kh3!) **67...g3 68 f4 Kh3?**

Black 'takes his revenge'. Better chances were offered by 68...Ra1, although even then White should not lose. But the comedy of errors continues.

69 Rd3 Kh4 70 Rd2(?).

A simpler way to draw was by 70 Rd8! g2 71 Rh8+ Kg3 72 Rg8+ Kf3 73 Ke6 etc.

70...Ra1 71 Ke5??

This move just before the time control proves fatal. 71 Kg6 would have drawn.

But now after **71...Kg4 72 f5 Ra5+ White resigned.**

The next position arose in the game **Suetin–Forintos** (Belgrade, 1977).

The position is an elementary win for White. He should play 48 Rb5+ Kc6 49 Rb4, and then after a3–a4 the white king heads for the K-side, to assist the advance of the h-pawn. But I 'automatically' played **48 a4?**, and after **48...Rf4 49 Kb3 Ka6 50 a5 Re4 51 Kc3 Rf4 52 Kd3 Rg4** the position on the board was a dead draw.

The list of such instances could, of course, be continued. All this merely indicates that technical endings should be known as well as the multiplication tables.

There is no need to demonstrate that a thorough study is also required of opening theory. Of course, there are a number of systems and variations which in the main require strategic understanding. But in theory there are also a number of sharp variations, where tactical points predominate. Here not only is logic not enough, but at times even the most keen positional feeling is inadequate. Exact knowledge is required. When deciding on such tactical play, you must retain in your mind a completely clear-cut set of opening moves.

Take for instance the Jaenisch Variation in the Ruy Lopez: 1 e4 e5 2 Nf3 Nc6 3 Bb5 f5. When playing this as Black, you must first of all study the sharpest continuation: 4 Nc3 f×e4 5 N×e4 d5 6 N×e5 d×e4 7 N× c6. And now—a whole series of variations: 7...b×c6 8 B×c6+ Bd7 9 Qh5+ Ke7 10 Qe5+ Be6 11 f4!, or 7...Qg5 8 Qe2 Nf6 9 f4 Qh4+ (9...Q×f4 10 N×a7+!) 10 g3 Qh3 11 Ne5+ (interesting is *11 N×a7+ Bd7 12 B×d7+ Q×d7 13 Nb5 c6! 14 Nc3 0-0-0 15 b3 Bb4! 16 a3 B×c3 17 d×c3 e3 18 0-0 Rhe8 19 Bb2 Qd2*, with very sharp play) 11...c6 12 Bc4 Bc5 13 c3! Ng4 14 d4 N×e5 15 Q×e4 etc.

Apart from the main variations, there are also many finesses of a tactical nature, which it is equally necessary to know. For example: 4 d4!? f×e4 5 N×e5 N×e5 6 d×e5 c6 7 Nc3!? c×b5 8 N×e4 d5 9 e×d6 Nf6 10 Qd4 N×e4 11 Q×e4+ Kf7 12 Bf4 Qe8 13 Be5 Qc6 14 Qf4+ Kg8 15 0-0-0, with boundless complications.

But what a large number of such tactical systems there are in opening theory! And each has a number of its own subtleties, which must be known and sensed to an equal extent.

Chess culture is not based on pure knowledge alone. It is also made up of a deep penetration into methods of play in typical positions. To the reader wishing to make a closer acquaintance with my methods of studying typical positions, I can recommend my book *Modern Chess Opening Theory* (Pergamon Press, 1965), where I examined ways of playing with different types of pawn centre, the formation of pawn weaknesses in return for piece activity, and so on.

But in the present section we will turn to examples from the play of two World Champions of different eras. Their mastery of play in typical positions is an indication of their extremely highly-developed chess culture.

Botvinnik–Kan
11th USSR Championship 1939

It is natural that White's plans should be associated with the weakness of the square d5, and the transfer of the knight to this square suggests itself: 14 e4 Nc6 15 Rfd1 Be6 16 Nf1 Rad8 17 Ne3. But after 17...Ne7 Black retains a very solid, defensible position. As soon as White places his knight on d5, there follows ...B×d5! followed by the transfer of the black knight to d6, when the advantage may even swing to Black.

The following decision by Botvinnik is highly instructive. He defers the occupation of d5, and first endeavours to extend his activity in the centre and on the K-side: **14 f4! Nd7 15 f5! Nf6? (15...f6 is better) 16 Ne4!**

Another instructive point. The knights have to be exchanged, since after this the activity of White's bishop increases sharply, while the black opposite-number remains passive.

16...Qd8 17 N×f6+ Q×f6 18 Be4 Rb8 19 Rad1 b6 20 h3 Ba6 21 Bd5 b5 22 c×b5 R×b5 23 c4 Rb6 24 Rb1.

White has an obvious advantage. Botvinnik plays the subsequent part of the game very exactly.

24...Rd8.

Black cannot occupy the b-file. After 24...

Rfb8 25 R×b6 Q×b6 there follows 26 f6!, with the very strong threat of 27 Qg6.

25 R×b6 a×b6 26 e4.

Parrying the threat of 26...R×d5, while at the same time 26...b5 27 c×b5 B×b5 28 Rb1 loses a pawn.

26...Bc8 27 Qa4! Bd7 28 Qa7 Be8 29 Rb1 Rd6 30 a4.

White has completely tied down the black forces on the Q-side, and now the threat of 31 a5! proves decisive.

30...Kh7 31 a5! b×a5 32 Q×a5 Ra6 33 Q×c5 Ra2 34 Qe3 Qa6 35 Rb8 Qa4 36 Kh2!

Right to the end White plays accurately. Now 36...Qc2 is refuted by 37 Qg3 Ra1 38 R×e8 Qd1 39 Qg6+!! f×g6 40 Bg8+ Kh8 41 Bf7+ Kh7 42 B×g6 mate!

36...Ra3 37 Qc5 Ra2 38 Ra8 Q×a8 39 B×a8 R×a8 40 Q×e5 Bc6 41 Qc7 Resigns.

In this game Botvinnik consistently carried out a stratagem, characteristic of modern strategy, of extending the scope of his operations on the basis of constant pressure on an organic weakness in the opponent's position.

Karpov–Parma
Caracas 1970

We have here a typical formation with a backward d6 pawn for Black. White's plan naturally involves trying to exploit this main weakness of Black's, but by the direct method of exerting pressure (Qd3, e3–e4 etc.) White cannot achieve a great deal. Karpov resorts to the device of extending his sphere of active operations.

29 f4! Re8 30 f×e5.

Karpov makes an instructive comment on this move: "30 f5 was also possible, but with the opponent having only one weakness (the d6 pawn) it would be more than difficult to win. But now, in addition to the weak pawn at e5, other advantages are added to my position, namely: occupation of the open file, and the possibility of starting combinational play".

30...d×e5 (30...R×e5 31 Qd4!) 31 c5! Re6 32 Qd3 b×c5 33 b×c5 (but not 33 Rd×c5 Rd8!, equalizing) **33...Qc6 34 Rb1 Qc7 35 Rf1 Rf8 36 Kh1 Qc6 37 Rb1.**

Although for the moment White has no clear plan for gaining a winning advantage, he has a strong hold on the initiative, and is skilfully maintaining the tension. All the time Black has to adjust to a range of white threats, and is doomed to a prolonged, gruelling defence. Black still has a chance of saving the game, but in practice it is very difficult to demonstrate this. We have one of those typical problem positions, where there is no clear win, but no clear draw.

37...Qc7 38 e4 Rb8 39 Rf1 Rb7 40 Qc3 Rb5 41 a4 Rb8 42 Rc1 Rc8 43 Rb1 Kg8 44 Rbd1 Qe7 45 Rf1 Rc7 46 a5 Rec6 47 Rc1 f6?

For a number of moves White has being trying to force this advance, which opens the 'sluice-gates' for an attack by the heavy pieces along the open lines. And here Black fails to stand the pressure, and makes this decisive weakening. Now White's initiative flares up into a powerful attack.

48 Qd2 Kf7 49 Kh2 Ke8 50 Rd6 Rd7.

Slightly better was 50...R×c5 51 R×c5 R×c5 52 R×a6, although even here it is not easy for Black to defend both his back rank and the d5 square.

51 Rd1 Rc×d6 52 c×d6 Qe6 53 Qd3 Qa2 54 Q×a6 Qc2 55 Qa8+ Kf7 56 Qd5+ Kg7 57 Rd2 Qc3 58 Ra2 h5 59 Rd2!

White's last two moves were not the most accurate, but now he reverts to the correct course, and confidently converts his advantage into a win.

59...h4 60 Rd1 Qc2 61 a6 Qa4 62 Qd3 g5 63 Rb1 f5 64 Rb7 g4 65 h×g4 f×g4 66 Qe2! Resigns.

Keep your cool!

It has long been observed that mistakes in a game of chess, like misfortunes in life, rarely happen in isolation. Very often the first error is followed by a chain reaction of mistakes, ending in defeat. Therefore it is especially important to maintain your composure and clarity of thought at that very moment when the game begins to go downhill. As the saying goes, know the edge, but don't fall over. By no means everyone, and by no means always, succeeds in doing this.

This position arose in the game **Ragozin–Keres** (Training Tournament Leningrad-Moscow, 1939). For Black it is highly promising, although it requires vigorous action on his part. 14...f5! was good, and after 15 e×f6 (or *15 Qd3 B×f3 16 g×f3 Ng5*) 15...R×f6 Black has strong counter-play along the f-file. But at this point Black deviates from the correct path, and then move by move worsens his position.

14...Na7?

A very slow manoeuvre. Black transfers his knight to b5, where it will be more stably posted, but in the meantime he loses his important outpost at e4.

15 Nbd2 Kh8.

Now 15...f5 is no longer good, in view of 16 e×f6, and Black is forced to capture with his knight on f6, when by 17 Qc2! White sets up strong Q-side pressure.

16 Bf4 f5.

A further inaccuracy. Black should have reconciled himself to a slightly inferior position, and played 16...N×d2. The pawn sacrifice which he makes proves to be unfounded.

17 e×f6 B×f6 18 N×e4 d×e4 19 R×e4 B×f3 20 g×f3! Nb5 21 Be3 Re8 22 Rg4 c6 23 Qd3 Ra7 24 Qc4 Qd5.

24...Qd6 25 Rc1 Rc8 was slightly better. The ending now reached is hopeless for Black.

25 Q×d5 c×d5 26 B×d5 Rd8 27 Bc4 N×d4 28 Kg2 Raa8 29 Rd1 Nf5.

An incurable weakness has been created in Black's position—his a6 pawn. At the same time, attempts to attack the a5 pawn prove unsuccessful, for example: 29...Nc6 30 R×d8+ B×d8 (*30...R×d8 31 Bb6*)

31 Bd5 Rc8 32 Rc4 Ne7 33 Bb6, and White wins.

30 R×d8+ B×d8 31 Bb6 Bf6 32 Bd5 Rb8 33 R×b4 g6 34 Bc4 Nh4+ 35 Kh3 N×f3 36 Bd4! Rf8 37 Rb8! Kg7 38 R×f8, and White soon won.

It is very much more rarely that one comes across the opposite picture, when a player succeeds in time in finding the necessary 'brake', enabling him to stop on the path to defeat.

Botvinnik–Romanovsky
11th USSR Championship 1939

In this complicated position White played **19 Rd2,** which is not the best. He achieves nothing by 19 Ne4 d5 20 Nc3 Bd7 21 e4 d×e4!, but he could have retained some pressure by continuing 19 a5! For example: 19...Ne5 20 Na4 Nc6 21 B×c6 b×c6 22 Nb6 c5 23 Qc3 Bb7 24 b4 etc. (pointed out by Botvinnik).

19...Ne5! 20 Rad1 Nf7! 21 Qe3.

Again a4–a5 followed by Na4 was stronger, retaining approximate equality.

21...Re8 22 a5 Bd7 23 b3 Bc6 24 Ne4 Rbd8 (with the threat of 25...d5 26 Nc5? d4) **25 Qc3 Rc8 26 Qb4!**

Here it is, the 'brake'. Seeing that in the middlegame Black's pressure is growing, White makes a sensible decision: he intends to take play into an ending, where he may be a pawn down, but will obtain an active position, sufficient for a draw.

26...B×e4 27 B×e4 d5 (White would probably have had more difficulties after 27...Rc7 followed by ...Rec8) **28 Q×e7 R×e7 29 Bg2 Rc3 30 e4!**

This energetic move would also have followed on 29...Nd6, with the possible variation 30 e4 N×e4 31 B×e4 d×e4 32 Rd8+ R×d8 33 R×d8+ Kf7 34 Rd4, when a draw is the most probable outcome.

30...d×e4 31 B×e4 R×b3.

This eases White's defence, but even after 31...Ng5 32 Bg2 R×b3 33 Rd8+ Kf7 34 R8d3! R×d3 35 R×d3 the draw would have been not far off.

32 Rd7 Kf8 33 B×h7! Rb5.

Nothing is achieved by 33...R×d7 34 R×d7 g6 35 B×g6 Ne5 36 Rd8+ Ke7 37 Re8+.

34 Be4 Ke8 35 R7d2!

Yet another important subtlety. After 35...R×a5 36 Bg6! Rc7 37 Rd8+ Ke7 38 B×f7 K×f7 39 Rd7+ White comfortably regains his pawn.

35...Rc7 36 Bg6 Ke7 37 B×f7 K×f7 38 Rd7+ R×d7 39 R×d7+ Kf6 40 h4 g6 41 Kg2 R×a5. Drawn.

We have examined a whole series of characteristic thinking deficiencies. It is readily apparent that all of them (loss of sense of proportion and flexibility, excessive self-confidence and restricting uncertainty, impulsiveness etc.) are closely allied one to another, and are sometimes simply interwoven. The eradication of these deficiencies requires first and foremost the development of creative thinking, in principle eliminating the routine and mechanical approach to the solution of complex chess problems. A far from minor role here is played by chess culture, the useful knowledge of a chess player.

Hand in hand with the development of thinking goes the education of a player's character. After all, the roots of many thinking defects lie equally in a player's character.

If, for example, at the board a player sins by overestimating his possibilities, and by a loss of objectivity, in life too he will often be noted for his superficiality. And, when working on overcoming the deficiencies in your play, you must in the first instance look into your own character, and think about what is hampering you, and what weaknesses have to be eliminated.

In a chess struggle there participates the entire intellect of a person, his spiritual world. And victory is yielded not only by thought, but also by will-power, composure, and an indomitable striving for the cherished goal.

5

DIRECT AND INDIRECT CONSEQUENCES OF TACTICAL MISTAKES

Up till now we have laid little emphasis on errors of a tactical or combinational nature, But it will have been readily apparent that, in a number of the illustrations given on various themes, we have encountered all sorts of tactical blows which decided the outcome of a game.

We will now dwell in more detail on mistakes of a tactical nature. Systemization is even more complicated here than with the mistakes examined earlier.

Mistakes which are difficult to rectify

It has long been known that tactical mistakes are the most punishable, and in many instances it is they that have a decisive influence on the fate of a game. Not without reason is it said that sometimes even forty best moves are not enough to win a game, whereas it only requires one tactical mistake for the fruits of lengthy effort to be completely ruined.

The causes of tactical mistakes lie not only in inadequate combinational vision or weakness in calculating variations. The number of additional causes giving rise to mistakes of this type is very great: impetuosity in time trouble, fatigue, carelessness, nerves, lack of natural attentiveness, and so on. We should also mention that on each occasion it is very difficult to establish the true cause of a particular oversight, since all the factors listed are closely interwoven.

Out of these causes we will especially single out excessive abstractness of thinking. Nearly always this leads to a loss of lively perception, and as a result of this to tactical oversights. In turn, abstract perception is promoted by the substitute methods examined earlier, namely: play on general considerations, 'reverse' thinking, thinking by analogy, dogmatism and so on. Constraint due to failure of abstract thinking can also result from distraction by some ephemeral strategic idea, or a radically incorrect evaluation of an initial position. Of course, with naturally highly talented, or well-trained players of the combinational type, the probability of a tactical 'defect' is small. But even brilliant combinational players are not insured against tactical oversights and even outright blunders.

As an example of this we will consider grandmaster Ratmir Kholmov. The basis of his strength has always been excellent combinational vision. He has to his credit a number of splendidly conducted combinations, arising not only during inspiring attacks, but also in the skilful application of tactical resources to defence (and this is a rather rare quality).

Here is one of his early creative achievements.

Kholmov–Filip
Bucharest 1953

18 Nc5 N×c5 19 d×c5 B×c4 20 Q×c4!

This looks like an oversight, since it permits a double attack. In reality, it is the start of a long, splendidly-calculated tactical operation.

20...Ng4.

The temptation is very great, especially since after 20...Nd5 21 B×g7 K×g7 22 Rd1 White's chances would be clearly preferable.

21 B×g7 Q×h2+ 22 Kf1 Qh4.

In the event of 22...Qh1+ 22 Ke2 Q×g2 24 Qf4 K×g7 25 Rg1 White wins a piece.

23 g3 Qh3+ 24 Ke2 K×g7 25 Rh1 Nh2 26 Qf4! Rd8.

Slightly better was 26...h6 27 Rag1 g5 28 Qe5+ Kg8 29 Qf6 Qg4+ 30 f3 Qh3, retaining certain drawing chances. The move made by Black involves a clever trap on the 30th move, which White, however, sees through.

27 Rag1 Qg4+ 28 f3 Qh5 29 g4 Q×c5 30 Rc1!

But not 30 R×h2? R×a2+!!, when it is Black who wins.

30...Qb5+ 31 Qc4 Qb8 32 Qf4 Qb5+ 33 Ke1 N×f3+ 34 Q×f3 Qd3 35 Rh2 Rd7 36 Re2.

Thus White has safely passed through the 'mine-field', and now reaps the fruits of his bold tactical raid. After **36...Rc8 37 R×c6 Qb1+ 38 Kf2 R×c6 39 Q×c6 Qd3 40 Bc2 Qd5 41 Q×d5 R×d5 42 e4 Re5 43 Bb3 Black resigned.**

Strangely enough, along with such examples there have been many instances in Kholmov's practice when in the heat of the struggle he has committed really childish oversights. And this comes from the harmful habit of casualness, from which, incidentally, many other well-known masters also suffer. When they begin to play quickly and by reflex, they sometimes overlook an elementary tactical point.

Instructive in this respect is the game **Suetin–Kholmov,** played in the Semi-Final of the 30th USSR Championship (Minsk, 1962).

1 e4 c5 2 Nf3 Nc6 3 d4 c×d4 4 N×d4 Nf6 5 Nc3 d6 6 Bg5 Bd7 7 Qd2 Rc8 8 Be2 N×d4 9 Q×d4 Qa5 10 f4 Qc5 11 Qd3 e6 12 0–0–0 Bc6 13 B×f6 g×f6 14 Kb1 h5 15 h4 a6 16 Bf3 b5 17 Ne2 f5!? 18 e×f5 B×f3 19 g×f3 Q×f5 20 Qd2.

From the opening Black has achieved a perfectly acceptable position, and by now playing 20...Qc5 he would have had definite prospects of counter-play. But in the heat of the battle, striving to seize the initiative as soon as possible, Kholmov makes a very significant tactical oversight.

20...Bh6? 21 Q×d6! Q×c2+ 22 Ka1 Bg7?

A further piece of carelessness, which leads to an immediate catastrophe.

23 Nc3!! Resigns.

23...B×c3 is met by 24 Qd7+, and 23... Ra8 by 24 Qc6+ Ke7 25 Rd7+ Kf6 26 Ne4+!

The next game shows clearly both Kholmov's perspicacity, and the deficiency we have just mentioned. Unfortunately, uneven play of this type is a hindrance to many strong players.

Kholmov–Deze
Zalaegerszeg 1977

1 Nf3 c5 2 c4 g6 3 d4 c×d4 4 N×d4 Nc6 5 e4 Nf6 6 Nc3 d6 7 Be2 N×d4 8 Q×d4 Bg7 9 Bg5 0–0 10 Qd2 Be6 11 Rc1 a6 12 b3 Qa5 13 0–0 Rfc8 14 Bf3!? Rab8 15 a4 Qb4 16 Qd1 h6 17 Bd2 Qb6 18 Nd5 N×d5 19 e×d5 Bf5 20 a5 Qc5 21 g4 Bd7 22 Re1.

The opening battle has concluded in favour of White, who has a spatial advantage in the centre and on the Q-side.

22...Re8 23 b4 Qd4! 24 Re4 Qb2! 25 c5 Rbc8 26 Qe1 Bb5 27 Kg2 Qa3 28 c×d6 e×d6 29 R×c8 R×c8 30 Re7 Rf8 31 R×b7 Re8 32 Qd1?!

Up till now Kholmov has played the game confidently, but here he is careless. He could have consolidated his positional advantage by 32 Re7! R×e7 33 Q×e7 Qa1 34 Qe1!

32...Qd3! 33 Bf4 Qc3 34 Qd2?!

Bad was 34 B×d6? Re1! 35 Rc7 Bf1+ 36 Kg3 Be5+, but the lesser evil was 34 Bd2. Now White finds himself in a difficult position.

34...Bf1+! 35 K×f1 (White loses quickly after 35 Kg3? g5!) **35...Q×f3 36 Be3 Q×g4?**

Black takes his revenge! Correct was 36... Re4!, when it is difficult for White to find a satisfactory defence.

37 Rc7 Qf3 38 b5!

After running into difficulties, Kholmov mobilizes himself, and begins playing with great tactical ingenuity. The conclusion of the game is highly instructive.

38...Re5? (38...Re4 is better) **39 b6 Rh5 40 Bf4 Be5 41 b7 Qh1+** (or 41...B×f4 42 b8=Q+ Kg7 43 Qc3+) **42 Ke2 Resigns.**

I should like to draw the reader's attention to one further problem, which, in my opinion, is of no small importance. Very often a veiled tactical idea must be 'grasped' immediately. Both from my own experience, and from the experience of other players, I have repeatedly been convinced that, if you do not see immediately a combinational situation on the board, and you sidestep it, you can overlook it altogether.

A curious case of tactical 'blindness' occurred in the game **Ebralidze–Ragozin** (10th USSR Championship, 1937).

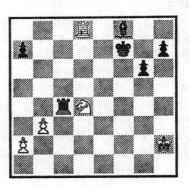

A pawn up in the ending, Black, who was in time trouble, planned the following tactical operation, which should have led to his immediate defeat.

39...Be7 40 Rd7 Rc7??

An optical illusion. On 41 R×c7 Black was intending to play 41...Bd6+, overlooking that this move is impossible. The control had now been reached, and White had more than sufficient time. And although Ebralidze not only thought for a long time, but could also hear the loud promptings of the excited spectators: "take the rook!", he nevertheless failed to 'see' that which had happened on the board. After lengthy reflection there followed **41 Rd5?? Bf6 42 Nb5 Rc2+ 43 Kg3 a6 44 Rd7+? Ke8 45 Rc7? Be5+**, and **White resigned.**

Of course, in such a unique form, chess blindness occurs extremely rarely. But many similar situations can be recalled.

All this, of course, does not mean that combinational vision 'operates' only in the first instant. On the contrary, in the majority of cases the full disclosure of the tactical essence of a position occurs by no means immediately, and depends on various factors. Many times I have had occasion to see and experience for myself how such 'illumination' came after long and tormenting searching, sometimes even in serious time trouble. And even so, I should like to recommend the reader not to forget the importance of the first glance at the position.

Dominating now in chess is a dynamic style of play, which sometimes acquires forms which are very sharp and full of combinational possibilities. And perhaps, one of the reasons for the popularity and promising nature of such a style is its effectiveness. Continually set the opponent specific problems, erect clever tactical barriers in his path—this is one of the mottos of this fighting strategy.

How many such examples can one count in the games of Mikhail Tal! He has the ability to start a tactical battle even in the most hopeless of positions.

Smyslov–Tal
*Candidates' Tournament,
Yugoslavia 1959*

Black's position appears desperate, and White's next strong move confirms this impression: **25 h4!**

The black queen has no convenient retreat square. 25...Q×c1+ 26 B×c1 B×c7 is bad because of 27 Ne7+ Kh8 28 N×c8 and 29 B×d7. Black finds the only practical chance.

25...Q×h4 26 N×e5 N×e5 27 R×c8 Nf3+!? 28 g×f3 Qg5+ 29 Kf1 Q×f5 30 R×f8+ R×f8 31 f×e4 d×e4.

Black's position is already so bad that it is difficult to hope even for a miracle. But, as the course of events shows, the game is by no means over.

32 Qe3 Rd8 33 Qg3 g5 34 Rc5 Rd1+ 35 Kg2 Qe6 36 b5.

White could have won more simply by 36 Qb8+ Kh7 37 Qc8!

36...Kh7 37 Rc6 Qd5 38 Qe5?

And here is the miracle for which Black was hoping. However, his desperate resistance is a good example for those who lose heart too soon. White could have won by 38 Qh2! e3+ 39 Kg3.

But in the heat of the battle White overlooks the threat of perpetual check, and loses control of the squares g1 and f3.

38...Rg1+! 39 Kh2 Rh1+ 40 Kg2 Rg1+.
Drawn.

Suetin–Tal
33rd USSR Championship 1965

The position is in favour of Black, who is a healthy pawn to the good. Wishing to increase his advantage, Black went in for a sacrifice of the exchange: **27...R×f3!?** 28 g×f3, and now incautiously captured the h3 pawn with his queen (28...Nf4 was much stronger). Now White begins a tactical counter-offensive, which, in turn, involves a sacrifice of the exchange.

28...Q×h3 29 R×d5 N×d5 30 Qe4 Nb6 31 Qb7 Bd8.

Events develop by force. There followed **32 B×e5! Qd7.** Black loses after 32...d×e5 33 R×e5 h5 34 Qf7.

33 B×d6?

Here it is—the instantaneous mistake! Correct, with the same tactical idea of exploit-ing the weakness of the 8th rank, was 33 Bd4!, after which White's threats are very dangerous. On 33...Kg8 there could have followed 34 Qe4 followed by Ng3, aiming for f5. After missing this tactical opportunity, White ends up in a lost position.

33...Kg8 34 Q×d7 N×d7 35 Re8+ Kf7 36 Rh8 Rc8 37 Kg2 Nb6 38 Ne3 Bf6 39 R×c8 N×c8 40 Bc5 Ke6.

The ending is hopeless for White. His Q-side pawns are doomed.

41 Kg3 Nd6 42 Kf4 Be5+ 43 Kg5 Bb2 44 Nc2 Nc4 45 Bd4 N×a3 46 B×g7 N×c2 47 B×b2 a3 White resigns.

Errors leading to positional concessions

Thus a serious tactical mistake, be it an error of calculation or a simple oversight, in many instances leads to retribution.

But is this the only way things happen? In many cases the consequences of a mistake assume a quite different aspect. A tactical error sometimes remains in the background, and one gains the illusory impression that there never was one, and that it was a positional mistake that was committed.

I will give yet another example from my bitter experience. In the game **Suetin–Kupreichik** (Daugavpils, 1978) Black played an eccentric opening variation: **1 d4 d5 2 c4 e6 3 Nf3 Nf6 4 Bg5 h6 5 B×f6 Q×f6 6 Nc3 d×c4?! 7 e4 a6 8 B×c4 b5 9 Bd3 c5.**

The most important stage of the opening battle has been reached. White has a big lead in development, but if he should fail to exploit it effectively, in time the potential advantages of Black's position may tell: the two bishops, and pressure on the centre.

In the game White failed to find the correct plan, and after **10 e5 Qd8 11 d×c5 B×c5 12 0–0 Ra7! 13 Qe2 Rd7 14 Rfd1 0–0 15 a4 b4 16 Ne4 Be7 17 Bc2 Bb7 18 R×d7 N×d7 19**

Ned2 Qc7 he not only allowed the opponent to equalize, but even incurred a rather inferior position.

And even so there was a way for White to gain a big advantage. I discovered this as soon as I arrived home, and cast a fresh glance at the critical position.

White should have played 10 Rc1!, when the rook comes very strongly into play along the c-file. The threat is 11 d×c5!, winning a pawn. On 10...Nd7 White has the unpleasant reply 11 e5 Qd8 12 d5! After missing this chance, White lost all prospect of retaining an advantage.

In the following example too, a tactical miscalculation by one of the players led to great positional inconvenience.

In this position from the game **Antoshin–Chistyakov** (Moscow, 1952) White, who was aiming for active play on the K-side, had just rashly played 16 g4? (*16 Rdf1 was better*). There followed a simple, but spectacular tactical blow: **16...Nd3!**, and to avoid the worst White had to agree to positional concessions: **17 N×e4 d×e4 18 Ba1 Bc5!**

It is important to exchange off White's centralized knight, and this, incidentally, will enable Black to penetrate along the only open file with his rooks.

19 Rdf1 B×d4 20 B×d4 e5!

There is no need to hurry with the intrusion on c2. Reckoning that the variation 21 B×e5

N×e5 22 f×e5 Q×e5 is completely unattractive for White, for the moment Black strengthens the positions of his pieces.

21 Bc3 b5 22 g5 b4 23 Ba1 Rc2 24 f5 Rfc8 25 f6.

Unsatisfactory is 25 Qg2 R×a2 26 Q×e4 R×a1! 27 Q×d3 e4 28 Qe2 Ra2 with a big advantage for Black. Thanks to his powerful knight at d3, Black has now completely tied down the enemy forces. All this is a consequence of White's tactical oversight on the 16th move.

25...Qe6 26 f×g7 R×a2 27 Rf6 Qh3 28 Rgf1 Rcc2 29 R×f7 R×a1!

But not 29...R×d2 30 Rf8+ K×g7 R8f7+, with a draw.

30 Rf8+ K×g7 31 R8f7+ Kg6 32 R7f6+ K×g5 33 R×a1 K×f6 34 Kg1 Qf3!, and Black won.

And now, for comparison, we will analyze an instance where a strategically lost situation arises as a result of purely positional inaccuracies.

Bagirov–Polugayevsky
45th USSR Championship,
Premier League 1977

1 d4 Nf6 2 c4 c5 3 Nf3 c×d4 4 N×d4 Nc6 5 Nc3 e6 6 e3 d5 7 c×d5 e×d5 8 Be2 Bd6 9 0-0 0-0 10 Bf3 Be5 11 N×c6 (11 Nde2 is better) **11...b×c6 12 Bd2 Qd6 13 g3 Bh3 14 Bg2 B×g2 15 K×g2 c5.**

Here Bagirov committed a typical mistake, incautiously weakening the white squares in his position by 16 f4?. Polugayevsky exploited his opponent's inaccuracy with the utmost precision to create an excellent text-book example.

16...B×c3 17 B×c3 Ne4 18 Qf3 Rfe8 19 Rfd1 Qb6 20 Rac1 Rad8 21 Rc2 d4!

A timely transformation of advantages. Now Black creates a strong passed pawn in the centre, which ties down White's forces still further.

22 e×d4 c×d4 23 Be1 Qa6 24 Qb3! h5 25 Qc4 Qb7 26 Qc6 Qe7 27 Ba5 Rd6 28 Qc7 Qe6 29 Qc4 Rd5 30 Bb4 a5 31 Be1 h4! 32 Qc6 h3+ 33 Kg1 d3 34 Q×e6 R×e6 35 Rc8+ Kh7 36 f5 Ree5 37 Rc4 d2 38 b4 Nc3! White resigns.

Incidentally, grandmaster Bagirov is an erudite player, and has a particularly good command of positional weapons. This game is completely unrepresentative of his style. As the saying goes: "every man has a fool in his sleeve!".

It seems to me personally that many positional errors in master games occur due to an incorrect calculation of variations, which indicates the indissoluble link between the elements of strategy and tactics in modern chess.

Of course, mistakes are by no means always as transparent, as was the case, for example, in the Antoshin–Chistyakov game. In order to disclose the bad side of this or that move, one frequently has to use the 'magnifying glass' of analysis.

Bronstein–Botvinnik
World Championship Match,
Moscow 1951

A complicated strategic battle is in progress. Black is aiming for active play on the K-side, while White intends to launch a minority attack on the Q-side, and in some cases to carry out the central advance e3–e4. Hoping to take the initiative as soon as possible, Black continued **14...g4?** He was counting on the variation 15 f×g4 N×g4 16 Nf4 Nf6! followed by ...Ne4, occupying with his knight a strong outpost in the centre. But the World Champion clearly underestimated the subtlety of White's 16th move. It should be mentioned that 14...Be6, completing his development, was better.

15 f×g4 N×g4 16 Bh3!

In view of the threat of 17 B×g4 f×g4 18 e4!, Black is forced to retreat his knight to a poor position, which allows White to quickly develop his offensive on the Q-side.

16...Nh6 17 Nf4 Bd6 18 b4 a6 19 a4 Qe7 20 Rab1 b5 21 Bg2 (21 Bd2 is more precise, keeping the knight at h6 tied down) **21... Ng4 22 Bd2 Nf6 23 Rb2 Bd7 24 Ra1 Ne4 25 Be1 Rfe8 26 Qb3 Kh8.**

Black defends against the threat of 27 a×b5 a×b5 28 R×a8 R×a8 29 N×d5! Nevertheless, he should have decided on 26...B×f4, since soon the white knight becomes highly active.

27 Rba2 Qf8 28 Nd3!

Although Black has succeeded in establishing his knight at e4, the general evaluation of the position is favourable for White. Having deployed his pieces actively, Bronstein prepares an intrusion along the a-file.

28...Rab8 29 a×b5 a×b5 30 Ra7 Re7 31 Ne5 Be8 32 g4!

A strong and unexpected tactical blow. White's hitherto inactive black-squared bishop comes very strongly into play.

32...f×g4 33 B×e4 d×e4 34 Bh4 R×e5.

This sacrifice is forced, since other continuations are no better. Thus after 34...R×a7 35 R×a7 the threat of 36 Nf7+ is immediately decisive, while 34...Rg7 35 Qe6 is winning for White.

35 d×e5 B×e5 36 Rf1 Qg8 37 Bg3! Bg7 38 Q×g8+ Resigns.

Often a player becomes carried away by the calculation of complicated variations, and forgets about the necessity for a correct evaluation of the position. Meanwhile he must evaluate correctly not only the initial position, but also all the positions which are reached in his mind during the calculation. By becoming involved in purely tactical problems, it is easy to lose one's positional orientation.

Here are some examples of this type.

This position was reached in the game **Faibisovich–Vorotnikov** (Daugavpils, 1978).

Not sensing the danger, Black played **11...Be7** (11...f6 is correct). Now White forcibly gains a clearly superior position. **12 d×e5! B×h3.** It was on this counter-blow that Black was counting, but... **13 Nh4 B×h4 14 Q×h3 Be7 15 Bf4 Nh6 16 Rfe1 Ng4 17 e×d6 c×d6 18 Rad1 0–0 19 Nd4.**

White's initiative develops quickly and effectively. Against the threats of 20 Nf5 and 20 N×c6 Black has no good defence.

19...Rfe8 20 N×c6 d5 21 N×e7+ R×e7
22 R×d5 R×e4 23 Be3 f5 24 Qf3 f4 25 Bd2 R×e1+ 26 B×e1 Re8 27 Rd1 Kh8 28 Q×f4 Q×c2 29 Qd2 Qc7 30 g3, and White soon realized his advantage.

Here, strictly speaking, Black did not commit any obvious oversight. The mistake of the Leningrad master was that, in considering his 11th move, he did not include in his calculations an evaluation of the position arising after 14 Q×h3. As a result, Black's badly placed pieces, and his weakness in the centre and on the white squares, quickly led to his defeat.

Such errors in evaluating the consequences of a move occur particularly often when a sharp tactical skirmish is replaced by purely positional problems. In such a skirmish, as they say, it is easy to lose one's head.

In the game **Kupreichik–Magerramov** from the same tournament, Black initiated very sharp tactical play in the centre: **1 e4 c5 2 Nf3 e6 3 d4 c×d4 4 N×d4 Nf6 5 Nc3 d6 6 Be3 a6 7 f4 b5 8 Qf3 Bb7 9 Bd3 Nbd7 10 g4 b4?! 11 Nce2 e5 12 Nb3 d5?! 13 Ng3 Be7 14 0–0–0 0–0 15 g5! d×e4 16 N×e4 B×e4 17 B×e4 N×e4 18 Q×e4 e×f4 19 Q×f4.**

The position has stabilized, and one can now make an evaluation of the complications which have occurred. They have proved clearly unfavourable for Black, and have merely created for White favourable conditions for storming the opponent's castled position. The young master playing Black must have been dispirited by the consequences of his apparently active play in the opening. Only this can explain why he should lose here within a few moves, without offering any resistance: **19...Qc8? 20 Nd4! Nc5 21 Nf5 Ra7 22 Qe5!,** and **Black resigned.**

In the majority of cases, calculating play is directly linked to the struggle for the achievement of positional gains. In turn, all positional manoeuvres must also first and foremost be specific and tactically justified.

Uhlmann–Larsen
Candidates' Match,
Las Palmas 1971

In this position White continued **14 Bb5+**.
This is certainly a natural move: it is tempting to deprive Black of the right to castle. And even so, there was plenty to think about here. Thus, 14 0–0 deserved serious consideration, and if 14...h6 *(14...0–0 15 B×h7+!* etc.), then 15 Qe2 0–0 16 Qe4! (recommended by Averbakh).

14...Ke7!

An interesting idea. Although Black's king is situated in the centre, it by no means prevents the mobilization of his forces. The co-ordination of his heavy pieces is maintained (which would not have been the case after the more 'logical' *14...Kf8*). Moreover, the white bishop at b5 is badly placed tactically, and there is already the threat of 15...Qb6. At the same time, White achieves nothing definite by 15 Bg5+ f6 16 e×f6+ g×f6 17 Bh4 Nf4!, or 17 Bh6 Qb6!

15 0–0 Qb6 16 Bd3.

16 Qe2 was slightly better. But White in this game is in the grip of natural moves, and as a result, their outwardly innocent banality becomes the cause of greater misfortunes.

16...h6! 17 Qe2 Rhd8 18 Bd2 Kf8.

Here, on the threshold of the middlegame, we can sum up. Black's pieces are very harmoniously and actively placed, and there is no longer any question of White having a lead in development. White's misfortune is that he has no good plan, and this allows his opponent to strengthen his position unhindered.

19 Rac1 Rac8 20 Rc2 a5 21 Rfc1 Kg8 22 h3 Ne7.

Although Black operates with the utmost simplicity, his threats continue to grow. He threatens not only 23...B×f2+, but also 23...Nf5 followed by B×f3 and ...Nd4!

23 Ne1 Bd4.

While improving the position of his black-squared bishop, Larsen radically breaks the pin on the c-file.

24 R×c8 R×c8 25 R×c8+ N×c8 26 b3.

This creates a serious weakening of the c3 square, but White is already doomed to a cheerless defence.

26...Ne7 27 Nf3 Bc5 28 Be1.

After 28 Be3 B×e3 29 Q×e3 Q×e3 30 f×e3 B×f3 31 g×f3 Nd5 the threat of 32... Nc3 is highly unpleasant.

28...Nf5 29 Kf1 Qc6!

The time for decisive action has come. The threat is 30...Nd4!.

30 Bb5 Qc7 31 Bd3 Nd4 32 N×d4 B×d4 33 f4 Qc1 34 Qd2 Qa1 35 Qc2 Bc3 36 Qb1 Ba6! A typical tactical blow to crown Black's excellent strategy. **White resigns.**

From the example of this game we have once again seen how important it is, even in a positional game, to think in concrete terms, taking account of the tactical peculiarities of the position.

6

THE PROBLEM OF CHOOSING A MOVE

For a long time chess literature has included a thorough study of the various principles and methods of strategy and tactics. But such a general problem as choosing a move, which is especially interesting from the psychological viewpoint, remains comparatively little studied. In the final analysis, ways of thinking essentially reduce to finding the best moves, and to the calculation of variations inevitably linked with this process. In Part I of this book, I devoted a special section to the problem of choosing a move. However, this theme obviously extends well beyond the bounds of a single section or article. Without attempting to encompass the unbounded, I should like to continue the discussion on this theme, and to dwell on certain questions which up till now have remained open.

Of course, there is an enormous number of positions where the choice of a move does not pose any problem. In a large number of cases the moves as though suggest themselves, since they are determined by the chosen plan, or by the development of a forcing variation. It is here, incidentally, that the scientific nature of chess is revealed, making it an intellectual skill.

Choosing a move is a fairly simple matter in well-known opening variations, in various exchanging operations, when parrying obvious threats, in theoretical endings, and so on. But at the same time there exists a vast number of positions, in which choosing a

move is a very difficult problem. The practical chess player realizes this in literally every game. When a real battle begins, there inevitably arise several genuinely creative moments, which demand not only knowledge and experience, but literally the full output of strength and energy. One such moment is generally regarded as the choice of a definite strategic plan at the transition into the middlegame. Similar problems often crop up at the transition into the endgame. And is it easy to find a move during a fierce tactical skirmish, abounding in complex variations?

It will be with difficult instances of choosing a move that this chapter will be concerned. Let us first dwell on the history of the question. A number of special studies have been written about the problem of choosing a move. A treatment of this topic has been suggested, for example, by grandmaster Kotov, and this can be found in the appropriate section of his book *Think Like a Grandmaster* (Batsford, 1971) and also in the section 'The calculation of variations' in *Paul Keres Chess Master Class*, by Neishtadt (Pergamon Press, 1983). It should be mentioned that Kotov approaches the problem mainly from the practical viewpoint. It was he who introduced such concepts as 'tree of analysis', 'candidate moves' and 'infiltrating' moves.

In recent years a number of interesting works have been published by N. Krogius, chess grandmaster and doctor of psychological sciences. His books, which are closely linked with the study of chess psychology, are well known, and are of topical significance for the problem we are considering.

But now we will dwell in more detail on the little-known, but interesting works of the Soviet master and methodologist B. Blumenfeld. Many of the points raised by him are unusual, and at the same time have not lost their theoretical significance to this day.

In considering them, we will draw parallels with modern opinions.

Visual imagination and the calculation of variations (based on material in an article by Blumenfeld in *Shakhmaty v SSSR*, 1936, No. 1).

In his interesting article, Blumenfeld emphasizes first of all the importance of the correct calculation of variations. "The correcting of defects in the thinking process is no less important that the perfecting of opening knowledge", he writes.

Blumenfeld attaches great importance to the question of the fixing with the visual imagination of all positions after each mentally made move (one's own and the opponent's). The reason for blunders in games is very often carelessness in fixing the intermediate positions.

We will consider an example on this theme which is given by Blumenfeld.

In this position from the game **Blumenfeld-Zhivtsov**, played in the Semi-Final of the 1935 Moscow Championship, Black placed his bishop *en prise*: **1...Be4??**.

It is curious that up to this point Zhivtsov had played well, and was not in time trouble. Before making his move, he considered the position for quite a long time. In making this move, he calculated that the bishop could not be taken, in view of the variation 1...Be4 2 B×e4 Q×e5 3 Bh7+ K×h7 4 Q×e5 Nd3+, regaining the queen, but he 'forgot' that after **2 B×e4** the rook at a8 was attacked.

This seems paradoxical: the player with Black calculated a fairly long variation, and at the same time made a bad blunder. Blumenfeld sees the reason for the oversight as being that his opponent did not fix in his mind the bishop from c2 on the square e4, but as though held it in mid air, aiming for the square h7, so as after the check to capture the queen. In Black's calculations there figured only one tactical idea: the bishop from c2 aiming for h7. But on the way to it there was the 'transit' point e4. But this 'stop' was not made by the visual imagination.

The author remarks that, in the majority of cases, such mistakes do not result from weakness of visual imagination, but as a result of nervous haste or insufficient intensity of will-power. Blumenfeld writes: "On mentally making a move, you may be too lazy to fix the change promptly with your visual imagination, and often you allow yourself the privilege of making a move as a result of a conversation with yourself, or by reproducing the notation of the move in your mind, or else by a spatial movement in the mind, but without firmly fixing with the visual imagination the position after the move".

It can be concluded that sometimes the impression created by the visual imagination supplants reality. Often movements in the mind during the calculation of one variation hinder the correct representation of a position reached in another variation. It follows that the greater the number of variations, and the longer they are, the greater is the probability of tactical mistakes.

Blumenfeld warns against excessive enthusiasm for calculating long variations when choosing a move. With each move made in the mind, the position created becomes more and more removed from reality, and the impressions arising from move to move of the intermediate positions become more and more faint. After all, the thinking of a player is inseparably linked with visual imagination. Therefore the clearer the visual picture, the easier and more accurately the thinking works.

Blumenfeld thinks that the calculation of lengthy variations also involves the danger of unnecessary mental exertion, the fatigue from which can affect the subsequent play.

Not without instructional value are the following conclusions and pieces of advice of the author. We give them in somewhat abridged form.

After a move by the opponent you should begin thinking not from preconceived conclusions, made beforehand, but as though anew, first impressing with a glance the resulting position on your mind. However strongly developed your visual imagination, it is obvious that the representation in your mind is weaker than the direct visual perception. Never be hasty, and don't, without thinking, make a reply prepared beforehand.

You should observe a strict inner discipline when considering variations, and in particular you should not jump in your thoughts from one variation to another, returning several times to the same ones, but should establish an order for considering the variations...

In establishing the order of consideration, you should proceed with the aim of reducing the number and length of the variations. In the first instance you should examine what on first impression seems to be the most dangerous reply to the proposed move... And only if a defence is found against this reply should you try to see whether or not the opponent has some other, less obvious path.

If there is the opportunity to choose between two continuations of roughly equal effect, it is better to select the path which contains the fewer variations, and, consequently, the less danger of a mistake.

Foreseeing objections on the part of admirers of beauty in chess, Blumenfeld makes the following comment: "The calculation of variations is only a necessary technique, and if it is possible to simplify or facilitate this technique, so much the better. The beauty of chess lies in its intrinsic logic and richness of ideas... And calculation is needed only to check the correctness of these ideas".

In our time, practice as a whole rejects the conception of a strict limitation of the calculation of variations. Even the most fervent rationalists, who strictly husband their calculating capabilities, in case of necessity will carry out truly brain-racking calculating work.

Without the calculation of 'superfluous' variations, it is impossible to get by in the modern dynamic struggle—such has been the evolution of chess thinking. It should not be forgotten that Blumenfeld expressed his views more than 40 years ago, and besides, he leaned almost exclusively on his comparatively slight practical experience. And if today his conception appears old-fashioned and rather naïve (a player who avoids calculations reminds one of an ostrich hiding its head in the sand when escaping from danger), certain of Blumenfeld's observations remain highly interesting. And in particular they can be addressed to young players of 1st or 2nd category (cf. p. ix) for work on the technique of calculation. Questions of 'fixing', discipline of thinking, attention to the visual image, the useful economizing of strength etc.—all these are important factors in the very difficult work of calculation.

Problems of time utilization when choosing a move

This problem was also studied by Blumenfeld, in an article published in *Shakhmaty v SSSR*, 1937, No.9.

Here are the main points raised by him.

The choice of a move is not the solving of a theoretical problem, but the taking of a decision in a conflict situation, taking into account all the important points, and in particular not only the objective virtues of the move, but also the balance of time for thought.

As an example he considers the position arising after 16 moves in the game **Alekhine-Reshevsky** (Kemeri, 1937).

In this position the exchange of queens suggests itself (17 Q×f5), after which White retains a clear advantage, since he essentially has an extra pawn on the Q-side. Alekhine, however, continued **17 Qg3!?**, thereby electing for a double-edged struggle. Jumping ahead, we should say that the game was won by him with a beautiful combination, after a mistake committed by the opponent in serious time-trouble. But let us see how this happened.

17 Qg3 e5 18 Be3 Bb4 19 Na4 Ba5! 20 f4! Bc7 21 b3 f6 22 f×e5 Qe6 23 h3 Rhg8 24 Bd4 N×e5 (24...f×e5 is better) 25 Qc3! Nd7 26 c5! Rge8 27 b4! Nb8 28 Nb6+ B×b6 29 c×b6 Q×a2 30 Qg3! Rd7 31 Bc5 Qf7 32 Ra1 Qg6 33 Qh2! Re5 34 Ra8 Rd2 35 R×b8+! K×b8 36 Q×e5+! Resigns.

Alekhine's choice on his 17th move, as Blumenfeld sees it, was motivated by an aggregate of specific reasons, where psychological factors played a far from minor role. There was his conviction of his superiority in such situations even over such a player as Reshevsky, and also the fact that Reshevsky was a fervent 'time-trouble sufferer', and that it was in double-edged, concrete play that he was likely to run short of time.

Blumenfeld links the amount of time spent in thought with the will-power factor in calculation. If a player feels a sense of uncertainty, a large part of his time may be wasted on regretting mistakes made earlier, or even the chosen plan as a whole. Much time can be fruitlessly wasted due to a lack of the necessary organization in the calculation of variations. The principle of economizing on time when considering a move should be an essential one for every practical player. But, as Blumenfeld sees it, simultaneously there should be a minimum time spent in thought. If, for example, you set yourself the rule of making even the most obvious moves only after five to ten seconds of thought, this can eliminate many mistakes. This is a sensible piece of advice. Incidentally, when spectating at a strong tournament where grandmasters and masters are playing, young players will find it beneficial to follow the truly majestic unhurriedness with which the players make the most obvious moves. As with an experienced driver of a car, in the most rapid movement of a master (apart from play in time trouble, of course) there is no convulsive haste. On the other hand, in games between inexperienced players we often observe hasty, purely reflex movements of the hands, for which they sometimes have to pay dearly, both in factors of play, and in time.

Blumenfeld warns against unproductive waste of time, arising as a consequence of vague fears: "Isn't there some unpleasant surprise lying in wait for me?" It should be mentioned, however, that this process can be evaluated in more than one way.

As we already know, a very large number of players see their own tactical possibilities incomparably better than unexpected moves on the part of the opponent. Therefore, avoiding groundless fears, it is nevertheless useful to check whether or not there isn't some hidden trick when, for example, the opponent makes what appears to be a losing move. In the heat of a game players sometimes forget about a highly important difference between chess and draughts: it is not obligatory to capture! Even during the most simple exchanges, there is the possibility of unpleasant intermediate moves, which must be foreseen.

In short, the distance between groundless and genuine fears is not always so great.

At the end of his article Blumenfeld raises a number of problems which, in his opinion, deserve special study: how to utilize the time when the opponent is thinking; training methods applicable to the problem of economizing on time; which time control is the most expedient; whether thinking is affected by the quality of the equipment and the conditions of play, etc. To this day certain of these questions remain open.

In connection with this I should like to dwell on the following point. Somehow, up till now little consideration has been given to a limit on the maximum time spent in thought on one move. Sometimes even the most experienced players can think over an individual move for a whole hour, and sometimes even longer.

In connection with this, I should like to share certain observations made by me of Fischer's play in 1971 during his match with Petrosian in Buenos Aires. What was striking was the following: even in the most complicated situations he set himself a rather strict limit on time for thought. The maximum was half an hour. Then he would cast off his doubts and come to a decision. Incidentally, Fischer endeavoured with enormous con-

centration of effort to utilize the time when it was the opponent's turn to move. Although Fischer himself played quickly, for literally the full five hours of play, apart from necessary pauses, he worked intensively at the board.

Of course, such thinking traits are strictly individual. And even so, the key to optimum solutions should be sought in the practice of the world's leading players. From them one must learn an economic attitude to one's reserve of time.

Combinational vision

Practice shows that the calculation of variations involves a highly complex mechanism. The 'heart' of it is a penetration into the combinational subtleties of the position, and in this respect calculation is a kind of function of combinational vision. It is necessary to possess this special vision in order to disclose the combinational harmony of a particular position. Without this, calculation would be transformed into a senseless, purely formal operation.

Combinational vision and the calculation of variations are very closely interlinked. The vision greatly facilitates, and sometimes replaces the calculation; in turn, a correct calculation checks the accuracy of the image seen by the player.

Even inexperienced players are attracted mainly by the beauty and inexhaustible nature of combinations. What combinational miracles we see happening in the game of chess! For this reason combinational vision is virtually the most necessary weapon of a chess player. Without possession of it, there can be no question of progress. It is no accident that such an outstanding methodologist as grandmaster Richard Réti said: "Before attempting to play positionally, you should learn to make combinations. You will perhaps lose a few games, but on the other hand you will learn to play chess!'"

At the same time, how often even the most experienced fighters are let down by deficiencies in combinational 'vision'. To give a detailed systemization of such deficiencies is a very complicated matter, since we are dealing with the most frail and delicate aspect of chess thinking. I should merely like to draw the attention of the reader to certain psychological factors, which influence the distortion of combinational vision.

With this aim it is useful to make the acquaintance of the section 'Mysteries of chess images' in Krogius's book *O Psikhologii Shakhmatnovo Tvorchestva* (Fizkultura i Sport, 1969).

Here are some of the points covered in considerable detail by the author. We will approach them from the viewpoint of purely tactical problems.

A residual image signifies the transference in immutable form of the evaluation of a previous position to a new situation. In this way the past obscures reality, distorting correct vision.

There is a vast number of examples of this type. It is the presence of a residual image which often leads to oversights, and even to blunders. I give the following instance from my own practice. The diagram position arose after White's 33rd move in the game **Kudryashov–Suetin** (Daugavpils, 1978).

It is easy to see that Black has a won position. He has an extra pawn, which is also passed, and without delay he sets it in motion: **33...e3! 34 Qf3 Rd2 35 Ne2 b4 36 Rc1 Bd6 37 Rh4.**

When I went in for this whole variation, I had planned 37...Rg4 here, which was in fact the correct path, leading most quickly to the goal. But expectedly the idea came to me of playing more simply, and, although I had sufficient time in reserve, I quickly played 37...Qd5?? It was here that, to my horror, I noticed that White could simply capture the e3 pawn, and that the fruits of my labour were completely ruined. There can be only one reason for this blunder. The e3 pawn was the basic pivot of Black's position, and until the last move it was more than adequately defended: But in the heat of the tactical struggle I first deprived it of the protection of my bishop (which, of course, had no consequences and was justified in concrete terms), and then, under the illusion that the passed pawn was defended, the 'nightmare' queen move was made. After **38 Q×e3 Rg4 39 Rh5! Rd1 40 Qh6 Rg7** the situation had sharply changed. It is true that subsequently I succeeded, as they say, in winning the game for the second time, but this lies entirely on the 'conscience' of my opponent.

Like many other features of chess thinking, the residual image can sometimes be a useful support, providing that there is conscious regulation and the necessary self-control. One can often follow how an experienced tactician, on noticing a clever combinational motif, like a true hunter will patiently 'shadow his victim': he will engage in diversionary manoeuvres, carefully mask the prepared trap, and lull the vigilance of the opponent.

For an example we will turn to the play of David Bronstein, which is rich in interesting ideas. Here are two curious episodes from his games.

This position arose in the game **Bronstein–Reshevsky** (Candidates' Tournament, Zurich, 1953).

In this game, which was of great competitive significance, both players were in serious time trouble. White, who was playing for a win, chose a risky path, which, however, involved a cunning trap.

38 Rc8?!

More cautious was 38 c4, to which Black should have replied 38...Re5!, holding the position.

38. . .N×f2! 39 c4 Ra5 40 Bb3.

Here it is—the 'bait'. In time trouble Black feverishly made the natural move, and fell into the prepared trap: **40...Ra3? 41 Bc5!**

This double attack (the threat of mate after 42 Bf8+ and the attack on the rook) immediately decides the game.

41...Be7 42 B×a3 B×a3 43 c5! e3 44 c6 Ne4 45 Re8 f5 46 Bc4 Bd6 47 c7 B×g3+ 48 Kg2 B×c7 49 Re7+ Kf6 50 R×c7 f4 51 Kf3 Resigns.

The following diagram shows a position from the game **Mikenas–Bronstein** (33rd USSR Championship, 1965).

Here too Bronstein prepared a veiled combinational blow. He played **23...Qe5!,** as though inviting White to make the natural move **24 Rb4,** by which he simultaneously guards his rook against the threat of 24... Qe1+, and also the b2 pawn. But it was this move that Black was hoping for! There followed **24...R×a3!!,** and **White resigned.** Mikenas 'forgot' about the tactical weakness of his back rank (24 Qd2 was correct).

In these examples the residual image played a positive role.

But let us not digress from our basic theme. Here we are talking mainly about negative features which distort our 'vision'. Let us now consider a kind of antipode of the previous image—the advance image. When it arises, the role of coming events in the game is overestimated. Sometimes the desired supplants the actual. Here I make use of the following truly staggering case, which is cited by Krogius.

We have here a position from the game **Capablanca–Ryumin** (3rd Moscow International Tournament, 1936) after White's 26th move. All the battle lies ahead, and what's more, Black's position looks the more promising. That is probably also what Ryumin thought. This most likely also influenced the following gross oversight. Carried away by searches for active possibilities, he conceived the idea of creating an immediate combinational threat—26...Nc5, planning an attack on f2. He confidently picked up his knight at d7, and only then remembered that his queen was *en prise!*

It will be remembered that Ryumin was a brilliant tactician, with great combinational talent. But in the course of the battle anything can happen. In the given instance the master of the situation became the negative advance image.

Of course this example is more of a caricature than an illustration of the theme in question. But even a caricature can sometimes present an effective lesson.

Note that an excessive striving to leap ahead can lead to a narrowing of the field of attention. But there must not escape from it the so-called intermediate moves of the opponent. Combinational ideas, even the most attractive ones, must not be carried out hastily and uncontrolledly.

As Krogius correctly emphasizes, in good hands advance images, like residual images, can be important factors in developing the ability to foresee events on the chess board. Indeed, who, for example, can deny that Ryumin's idea in the example considered was tactically attractive? It could have become formidably strong, if Black had first retreated his queen, say, to a7...

The distortion of combinational vision is closely linked to disturbance of a player's attention. Of course, attention depends upon strictly individual features. At the same time there are general principles which are obliga-

tory for all players. During play a player must concentrate only on his own game, and has no right to allow his attention to wander. This will enable him, if not to eliminate oversights completely, then at least to avert many of them.

The reader wishing to make a closer acquaintance with the causes of disturbance of combinational vision is directed to the aforementioned work by Krogius.

It should be remembered that deficiencies of attention and lack of composure can be overcome only by constant and tireless training and systematic self-education. Normally such work includes both main components of the process of concrete thinking. 'Vision' is inseparable from calculation!

This applies especially to modern dynamic battles, which are literally sated with calculating play.

Timman–Sigurjonsson
Geneva 1977

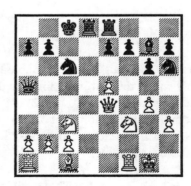

Right from the opening in this game there began a very tense battle, demanding first and foremost sharp combinational vision and deep calculation of variations. Objectively, White has gained a certain advantage, but on the way to his goal there are numerous dangers to be avoided.

16 Re1! Ng8 17 a3 f5 18 e×f6?!

White fails to investigate thoroughly into the essence of the position. Much stronger was 18 Qc4!, with the unpleasant threat of b2–b4, when it is difficult for Black to find a satisfactory defence.

18...N×f6 19 Qe6+ Nd7 20 Nd5 Rf8 21 Bf4 Qc5+ 22 Kg2(?).

A further inaccuracy. It was better to keep the king on the back rank—22 Kh1. At g2 in a number of variations it allows an unpleasant check along the second rank.

22...g5!? 23 Be3?

Here too White fails to find the correct reply. However, there has now arisen a complex labyrinth of variations, where White is really required to rack his brains. Bad, for example, is 23 B×g5?? R×f3!, or 23 N×g5? R×f4 24 N×f4 Q×g5, when Black wins. The correct move was 23 b4!, with the possible continuation 23...Q×c2+ 24 Re2 Qg6 25 Q×g6! h×g6 26 Rc1 g×f4 27 b5.

23...Q×c2+ 24 Nd2 Kb8! 25 N×e7?

And this is already the decisive oversight, leading to White's defeat. Comparatively better was 25 Rac1, although even here after 25...Qg6 Black has the advantage.

25...N×e7 26 Rac1.

White also loses after 26 Q×e7 Ne5 27 Re2 R×d2 28 B×d2 Qc6+ 29 Kh2 Re8 etc.

26...Nc5! 27 Q×e7 R×d2+ 28 B×d2 Q×d2+ 29 Qe2 Q×e2+ 30 R×e2 Nd3 White resigns.

Up till now in this second part of the book I have been aiming to study the practical thinking of a chess player, proceeding from various characteristic mistakes, both of a positional and a tactical nature. I think that this comparatively little-used methodological approach is lawful, and, moreover, that it

should stimulate independent work by those wishing to improve.

I should also remark that in many ways a chess player is similar to an inventor. And is the work of an inventor easy? Remember Edison, for instance. He carried out more than a thousand unsuccessful experiments before making a great discovery.

A young player should have a clear impression of the numerous delusions and devious paths that he will encounter on the road to mastery, against which I have warned in the basic material compiled in this second part of the book.

The time has come to turn to positive aspects of thinking. But before doing so, let us dwell specially on one particular 'weed'. We have in mind the all-corrosive 'mildew'—banality. We have already referred to it in previous sections. Let us consider this problem as it applies to choosing a move.

The harmfulness of routine moves

Chess players well know that it is much simpler to lose a game than to win it! To do so it is by no means necessary to make bad mistakes. One can lose, and fairly quickly at that, without making any obvious errors.

Here is a brief example on this theme. The diagram position arose in the game **Fokin–Suetin** (Daugavpils, 1978) after Black's 12th move.

The opening was a double-edged and comparatively little-studied branch of the Meran Defence. Theory evaluates the position as slightly more favourable for White, mainly on account of the organic weakness of the e6 pawn. At the same time Black has no difficulties over his development, and is ready, in the absence of any specific hindrances, to deploy his forces actively (as in fact occurred in the game).

13 Bg5 (preferable is 13 0-0, not determining for the moment the position of the black-squared bishop, and intending in some cases to advance the knight to g5) **13...Bc5 14 Qe2 Bb7 15 0-0 0-0 16 Rad1?**

White, who appears to have positioned his pieces securely, but who has played without a definite plan, turns out to be in a difficult position. Now, strangely enough, Black wins virtually by force.

16...Ng4! 17 h3.

Also bad is 17 g3 Nde5 18 Bf4 N×f2! 19 R×f2 N×f3+ 20 Q×f3 e5 etc.

17...Nde5!

The decisive tactical thrust. As in a summer storm, the thunder clouds gather instantly over the white king.

18 N×e5.

White also loses after 18 h×g4 N×f3+ 19 g×f3 Qg3+! 20 Kh1 Qh3+ 21 Kg1 R×f3, or 18 Nd4 B×d4 19 R×d4 Nf3+.

18...N×f2! 19 Rd7 Q×e5 20 Be3 N×h3+, and **White resigned.**

The cause of White's defeat was his routine, although apparently perfectly good moves, which were lacking in any intrinsic logic. In making them, my opponent completely overlooked that, at an early stage of the game, Black could launch a very dangerous combinational attack on his king. Routine became the cause of great misfortunes.

Highly interesting in this respect is the game **Sämisch–Alekhine** (Dresden, 1926).

1 d4 Nf6 2 Nf3 b6 3 c4 Bb7 4 e3 e6 5 Bd3 Bb4+ 6 Bd2 B×d2+ 7 Nb×d2 d6 8 0-0 Nbd7.

At this point Sämisch made the perfectly natural move **9 Qc2.** At first sight, for the moment there is no need for White to be concerned with tactical nuances. At the same time he is guided by what is in general the correct strategical aim: control of e4. And nevertheless, after 9 Qc2 Black succeeds in consolidating his position and averting the exchange of his important white-squared bishop. Alekhine therefore recommends the interesting move 9 Ng5, with the possible continuation 9...h6 10 Nge4 0-0 11 f4 d5 12 Ng3 c5 13 Qe2 followed by Rad1, assessing this position as favourable for White.

Regarding this point, Alekhine makes the following comment in his book *On the Road to the World Championship 1923–1927* (Pergamon, 1984): "Small causes can have great effects! Thus we see how important it is to take the greatest care in planning the early layout of one's game. In this connection nothing is more damaging than a stereotyped approach, for it always conceals the danger of incurring a direct disadvantage, and in any case tends to deprive the game of all meaning. This attribute certainly had a lot to do with the appearance, a few years ago, of the spectre of the 'drawing death', an apparition which, thank God, was pretty quickly exorcised by the arrival of a number of talented young players who preferred to think for themselves."

The game continued **9...0-0 10 Rad1 Qe7 11 Ng5.**

With a delay of two moves. Alas, White has 'missed the boat'.

11...h6 12 Nh7 Rfd8 13 N×f6+ N×f6 14 Ne4 c5 15 N×f6+ Q×f6 16 d×c5.

As before, White plays sluggishly and routinely. Now Black gains a further trump—the half-open b-file. Better was 16 Rfe1!

16...b×c5! 17 Rd2 Rab8 18 Rfd1 Bc6 19 b3 Qe5! 20 Qb2 Q×b2 21 R×b2 a5 22 Rbd2 Kf8 23 Bc2 Ke7 24 f3 a4!

In contrast to the previous example, the retribution for White's routine play does not follow immediately. The ending is unpromising for White, a factor which Alekhine very accurately exploits.

25 Kf2 a×b3 26 B×b3 f5 27 Ke2 Rb4 28 Kd3 Ba4 29 B×a4 R×a4 30 Rb1 Ra3+! 31 Ke2 (31 Rb3 Rda8!) 31...Rc3 32 a4 Ra3! 33 Rb7+ Rd7 34 Rdb2 R×a4 35 R×d7+ K×d7 36 Rb7+ Kc6 37 R×g7 R×c4 38 Rg6 Kd5 39 R×h6 Rc2+ 40 Kf1 c4 41 Rh8 c3 42 h4.

Also after 42 Rc8 f4! 43 e×f4 Kd4 44 h4 Ke3 45 Kg1 K×f4! 46 h5 Kg5 47 g4 d5 Black wins easily.

42...Rd2! 43 Ke1 R×g2 44 Rc8 c2 45 h5 Rh2 46 h6 R×h6 47 R×c2 Rh1+ 48 Kd2 Rh2+ 49 Kd3 R×c2 White resigns.

A curious analogy. As we have already seen, tactical miscalculations or oversights are punishable both in the direct, and in the indirect sense. In certain cases they entail immediate retribution, while in others this can be avoided, but as a consequence of the mistake the position is significantly weakened. We see a similar picture in the event of routine thinking, although in character this is a defect of a different type. Different mistakes can result in identically sad consequences.

The most difficult move in the game

I first met this concept in my youth, when I was studying Alekhine's games with his wonderful annotations. I think that it was he who brought into widespread use the concept of the most difficult move in the game. For the great artist of chess, this term had a very wide range: from a brilliant combinational blow and its associated volcano of fantastic variations, to the most subtle positional manoeuvre.

Alekhine–Koltanowski
London 1932

In this game, where up till then there had been strictly positional play, White unexpectedly played 22 N×c7!

Regarding this move, Alekhine writes: "As a rule, so-called 'positional' sacrifices are considered more difficult, and are rated more highly, than those based on the exact calculation of tactical possibilities.

I think that the present position represents an exception, since the great number and the complexity of the variations associated with the knight sacrifice demanded considerably greater intensive mental work than any overall evaluation of the mutual possibilities".

22...R×c7 23 R×d6.

Here Alekhine gives a detailed analysis, in which splendid calculation is combined with penetrating combinational vision:

I. 23...B×b3? 24 Q×f6+ and then 25 R×b3;

II. 23...Nd4? 24 N×d4;

III. 23...Qc4 24 N×c5!;

IV. 23...Nd8 24 Rf3 Rf7 25 N×c5;

V. 23...Bf7 24 R×f6! Nd4 25 N×d4 c×d4 26 Q×c7+ K×f6 27 Rf3+;

VI. 23...Re8 24 N×c5 Nd8 25 b4 Nf7 26 R×e6;

VII. 23...Kf7 24 Rf3 Ke7 25 a4 Qb6 26 R×e6+ K×e6 27 N×c5+ Kd6 (or 27... Kf7 28 Q×f6+ Kg8 29 Ne6!) 28 Q×f6+ K×c5 29 Rc3+ Kb4 30 Qd6+.

The game went **23...Bc4 24 a4! Q×a4 25 N×c5 Qb5 26 Q×f6+ Kg8 27 Nd7! Rd8 28 Rf3 Qb4 29 c3 Qb5 30 Ne5! Rdc8 31 N×c6 Resigns.**

Stahlberg–Alekhine
Hamburg, 'Tournament of Nations', 1930

In this example Alekhine finds a 'quiet' move which decides the game.

30...h6!

Black prepares the spectacular combinational blow 31...R×f3! 32 Q×g5 R×f2. In the event of 31 Qd2 he wins by 31...B×f3 32 N×f3 N×f3+ 33 R×f3 R×f3 34 Q×g5 R×f1+ 35 R×f1 R×f1+ 36 K×f1 h×g5

37 Ke2 Kf7 38 Kf3 Ke6 39 Ke4 b5!, when the pawn ending is won for Black.

31 Kh1 R×f3!! White resigns.

Such moves, 'imperceptible' but powerful in their consequences, are a sign of intricate mastery of tactical skill. In the given instance the pawn move was the introductory chord to an attack on the king. But, of course, the aims of such quiet moves can be the most varied.

Karpov–Savon
Alekhine Memorial,
Moscow 1971

One gains the impression that the energetic advance of the a-pawn has given Black active counter-play on the Q-side. Now 18 Qb3 looks the most natural, but then Black replies 18...Nc6, and the threat of ...N×d4 retains him good chances. This is possibly what Savon had been counting on, but Karpov made the quiet, 'short' move **18 Qc1!**, which cast doubts on Black's plan. With one exact move White takes control of the squares b2 and c6.

Now all the specific variations lead to an advantage for White. Possibly the lesser evil was 18...c5 19 b×a3! c×d4 20 a×b4 d×e3 21 N×e4 d×e4 (or *21...B×e4 22 Q×e3 B×b1 23 Rf×b1*) 22 Q×e3, when White comes out a pawn up and with good winning chances.

In the game it was all over much more quickly: **18...Ra6?! 19 b×a3 Rc6 20 Qb2 Nc2** (bad is 20...N×d2 21 B×d2 Nd3 22 Qb3!) **21 Rc1 N×e3 22 R×c6 N×f2 23 Nf1 Qd7 24 N×e3 Resigns.**

Incidentally, the twelfth World Champion is noted for his amazing ability to find outwardly imperceptible, but highly exact moves. I should like to give a further example from this series. If up till now we have been examining positions where the correct choice of move consolidated an advantage already achieved, we will now dwell on an equilibrium situation. The responsibility and difficulty of finding a move here are by no means less, if not more, than in positions with an obvious advantage.

Karpov–Portisch
Portoroz 1975

A tense struggle for space and the initiative is in progress. By his last move, ...Nd7–b6, Black attacked the bishop, so as on the natural 16 Bd3 or 16 Be2 to carry out the freeing advance ...c6–c5. White's next intermediate move, however, considerably hinders the realization of this plan: **16 Na2!**

An excellent reply. On 16...N×c4 White replies 17 N×b4!, depriving Black of counter-play. At the same time after 16...Bd6 17 Be2 the threat of a4–a5! is very strong.

16...Ba5 17 Be2 e5.

Again the best chance. 17...c5, as planned beforehand, is not good because of 18 d×c5! Q×c5+ 19 Be3.

18 Qc2!

The series of short thrusts continues. The threat is 19 b4, and at the same time the c5 square is attacked.

18...N6d7.

18...e×d4 fails to 19 b4! B×b4 20 N×b4 Q×b4 21 Ba3 Qa5 22 B×f8 Q×g5+ 23 Kh1 K×f8 24 a5 N6d7 25 Qb2 Nc5 26 Q×d4, with a material advantage for White.

19 d×e5 Q×e5 20 Kh1! Re8 21 Bc4.

Another important subtlety. White has made a useful prophylactic move, by removing his king from the a7–g1 diagonal. The most convenient post for his white-squared bishop is at d3. But if immediately 21 Bd3, then 21...Nc5. Therefore, so as to divert the knight, White resorts to the tactical threat of Qb3. To defend against it, Black must move his knight to b6, but then the d3 square can be occupied.

21...Nb6 22 Bd3 Na6 23 B×a6 b×a6 24 Rd1!

A by no means obvious move, but specific analysis shows that it is the strongest in the position. For example, on 24 Rb1 there follows 24...c5, 24 Be3 is parried by 24...Nd5!, and finally, 24 Nc3 c5 25 Be3 meets with the adequate counter 25...Nc4. Such short but exact variations are typical of a situation where positional factors are predominant. The ability to see them also characterizes the strength of a player's specific thinking, just as the ability to find a combination and calculate long variations in a sharp tactical struggle.

24...c5.

On 24...Rad8 there could have followed 25 Be3 Nd5 26 Bd4!

25 Be3 Rac8 26 Nc3 Nc4 27 Bc1 Rb8?

Up till this point Portisch has competed most worthily in the art of seeking the best moves, but here he fails to stand the tension (it is at such moments that one gains a clear impression of the great intensity demanded by highly subtle mental work of this type) and overlooks White's obvious reply. It was essential to play 27...B×c3, and after 28 Q×c3 Q×c3 29 b×c3 White would merely have slightly the better ending. At the same time, as Karpov points out, White fails to achieve his goal after 28 Rd5 Q×d5! 29 e×d5 Re1+ 30 Kg2 B×b2 31 Q×c4 B×a1, with unclear consequences.

28 Nd5! N×b2 29 Bf4 Qe6 30 Rdb1 Qh3 31 B×b8 R×b8 32 R×b2 Resigns.

A curious fact about this game is that Karpov, who was already World Champion, was playing against the Slav Defence for the first time in his career.

The art of finding the most difficult, sometimes unusual moves is no less valuable in defence.

Adorján–Vaganian
Teesside 1974

Here a very sharp position has arisen. White has sacrificed the exchange, and has seized strong outposts in the centre with his minor pieces. It is true that the position of the white king does not appear very secure, but with his following move White also intends to worry the enemy king.

19 Bb5+ Kd8!

But not 19...Bd7 20 B×d7+ K×d7 21 Qa4+ Kd8 22 Re1, with a strong attack for White.

20 Qe2 Bd7 21 Bd3 Kc8! 22 Nf3 (bad is 22 B×h7 R×e5! 23 Q×e5 Bf6!, when Black wins) **22...Rg8 23 c4! Kd8!**

Black's play with his king in the centre at the very height of a sharp middlegame is most surprising. The move made by Vaganian is accurately based on the specific situation. Bad now would be 23...Bd6 24 Rc1 B×e5 25 N×e5 d4 26 c5!, with advantage to White.

24 B×h7 Rf8 25 Qd2 Rc8 26 b3 Rc5! 27 Rd1 Kc8!

Another important step in Black's plan. Before turning to an attack on the white king, Black prudently removes his king from the d-file, where it may have come under a frontal attack. The king manoeuvres (...Ke8–d8–c8–d8–c8) appear paradoxical, and are undoubtedly an enrichment to our ideas on tactics. One cannot help drawing a comparison here with the actions of a top-class ice-hockey goal-minder, who with his barely perceptible movements in a small goal exerts an enormous influence on the entire game.

28 Bd3 d×c4 29 B×c4 Qc6!

And now comes the long-awaited moment when Black switches to a counter-attack against the white king's flimsy defences.

30 Be2 R×e5! 31 N×e5 Rh8+ 32 Kg3 Bh4+ 33 Kf4 Rf8+ White resigns.

There has passed before the reader a rather brief exposition of moves which are difficult to find, in various playing situations. I hope that these examples will once again remind him that it is much easier to make errors than to find a good move, to say nothing of the best move.

PART III

The Master Level

7

DYNAMICS OF THE STRUGGLE, AND A CONCRETE APPROACH TO THE EVALUATION OF A POSITION

A modern panorama of the chess battle

One of the first conditions for attaining a high class of play is the creation of an accurate conception of the principles and regularities of the modern way of conducting the struggle. The thinking chess player must be armed with a conception of the views which correctly reflect a panorama of the chess battle. And in this respect it is especially important to sense the complex dynamic nature of the modern chess game.

At the end of the last century the wonderful Russian player Mikhail Chigorin spoke out determinedly against the dogmatism of the Steinitz theory, and demonstrated in practice the enormous role of fantasy in chess. The development of theory has confirmed still further the correctness of Chigorin's viewpoint. The inexhaustible richness of chess cannot be confined within the bounds of dry rules.

Modern theory and practice demonstrate the boundless possibilities for obtaining complicated positions, full of combinational motifs. The play in such positions is notable for its richness and diversity of ideas, which extend beyond the bounds of formal logic. The result is that in many instances the purely positional factors become a subsidiary factor in the play, and the struggle for them proceeds by no means as logically as was 'prescribed' by the rules of the old positional school.

From this it follows that playing for the accumulation of small positional advantages has its limits, beyond the bounds of which it loses force. In practice, situations often arise where a purely positional conduct of the struggle becomes clearly inadequate. In this connection, an ever increasing role is played by dynamic factors, which have considerably enriched the strategy and tactics of chess.

Advocates of the dynamic handling of a position proceed from the viewpoint that, in a whole series of complex positions, apart from stable factors resulting from the contours of the positions, an important role is also played by highly mobile and concealed factors. These include, for example, the co-ordination of the forces and their specific disposition. In the evaluation of such positions the primary role is often played by individual peculiarities, characteristic only of the given set-up.

Strategy based on dynamics is notable for its maximum approach to reality. A player does not endeavour at all costs to make his actions subject to a plan, but all the time weighs up the two together, absorbing the entire wealth of ideas from the chess 'life' on the board.

Instructive in this respect is the game **Tukmakov–Geller** (Zonal Tournament, Lvov, 1978).

We have here a typically dynamic situation, which it is hardly possible to evaluate on general positional grounds. The wealth of ideas contained in the position is revealed in the following sharp tactical battle which develops in the centre.

17 . . . Bf5!? 18 e5!

But not 18 e×f5? R×e3 19 Q×e3 Q×d4, with advantage to Black. White is obliged to force matters, since otherwise he cannot defend his e4 pawn.

18 . . . d×e5 19 N×f5 Q×f5 20 B×c5 e×f4 21 B×b6 a×b6 22 Rbc1!

The only way. Unfavourable for White, for example, is 22 g×f4 Rad8 23 Qc1 Rd3 24 Na4 Re2.

22 . . . Qc5+ 23 Kh1 Qe3 24 Qc2 f×g3?

A serious mistake. The logical continuation was 24...B×c3 25 Q×c3 f×g3, when it would seem that Black can maintain the dynamic balance.

Now the crisis ensues: **25 Ne4 Be5 26 Rf3 Qh6 27 Rcf1 f5 28 N×g3**, and White soon realized his material advantage.

Thus the dynamic approach to chess enhances the importance of tactics, and of combinational methods in particular. In a modern game one often encounters, for example, a positional sacrifice for the sake of attaining dynamic gains.

This wonderful, as grandmaster Rudolf Spielmann expressed it, feature of chess—the conversion of material into force—extends considerably the ways of battling for the attainment of positional superiority.

Kasparov–Panchenko
Daugavpils 1978

In a well-known variation of the Rauzer Attack in the Sicilian Defence, White chooses an interesting plan involving the sacrifice of a pawn: **12 e5!? d×e5 13 f×e5 Nd7 14 B×e7 Q×e7 15 Be4 B×e4 16 N×e4 N×e5.**

Black accepts the challenge, but then did he have anything better?

17 Qd4 f6 18 Nd6+ Kf8 19 Rhf1 Kg8 20 g4!

For the pawn White has gained a whole series of dynamic advantages. The point is not only that the black king has been prevented from castling, but also that there is a lack of harmonious co-ordination among the black pieces, a factor which is emphasized by White's subsequent tactical manoeuvres.

20 . . . h6 21 h4 Nf7 22 Qe4!

An important intermediate move, enabling

White to transfer his knight to a good square with gain of time.

22...Rf8 23 Nf5! Qe8 24 Nd4 e5 25 Nf5 h5 26 Rg1 Rh7 27 Qb7! Kh8 28 g×h5 Qe6 29 N×g7! Q×a2 30 Qe7 Rg8 31 Q×f6 Qa1+ 32 Kd2 Qa5+ 33 Ke2 Rg×g7 34 R×g7 R×g7 35 Rg1 Resigns.

It is appropriate to give here the following pronouncement by Karpov in his book of selected games: "Every player should be able to use such a subtle strategic weapon as a pawn sacrifice".

Undoubtedly one of the most effective methods in the dynamic struggle is the positional combination. In recent times this concept has been considerably enriched.

Here is an example of the modern positional combination, demanding both far-seeing calculation, as well as a keen evaluation of the resulting positions.

The diagram position is reached in a sharp variation of the Sicilian Defence after 1 e4 c5 2 Nf3 d6 3 d4 c×d4 4 N×d4 Nf6 5 Nc3 a6 6 Bg5 e6 7 f4 Qb6 8 Qd2 Q×b2 9 Rb1 Qa3 10 f5 Nc6 11 f×e6 f×e6 12 N×c6 b×c6 13 e5 d×e5 14 B×f6 g×f6 15 Ne4 Be7 16 Be2 h5 17 Rb3 Qa4.

This is a position of continuous searchings, which are mainly of a combinational nature. One of the topical continuations here is the following piece sacrifice, which was made in the game **Timman–Ribli** (Niksic, 1978).

18 N×f6+!? B×f6 19 c4 Bh4+.

Black provokes the move g2–g3. In the game Kengis–Mankus (1977) Black played 19...c5 here, but after 20 0–0 Qd7 21 Q×d7+ K×d7 22 R×f6 Ke7 23 Rg6 Kf7 24 Rbg3 White gained a marked advantage.

20 g3 Be7 21 0–0 Bd7?!

A serious error. Better is 21...Ra7 22 Rb8 Rc7 23 Qd3 Bc5+ 24 Kh1 Ke7 25 Qg6 Kd6 26 Qf6 Re8 27 B×h5 Rce7 28 Rd1+ Bd4 29 R×d4+ e×d4 30 Q×d4+ Kc7, with equal chances (Vitolins–Gavrikov, 1977).

Now White's attack begins to 'entwine' Black.

22 Rb7 Rd8.

It is already not easy for Black to find the correct path. Thus, 22...0–0–0 is bad because of 23 Rfb1 Bc5+ 24 Kh1 Bd4 25 c5! White also has a very dangerous attack after 22...c5 23 Bd1 Qc6 24 Bf3!

23 Bd3 Bc5+ 24 Kh1 Rg8 (White wins after 24...Rf8 25 Bg6+ Ke7 26 R×f8 K×f8 27 R×d7 R×d7 28 Q×d7) **25 Be2 Ke7 26 B×h5 Rg7 27 Qh6 Q×c4 28 Q×g7+ Kd6 29 Qf6 Bd4 30 Rfb1 Qd3.**

The fate of the game is decided. Now it is White who gains a decisive material advantage.

31 R7b3 Qf5 32 Q×d8 Q×h5 33 Qb8+ Kd5 34 Qc7 Qh7 35 Re1 Qf7 36 Rd3 Kc4 37 Rd2 Bc3 38 Q×d7 Qf3+ 39 Kg1 Resigns.

In these last examples, dynamic handling enabled the winner to exploit the latent advantages of the position. The positional sacrifices revealed advantages which were already present, and in an equal struggle allowed one player to gain the upper hand, when his opponent failed to withstand the tension in a sharp tactical battle.

We will consider a further example of the skilful exploitation of dynamic factors.

Smyslov–Radulov
Leningrad 1977

The position is evenly balanced. On the K-side Black has set up strong defences, and it appears that White's initiative has reached an impasse. But Smyslov finds an interesting plan: **25 Bh5!? N×e4 26 N×e4 B×e4 27 Nd4!?**

After 27 B×f7 N×f7 28 R×f7 Qc8 29 Qf4 R6e8! 30 Kh2 d5 or 30...Bg6 Black would have a clear advantage. But White is by no means bound to regain his pawn, but must in the first instance build up his threats on the K-side. The result is a double-edged, dynamic game, in which the loss of the pawn is unimportant.

27...Re7 28 Qh4 Qb7 29 Nf5 Red7 30 Be2 f6 31 Ng3 Bc6 32 Nh5 Re8 33 Qg3 Rc7 34 Bd4 Be4 35 Nf4 R7c8 36 c3 Nc6?

Black fails to withstand the strain of a difficult, 'calculating' defence, and commits a decisive error.

37 Ng6+ B×g6 38 Q×g6 N×d4 39 Bd3!

Black missed this move in his calculations. Now on 39...f5 there follows 40 R×f5! N×f5 41 R×f5, when mate is inevitable.

39...Kg8 40 R×f6! Resigns.

The dynamic treatment has enriched the approach to basic factors: material, space and time, by closely linking them with specific ideas for achieving particular advantages in the position. Thus the time factor is evaluated not by a mechanical counting of tempi, but by specific goals, on the attainment of which moves must be spent. In the light of this, time is an invisible positional factor.

Thus the dynamic treatment presupposes the taking into account of future operations on the board, giving consideration not only to external, but also latent, individual characteristics of the position. Moreover, each time it is necessary to seek the most important mobile element of the struggle in this or that specific situation.

It would be quite incorrect to oppose one against the other the positional and dynamic treatments. What is more, the one supplements the other.

When speaking of the correlation of positional and dynamic factors, it must not be forgotten that the dynamic approach developed on a sound positional basis, even though it was an expression of protest by lively chess thought against those canons of dogmatism which deadened chess creativity.

Of course, it is by no means always that the major role in the struggle is played by 'latent' individual factors. On the contrary, in practice one must be guided in the main by the external features of the position. There is, nevertheless, more severe everyday logic in chess than elements of fantasy. As Mikhail Tal aptly put it, otherwise chess would be too beautiful a game.

In a very great number of instances, positional principles have genuine strength. The dynamic treatment not only does not reject positional elements and principles, but, on the contrary, takes account of the most essential, viable peculiarities of the struggle, thereby deepening our understanding of positional principles.

What should indeed be contrasted with dynamics is routine. In dynamics the basic method is to search inquisitively, to be daring, and to reach the true depths of the position. The dynamic treatment essentially signifies an efficient, realistic approach to the struggle in chess.

Modern dynamic positional play is undoubtedly more complex and more complete than its forerunner. In order to determine the basic driving factor of the struggle, the true master should have a complete command both of the art of positional play, and of combinational mastery. And this is always in synthesis, since one must be prepared for the most diverse tests at the board under conditions of limited time for thought.

In the following interesting game, which appears to develop along positional lines, a considerable role was also played by dynamic factors.

Smyslov–Tal
Candidates' Tournament,
Yugoslavia 1959

In view of the threat of ...e5–e4, Black's position at first sight appears promising. But White's following original move sharply changes this assessment.

15 Qd3!

Apart from an understanding of positional subtleties, this non-routine idea also demanded lengthy calculation, since the outcome of the subsequent endgame battle depends largely on which side is able to activate his rooks more quickly. White voluntarily allows the doubling of his pawns on the d-file, reckoning that his opponent's weakness—the b7 pawn—is the more real.

15...Rfc8 16 Rfc1 Q×d3.

The threat of 17 c4 persuades Black to go into the ending. But a possibly better chance was the pawn sacrifice 16...e4 17 B×e4 N×e4 18 Q×e4 Bf6.

17 c×d3 g6 18 Rc3 R×c3 19 b×c3 Rc8 20 c4 e4 21 d×e4 R×c4.

And again it may seem that Black, who has activated his rook, has seized the initiative. But White's calculation has been the more exact.

22 Nd2 Rc2 23 Bd1 Rc3 24 Kf1 Nc5.

White intends to strengthen his position by Ke2, Bd4, Rb1 etc., so Black decides to change the course of the struggle by an exchange sacrifice.

25 Bd4 Rd3 26 B×c5 d×c5 27 Ke2 R×d2+ 28 K×d2 N×e4+ 29 Kc2.

Strategically White has won the battle, although it is true that realizing his advantage proves to be a difficult matter.

The game concluded: **29...Nd6 30 Be2 Bf6 31 Rb1 Kf8 32 Kb3 Ke7 33 Bd3 Kd7 34 f4 Bd4 35 Rf1 Be3 36 f5 Bd2 37 f×g6 h×g6 38 Ra1 Ke7 39 Ra2 Bb4 40 h4 Kf6 41 g4 Be1 42 h5 Kg5 43 Ra1! Bd2 44 Rh1 g×h5 45 g×h5 c4+.**

Also after **45...Kh6 46 Rf1 Bg5 47 Be2** Black's position is hopeless.

46 B×c4 Kh6 47 Rf1 K×h5 48 Rf6 Ne4 49 Be2+ Kg5 50 R×f7 Be3 51 Re7 Kf4 52 Bd3 Nd6 53 Kb4 b6 54 a×b6 B×b6 55 B×a6 Bd4 56 Re6 Be5 57 Kc5 Nf7 58 Bd3 Bb2 59 Bg6 Ng5 60 Re8 Ba3+ 61 Kc6 Nf3 62 Re4+ Kg5 63 Bh7 Kh6 64 Bf5 Kg5 65 Bg4 Resigns.

It should also be noted that often the moments when dynamic factors come into play are very difficult to grasp. For this reason their timely utilization can produce a great effect.

Portisch–Petrosian
Lone Pine 1978

Right from the opening White outlined a solid positional plan, involving the creation of a pawn centre, which he now begins to put into effect.

17 f3 e×f3 18 B×f3 B×f3 19 N×f3 Ne4 20 N×e4 Q×e4 21 Q×e4 R×e4 22 Nd2 Re6 23 e4?

It appears that White has achieved his aim, but, alas, he has failed to take account of the latent dynamic resources of Black's position. And it is they that play the main role in the subsequent course of events.

23...Nc5!!

The point! Otherwise White's idea would have been fully justified, and Black would have incurred a cheerless position. But this dynamic stroke sharply changes the situation.

24 Nc4 (24 d×c5 B×c5+ or 24 e5 B×e5! is unsatisfactory for White) **24...N×e4 25 Rac1 Bf8 26 Ne5 Nd6 27 a4 f6 28 Nf3 R×e1+ 29 N×e1 Rd7 30 Nf3 Nf5 31 Kf2 h5.**

It is readily apparent that White has a completely lost position. Petrosian energetically realizes his advantage.

32 Rc2 g5 33 Rc4 Bd6 34 g3 Kf7 35 Ng1 Ne7 36 Ne2 Nd5 37 Bc1 Ke6 38 Rc2 Kf5 39 Kf3 g4+ 40 Kf2 Rh7 41 Rd2 h4 42 Kg2 Ke4 43 Rd1 Ne3+ 44 B×e3 K×e3 45 Nc3 h3+ White resigns.

Of course, in practice, under conditions of restricted time, it is often difficult to determine which path is the more correct: the strictly positional, subject only to logic, or the dynamic, taking account of individual factors and leading to a double-edged game. Many positions give equal scope for logical thinking and for fantasy. In such instances the choice of method depends upon the taste and style of the player.

The dynamic treatment by no means reduces play to some standard pattern. We know prominent masters who prefer playing in situations where elements of logic predominate. Others, in contrast, aim for intricate play, containing a large number of diverse ideas, with a predominance of an element of fantasy and combinational creativity.

And, of course, players of high class have a command of different methods of play, and employ them depending on the specific situation in the game or tournament.

Such are some of the most general features of dynamics. Inseparable from them are also such important concepts as the initiative, the 'transformation' of positional factors, the harmonious co-ordination of the forces, and so on.

For example, the modern understanding of the initiative implies a study of its duration and stability, the role of tempi, and the possibility of counter-play—the most attractive and promising method of countering a growing initiative. And the 'transformation' of positional factors emphasizes the role of the transition periods from one stage of the game to another.

The harmonious co-ordination of the forces is one of the most important and most general principles of play. Co-ordination is inseparably linked to factors of time and the initiative. The modern dynamic treatment of the principle of co-ordination demonstrates more and more persistently that, in many instances, the existence of external positional gains by no means ensures the harmony of the forces, and, on the contrary, at times it can be achieved only at the cost of positional or even material concessions.

Modern practice shows that, under the powerful pressure of harmoniously co-ordinated forces, it is not only immobile weaknesses that can become vulnerable objects of attack, but also factors which in themselves are positionally strong (for example, a centre, or pawn chain). In many instances an attack is made on mobile enemy targets. In this respect several games by Karpov, for example, are instructive, where he carries out his favourite method of restricting an enemy knight.

Such in the most general outline is a panorama of the modern dynamic chess battle.

We will now turn to questions of positional evaluation.

A concrete approach to the evaluation of a position

The thinking of a chess player must first and foremost be specific. To think specifically means to take thorough account of the individual peculiarities of the given position, and to be able to combine them with general principles.

Specific thinking cannot be cultivated quickly and simply. Its development is preceded by the acquisition of experience in combinational vision, of which we have already spoken. I should like once again to emphasize that work on the perfecting of this skill must be done constantly. In parallel with it (as experience shows, it is even better with a short time lag) a player must master the different positional principles, and the typical tactical and strategic methods.

At a certain stage of a player's development, great importance is acquired by his general range of interests, and by his mastery of chess culture. Enormous benefit can be gained from a systematic study of the games of the outstanding masters of different times, the classic models of chess art. Conscientious work on all the components of chess science will enable one to avoid those deficiencies of thinking which were described earlier in this book. It should be remembered that the positive qualities of a player constitute a frail and delicate material, created by purposeful practice and training.

Of course, in life complete harmony does not exist. By nature a player normally inclines either towards combinational, or towards positional play. And it is very dangerous to trifle with one's nature. But, while leaning on your strong natural qualities, you should not forget about the other aspect of thinking.

Otherwise, from being a valuable support, it may turn into an evil antipode. And there is nothing worse than an antipode sitting inside you yourself.

But let us return to the basic theme of this section.

It is the study of questions associated with concrete thinking that has been the main idea of this work. Although earlier in the book the main discussion concerned unfavourable and negative aspects of thinking, on the background of them we each time sought an approach to the correct method. And it lies only in the development of concrete thinking.

Only with a concrete approach to a position can one reach its essence. The basic aim of concrete thinking is to study the dynamics of the critical position and find the most effective path. Here every individual move, while corresponding to the general plan, must solve the most vital problem in the given concrete situation.

The evaluation of a position is the main criterion on which a player bases the choosing of a move. The thinking act of evaluating a position proceeds involuntarily, and does not require any accentuation. We will recall a further pronouncement by Blumenfeld: "Evaluation is linked to the perception of the position, and is basically a sub-conscious act, in the sense that intermediate stages for the most part, if not completely, do not pass through the centre of consciousness".

The strength of a player has long become synonymous with his evaluating capability. Even in strictly concrete instances, when tactical elements dominate, the evaluation of position not only always becomes the starting point for calculation, but also accompanies the tactical play through the intermediate stages, and acts as a kind of 'stop lever' at the conclusion of the calculation. Control over the calculating operations lies in the evaluation of the final position, which for the moment exists in the mind.

Thus in the course of a game a player has very many times to evaluate a position. At the same time this is a single process, which is as though divided into a number of stages. It is for this reason that at the intermediate stages there should be a very rapid, sometimes instantaneous evaluation. The problem of such rapid evaluations is undoubtedly facilitated by the fact that they are based on a considered evaluation of the initial critical position. Initially we look as deeply as possible into the heart of the position with which the analysis begins. Then up to a certain point, if there are no 'sharp turnings' of a tactical nature, the thinking process proceeds in the main automatically. One can carry out, for example, the following interesting experiment. Ask two players of roughly equal standard to evaluate in parallel the course of the struggle in one and the same game over a phase of five to six moves, between which there does not occur any fundamental change in the character of the position. As a rule, at the first initial point of the evaluation there follows a rather prolonged consideration, but then (in the event of an identically correct evaluation) the thinking process develops almost identically, both in the course of play, and in time.

At intermediate stages the brain records changes in position, which in a number of cases must not only be registered by reasoning of a general nature, but also reinforced by concrete variations, if only short ones. It is such variations which illustrate the essence of the position, a fact which was repeatedly emphasized by Alekhine. Hence the necessary, if minimal expenditure of time. Even the most obvious moves must be checked.

While the calculation of variations in the final analysis is based on a correct 'vision' of the combinational essence of a position, the concrete approach to evaluation has the aim of grasping an even more important creative process—foresight.

The gift of foresight is one of the most treasured in chess mastery. Once the great Lasker had this to say about a certain young master, who had a certain promise: "While undoubtedly gifted strategically and tactically, he does not have that special fantasy, which is necessary so as to imagine to yourself the approximate contours of a complex operation in preparation". While one of the outstanding chess theorists, Nimzowitsch, asserted that one can guess the course of events in a game only if possessing creative fantasy!

This ability to foresee coming events appears only during a dynamic evaluation of position, which normally is rightly contrasted with a static evaluation, based on a study of the purely external factors. In comparing these two approaches to evaluation, the following discussion by Alekhine is highly instructive. We refer to his article *The battle for the world championship*, written directly after his return match with Euwe (1937).

Comparing his method of thinking with that of the opponent, Alekhine wrote: "Euwe's chess talent is purely tactical, in contrast to such masters as Steinitz, Rubinstein, Capablanca and Nimzowitsch. But he is a tactician who decided at all costs to make himself a good strategist. Thanks to intensive work on himself, Euwe has achieved a certain degree of success. A sure sign by which one can distinguish a genuine strategist from a 'fake' strategist is just how original is his resourcefulness.

In all Euwe's games we see one and the same picture: the plan conceived by him is based on the *external form of the position* [my italics—A. S.]. For example, on a Q-side pawn majority, on the opponent's isolated pawn, on the advantage of the two bishops, and so on [in other words, on static factors—A. S.]. Generally speaking, this is a good method, but, depending on the tactical possibilities in a particular position, in any plan exceptions can occur, and they occur fairly often. Euwe as a strategist is the complete antithesis of Réti. The latter in his well known book *New Ideas in Chess* stated that he was interested only in exceptions. With Euwe it is just the opposite—he believes too religiously in the immutability of rules.

It is curious that, in an article entitled *Obituary* which appeared at the same time, Euwe expressed exactly the same opinion: "I was unable to devise a single good plan, and my defeat must be put down more to illogical moves than to bad ones".

There can be only one conclusion: the dynamic evaluation (or treatment) of a position is the only correct method in chess. A static evaluation can be acceptable only in the preliminary stage of examining a position.

Let us consider some examples in which the evaluation is based on concrete thinking.

Tarrasch–Alekhine
Baden-Baden 1925

Here Alekhine played **11...Qd8!!**, about which he wrote: "The most difficult move in the entire game! Black forces the opponent to determine the position of his well-placed bishop at c4, since, on the one hand, Black threatens (either immediately or a little later) to free his game by ...e×d4, c×d4 d5!, while, on the other hand, to the natural reply 12 Nbd2 Black has prepared 12...N×e4 13 N×e4 d5, and in both cases he gains a highly comfortable game. Finally, the move played also has the advantage that the e-file is vacated for the rook at f8''.

Clearly reflected in this comment is an evaluation taking account of future concrete prospects, i.e., a dynamic evaluation. Since the play is not of a forcing nature, the author considers only essential continuations, so as to present as accurately as possible what can result from his intended plan.

12 Bd3 Re8 13 Nbd2 Ba7! (averting the possible threat of 14 Nc4) **14 Qc2 e×d4 15 N×d4 Ne5 16 Bf1 d5! 17 Rad1 c5 18 Nb3 Qc7 19 Bf4.**

Slightly better is 19 e×d5 N×d5 20 Nc4 N×c4 21 B×c4 N×e3 22 R×e3 R×e3 23 f×e3 Qe7!, although even in this case Black's advantage is undisputed.

19...Nf3+ 20 N×f3 Q×f4 21 e×d5?

Essential was 21 e5 Bf5 22 Qd2 Q×d2 23 R×d2 Ne4 24 Rdd1 Rad8, when White can still hold on.

21...Bf5! 22 Bd3 B×h3 23 g×h3 Q×f3 24 R×e8+ R×e8 25 Bf1 Re5 26 c4 Rg5+ 27 Kh2 Ng4+ 28 h×g4 R×g4 White resigns.

Alekhine–Capablanca
34th game of the World Championship Match 1927

In this almost symmetrical position there is not even a hint of immediate danger. But appearances are deceptive. It only required Black to make one move on general grounds—**20...h6?**, and after **21 Qd2!** he was in serious difficulties. The manoeuvre of the white queen is linked with a concrete idea, and at the same time is based on deep foresight. The main threat is 22 Qa5. If Black attempts to parry it by 21...Bc6, White decides the game with a spectacular blow on the K-side: 22 Nh4! N×e4 (or *22...B×e4 23 Qe3!*) 23 Nhf5+ g×f5 24 N×f5+ Kf6 25 Q×h6+ K×f5 26 g4 mate!

Strangely enough, Black had just one move which would have given him some chance of a successful defence: 21...Na4!, as pointed out by Lasker. Then White would have simply strengthened his position by 22 Rfd1.

21...Be6?

This is equivalent to capitulation not only in the game, but also in the match. Alekhine wins a pawn, after which the stage of realizing the advantage begins.

22 B×e6 Q×e6 23 Qa5 Nc4 24 Q×a7 N×b2 25 R×c8 R×c8 26 Q×b7 Nc4 27 Qb4 Ra8 28 Ra1 Qc6! 29 a4! N×e4 30 N×e5.

Here 30 N×e4 Q×e4 31 Rc1 Rc8 32 N×e5? fails to 32...Ne3! 33 Q×e4 R×c1+ 34 Kh2 Nf1+ followed by ...Ng3+ and ...N×e4.

30...Qd6 31 Q×c4 Q×e5 32 Re1 Nd6 33 Qc1! Qf6 34 Ne4 N×e4 35 R×e4.

The realization plan consists of combining the advance of the passed pawn with an attack on the slightly weakened position of the black king. In the first instance White takes possession of the important a1–h8 diagonal.

35...Rb8 36 Re2 Ra8 37 Ra2 Ra5 38 Qc7 Qa6 39 Qc3+ Kh7 40 Rd2 Qb6 41 Rd7 Qb1+ 42 Kh2 Qb8+ 43 g3 Rf5 44 Qd4 Qe8 45 Rd5 Rf3 46 h4! Qh8 47 Qb6! Qa1 48 Kg2 Rf6 49 Qd4 Q×d4 50 R×d4, and in the rook ending Alekhine confidently realized his advantage, thus winning the concluding game of the match for the World Championship.

Karpov–Gligoric
San Antonio 1972

42 Qg1!

Regarding this manoeuvre Karpov wrote: "Such moves are very difficult to find! White has an obvious spatial advantage, plus the resultant positional gains. So as to increase them, he must find an exact plan for regrouping his pieces. Here are my basic thoughts about the position: 1) Black has only one weakness—his c5 pawn; White must quickly organize an attack on it, since this will enable him to restrict the manoeuvrability of the opposing pieces; 2) the best place for the king is at f3, where it is not liable to be checked, it over-protects the bishop at g4, and opens the g1–a7 diagonal for the bishop-queen battery and the second rank for rook manoeuvres; 3) White must battle for possession of the h-file and to develop an initiative on the K-side. At an opportune moment he can initiate play on the opposite wing,

and transfer there the weight of the struggle, utilizing the great mobility of his forces. White's last move meets all these conditions".

The subsequent development of the game illustrates the power of foresight of Karpov's initial dynamic evaluation.

42...Nb6 43 Rh2 Qe7?

Black dogmatically clings to his possession of the h-file, and fails to see the impending danger on the Q-side. Better was 43...a5.

44 Nb3 Kc7 45 Kf3!

A subtle move, and an important step in White's plan. On the one hand, the way for the rook is opened, and on the other—a tactical attack on c5 becomes imminent.

45...Nd7 46 a3! b×a3 47 Ra2! Rh4 48 R×a3 Rgh8 49 Rb1 Rb8 50 Qe1 R×g4 51 K×g4 Bc8 52 Qa5+ Resigns.

Inductive and deductive methods of thinking

The style of any chess player will bear in it features of individuality. In chess, as in other forms of creative activity, the character and general intellect of a person are expressed, and this leaves its mark on the play.

And even so, in the whole diversity of chess styles, two regularities can be picked out. In players of fairly high standard (candidate masters or first category players) one notices two basic types of thinking. Possessors of the first of these like to rely on fantasy. Their creed is combinations, and tactics; they do not like playing on general grounds. They conclude the evaluation of a position out of variations. In other words, players of this type prefer to go from the particular to the general, giving clear preference to the study of latent combinational resources. On the other hand, generalizations do not come easily to them, so that they do not like making them, and do so comparatively rarely.

Such a method of thinking we will call inductive.

It should also be mentioned that such players are normally unable to stand a gruelling defence, and feel uncomfortable in conditions of lengthy manoeuvring, while sometimes they are also weak in technique.

The antipode of this is a different type of thinking, which gives preference to evaluations of a general character. Players of such a stamp are unfavourably disposed to endless calculating searches. Calculation must support the general evaluation—this is their motto. They dislike perplexing situations, where everything hangs by a thread, and attempt to avoid 'irrational' positions. They normally have a good mastery of general principles, and endeavour to follow them constantly. In addition to their basic description, it can be added that they are more inclined towards painstaking work, and therefore normally display great tenacity in defence.

We will call such a method of thinking deductive.

On the basis of my considerable experience, I can state that both of these types of thinking are promising. I am convinced that very many young chess enthusiasts, who have one or the other thinking characteristic, with correct training can successfully raise the level of their play. Perhaps the only type who is devoid of prospects is the 'dogmatist'. Such players normally direct all their efforts towards the study of an enormous number of opening variations (and in our time also to the creation of 'home-spun' card-indexes— since there is now more than enough chess information). On this they expend an enormous, completely unjustified, amount of energy, since the memory becomes overloaded, and the thinking 'dozes off'. Usually such

players do not achieve much, and any successes that they do have are in fact indebted to other qualities . . .

Thus both the inductive and the deductive types of thinking are lawful. Each of them has its positive aspects, which serve as a basis for fruitful growth. And even so, every player should aim for a greater universalization of his play and, at any rate, for the elimination of obvious deficiencies in his weak link. In doing so, it is not necessary to direct all your efforts into the battle with your weaknesses. While eliminating your shortcomings, you should not forget that the strong aspects of your thinking are embodied in your very nature. And this will always remain your 'creed'. As an example, take the style of Mikhail Tal. His striking combinational talent appeared right from his early years. And although he works tirelessly on his positional mastery, even so his main weapon was, and still remains, his combinational creativity. In other words, the striving for balance in your play should be combined with a careful attitude to your natural capabilities.

Visual and verbal ideas

The language of chess has its own specific nature, but in our time, when cybernetics and other branches of science are becoming more and more interested in chess, many chess terms are acquiring a perfectly justified scientific transcription.

Thus in Blumenfeld's works we find designations of the two basic components of chess thinking, given in a purely scientific manner. He distinguishes visual and verbal ideas. Visual ideas are exclusively concrete, and are expressed in the language of calculational vision. As the author remarked, such a type of idea in the thinking process of a player 'comes to light' as though automatically. Compare this with the pronouncement by Euwe: "Tactics demand a penetrating glance"—this is already the normal chess interpretation.

The verbal idea basically contains reasoning, and can readily be formulated in words. In chess language, we are talking about strategical, positional thinking.

Between visual and verbal ideas there exists an inseparable link. A certain set of visual ideas will in the end lead to the appearance of new verbal ideas. We have only to glance at the history of the development of chess theory, and we see that very often a bold practical experiment later becomes a principle, a method. The great Morphy did not write any teaching works, but, acting with amazing purposefulness and energy from the very first moves of a game, in practice he initiated the creation and subsequent formulating of opening principles, which are unshakeable even to this day.

The original and at times fantastical and exclusively concrete analyses of the great Chigorin, who with rare persistence strove for a complicated, dynamic struggle, led to the emergence of the most promising method of thinking. In our time we already formulate perfectly exactly the various aspects of dynamics (for example, the sacrifice of a pawn for the initiative, or the positional combination).

Thus verbal ideas are the 'quintessence' of the development of a particular set of visual ideas. At the same time a deep knowledge and understanding of verbal ideas comprises not only a part of the elevated culture of a player, but also his creative potential, enabling him to find new, unusual visual ideas.

Also of interest is the following observation. It is noticeable that, with the years, a mature player displays a more and more marked tendency towards verbal ideas. On the contrary, the adherence to visual ideas diminishes with age. The flourishing of visual thinking is the destiny of youth. This example demonstrates once again how closely the problems of chess thinking are linked with heuristic regularities in general. In many fields of creative activity we can observe a similar age-dependent process.

Planning and strategic threats

Speaking about problems of evaluating a position, one cannot avoid touching on questions associated with the choice and implementation of a plan. Relying on the plan worked out, from the large number of possible continuations a player considers only a certain part of them. The plan not only sensibly restricts the mass of possibilities and the number of variations to be calculated, but also purposefully directs the player's thoughts.

A plan in a chess game is usually conceived under difficult 'working' conditions. Depending on the actions of the opponent, it can often be modified. At the same time, the implementation of the plan demands of the player enormous persistence. Otherwise very soon momentary concerns will divert him from the main strategic line.

Important component elements of a plan are various threats. Of course, the greater part of them are of a tactical nature. The range of them is very wide: from direct attack on some target or other, to all kinds of combinational ideas. But beyond the kaleidoscope of constantly changing threats, one must not lose sight of the more stable strategical threats.

In a number of situations, where the struggle is of a manoeuvring nature and constant positional factors predominate, it is not difficult to see a strategic idea of the opponent. But very often, just like unpleasant tactical surprises, strategic threats may be veiled, and this makes them dangerous.

Consider the following example from the game **Larsen–Geller** (Copenhagen, 1960).

The natural move looks to be 18 b×c6, with the aim of mounting pressure down the b-file. But White's following non-routine decision sharply changes the outline of his plan.

18 Ra1!

White plans an attack on the central square e5, which in a number of concrete variations is linked to the battle for the a-file. Thus if Black moves his rook to b8, there follows 19 d4!

18...R×a1 19 Q×a1 c×b5.

Apart from this, White also had to reckon with the following variations:

19...B×d3 20 Rd1! Be2 21 N×e5 R×e5 22 R×d6 Q×d6 23 B×e5, with a clear advantage to White;

19...Qc7 20 d4 e4 21 Nh4 c×b5 22 c5 Be7 23 d5! Q×c5 24 Rc1 Qd6 25 Nhf5 B×f5 26 N×f5 Qa6 (unsatisfactory is *26...Qd7 27 Bh3*, or *26...Q×d5 27 N×e7+ R×e7 28 Rd1* etc.) 27 d6 Q×a1 28 B×a1 Bf8 29 B×f6 g×f6 30 Rc8, with a won ending for White.

20 N×e5 Qc7 21 Nf3 Be7 (21...B×d3 fails to 22 B×f6 B×f1 23 Nd5! Q×c4 24 Nd2!) **22 Rc1!**

In his comments Larsen describes this move as the most difficult in the game. After a deep investigation of the concrete peculiarities of the position, White finds an excellent plan, consisting of occupying the square d5, which consolidates his advantage.

Now 22...B×d3 is very strongly met by 23 Nd5!, for example: 23...Qd6 24 Be5 Qa6 25 Qd4 etc. In a number of variations a typical strategic point is seen: with the exchange of the knight at d5, the white pawn which ends up on that square restricts the action of the knight at d8, and the threat of Rc8! becomes very dangerous, for example: 22...Qb6 23 Nd5 N×d5 24 c×d5 Bf8 25 Ne5 Qa6 26 Q×a6 b×a6 27 Bh3! Nb7 28 Rc7 Nd6 29 Ra7, with a big advantage for White.

22...b×c4 23 d×c4 Qb6 24 Nd5 N×d5 25 c×d5 Bf8 26 Bd4 Qb3 27 Ne5 b5 (27... Bf5 28 g4!) 28 Nd7! Ba3.

Black's position is already unsatisfactory. Thus 28...f6 is decisively met by 29 B×f6!, and 28...Qa3 by 29 B×g7!. Also bad is 28...Qa4 29 N×f8 Q×a1 30 R×a1 K×f8 31 Bc5+ Kg8 32 Bb4 Nb7 33 d6!

29 B×g7! B×c1 30 Nf6+ K×g7 31 N×e8++ Kf8 32 Qh8+ Ke7 33 d6+ Kd7 34 Nf6+ Kc8 35 Bh3+ Kb7 36 Q×d8 Qd1+ 37 Kg2 Bd3 38 Bc8+ Ka8 39 Qa5+ Resigns.

Every era produces its own heroes! This well-known saying can also well be applied to the modern development of chess strategy. There have now come to the forefront a whole series of such systems, where a very sharp struggle develops right from the opening, with eccentric turns and changes in the plans of the two sides.

One of the fashionable variations of the Sicilian Defence was employed in the game **Matulovic–Rajkovic** (Belgrade, 1977): 1 e4 c5 2 Nf3 e6 3 d4 c×d4 4 N×d4 Nf6 5 Nc3

Nc6 6 Ndb5 d6 7 Bf4 e5 8 Bg5 a6 9 Na3 b5 10 B×f6 g×f6 11 Nd5 f5 12 e×f5 B×f5 13 Bd3 e4! 14 Qe2 Nd4 15 Qe3 Bg7 16 f3 Qh4+ 17 g3 N×f3+! 18 Q×f3 e×f3 19 g×h4 B×d3 20 c×d3 B×b2 21 Rd1!

Weaker is 21 Nc2?! B×a1 22 N×a1 Rc8 23 0-0 Rg8+ 24 Kh1 Rg2!, with advantage to Black.

21...B×a3 22 Nc7+ Kd7 23 N×a8 R×a8 24 0-0 Rg8+ 25 Kh1 Rg2 26 Ra1! Bb2 27 R×f3 Rd2 28 Raf1 Bd4! 29 Rf4 R×d3 30 R×f7+ Ke6 31 R7f3! Rd2 32 Ra3 Be5 33 R×a6 R×h2+ 34 Kg1 R×h4 35 Rb1 b4 36 a3 Rg4+ 37 Kh1 b×a3 38 R×a3 h5 39 Rg1 Rh4+ 40 Kg2 Rh2+ 41 Kf1 Bd4 42 Rg6+ Kd5 43 Rd3 Rf2+ 44 Ke1. Drawn.

In this game, which abounds in forcing, combinational play, it is not easy to find a strategical line. And even so, Black's decision to make a positional sacrifice of the exchange on the 21st move is in the first instance a strategic one, and is linked with a definite plan of active defence, where account is taken both of his equivalent in pawns, and the role of his strong bishop.

These examples once again demonstrate strikingly that the plan in a chess game is normally a concrete one, and in many cases must be based to the end on the 'calculating part'. And notice how the plan can be literally overflowing with tactical elements!

Without strategical threats and the plans inseparably linked with them, there is no life on the chess board. If the main strategical threat is the leitmotiv of the plan, then along with it are often contained other, less obvious, but strong enough threats. This relates in particular to modern dynamic middlegame set-ups, of which the observant reader will have convinced himself and will be able to do so on many occasions in the future.

The strategic problems of the two sides often stem immediately from the opening set-up. Consider the position arising in one of the topical variations of the Nimzo-Indian Defence: 1 d4 Nf6 2 c4 e6 3 Nc3 Bb4 4 e3 c5 5 Bd3 0-0 6 Nf3 d5 7 0-0 Nc6 8 a3 B×c3 9 b×c3 d×c4 10 B×c4.

It is readily apparent that the leitmotiv of the subsequent struggle here is the distinctive duel between the two pairs of different minor pieces, the white bishops and the black knights. Black's problem is to blockade securely the centre, and to restrict to the utmost the action of the white bishops. Then his 'cavalry' will acquire good manoeuvring prospects, for example, on White's weakened squares on the Q-side. At the same time it would be a serious mistake to exchange in the centre: 10...c×d4? 11 c×d4. In this case not only is the 'gate' opened wide for the white bishops, but also the strength of White's pawn centre becomes much more of a reality.

From this viewpoint let us analyze more deeply the structure characteristic of the Modern Benoni: 1 d4 Nf6 2 c4 c5 3 d5 e6 4 Nc3 e×d5 5 c×d5 d6 6 e4 g6.

The battle here is highly complex in nature, and many plans are possible. But even so White's main threat is e4–e5! At the same time Black intends in time to carry out a Q-side pawn offensive by ...b7–b5, ...c5–c4 etc. The effective achievement of the strategical aim can in a number of cases involve a positional sacrifice. Typical sacrifices of this kind are, for example, the e4–e5!? break-through for White, and ...c5–c4!? for Black.

One of the most dangerous and typical mistakes for Black here is losing control of e5, after which the e4–e5 break is very dangerous. For example, 7 Bf4 Bg7 (7...a6 is more cautious) 8 Bb5+ Bd7 9 Be2 Qc7? (9...Qe7 is better) 10 Nf3 a6 11 0-0 0-0 12 e5! d×e5 13 N×e5 Qd8 14 Bf3, and Black is already in a strategically hopeless situation.

But even if Black should succeed in neutral-

143

izing the threat of e4–e5, he should not forget that it is always in the air. In a practical struggle the threat of such a break-through is highly unpleasant.

This position was reached in the 3rd game of the Candidates' Match **Polugayevsky–Mecking** (Lucerne, 1977). It is readily apparent that Black has thoroughly outplayed his opponent, and has won a pawn, for which White has no apparent compensation. But even so, the struggle is far from over. White's hopes are associated with pressure on the d6 pawn, and if possible, with the pawn break-through familiar to us.

There followed **26 g4?! Qd8!**

Indirectly defending the knight (*27 g×h5? Qg5+*), and bringing the queen into active play.

27 Re3 Nf6 28 Qf4 Qe7 29 Nc4 Rd8 30 Qg5 Kg7 (30...h6! is probably stronger) **31 e5!**

Here it comes, the long-intended blow by White in the centre, giving him possibilities of active counter-play.

31...d×e5 32 R×e5 R×d5 33 R×e7 (bad, of course, is 33 R×d5? Qe1+ 34 Kg2 Qe4+, when Black wins) **33...R×g5 34 h3 h5?**

Black loses his way in the face of the rapid change of scene. Winning chances were of-

fered by 34...Rd5 35 R×b7 (*35 Ne5 Ne4!*) 35...Ne4 etc.

35 Nd6! Kg8 36 N×f7 Rd5 37 Nh6+ Kh8 38 Nf7+ Kg7 39 Ne5+ Kg8 40 g5! Nh7 41 Re8+ Kg7 42 Re7+ Kg8 43 Re8+, and White gained a draw.

We will consider one further example, in which Black succeeds not only in eliminating the threat of a central offensive, but also successfully implements his plan of a counter-offensive on the Q-side. It should be noted that this is a typical instance. If White's initiative in the centre should misfire, then Black's counter-attack on the Q-side will develop, and what's more the e4 pawn will often become a weakness.

Ebralidze–Suetin
Moscow 1955

1 d4 Nf6 2 c4 c5 3 d5 e6 4 Nc3 e×d5 5 c×d5 d6 6 e4 g6 7 Bd3 Bg7 8 Nge2 0–0 9 0–0 Re8 10 Ng3 b6 11 h3 Ba6! 12 B×a6 N×a6 13 Bf4 Nc7 14 a4 Qe7 15 Re1 Nd7 16 Nf1 a6 17 Bg3 Qf8!

An instructive point. Black is slowly preparing a Q-side offensive, and would appear to have secure control over e5. But it was just at this point that the tactical threat of 18 e5! had arisen, since neither 18...N×e5 19 f4, nor 18...d×e5 19 d6! was possible. For this reason the modest queen move was very timely. Such moves are called consolidating moves, and their role in the implementation of any plan is very important.

18 Qc2 (18 Qb3 is better) **18...b5 19 a×b5 a×b5 20 Ne3 c4 21 R×a8 R×a8 22 Rb1 Nc5 23 Ne2 N7a6 24 Ra1 Nb4 25 R×a8 Q×a8 26 Qb1 Nbd3 27 f3 Qa7!**

In contrast to Black, White has failed to find any consolidating measures which could have halted Black's counter-offensive on the Q-side, and as a result has obtained a strategically lost position. The realization of the advantage is a matter of simple technique.

28 Kh2 N×e4 29 f×e4 Q×e3 30 Nc3 b4 31 Nb5 Q×e4 32 N×d6 Q×d5 33 Qa2 Be5 34 N×c4 B×g3+ 35 K×g3 N×b2!, and Black won.

Of course, 'smooth' strategy such as this occurs rarely in master games. More often Black's searches for counter-play in this system involve dynamic measures, such as the positional sacrifice of a pawn. The following variation is instructive: 1 d4 Nf6 2 c4 c5 3 d5 e6 4 Nc3 e×d5 5 c×d5 d6 6 e4 g6 7 Nf3 Bg7 8 Be2 0–0 9 0–0 Re8 10 Nd2 a6 11 a4 Nbd7 12 f4? (correct is *12 f3* followed by *Nc4*) 12...c4! 13 B×c4 Nc5!, and Black firmly seizes the initiative.

Observe how, as if at the wave of a magic wand, White's 'ideal' centre became a significant weakness. The point is that all the efforts of both sides were directed towards the centre, and it only required White to relax his attention for Black's pressure to triumph.

The given examples have in the main illustrated the basic plans embodied in the very opening structure of the Modern Benoni. But in practice the struggle is by no means bound to develop according to the basic scenario. A number of parallel topics can also be found. Black, for example, can firmly establish a knight at e5.

This plan was preferred in the game **Gligoric–Campos-Lopez** (San Antonio, 1972): **1 d4 Nf6 2 c4 c5 3 d5 d6 4 Nc3 g6 5 e4 Bg7 6 Nf3 0–0 7 Be2 e6 8 0–0 e×d5 9 c×d5 a6 10 a4 Bg4 11 Nd2! B×e2 12 Q×e2 Nbd7 13 Nc4 Nb6 14 Ne3 Re8 15 f3 Rb8 16 Kh1! Nh5 17 g4! Nf4 18 Qc2 Nc8 19 Nc4 g5?! 20 a5 Ne7 21 Nd1 Neg6 22 Nde3 Ne5.**

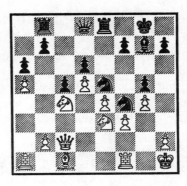

Black has securely averted White's possible break in the centre, but at the cost of serious positional concessions. He has considerably weakened the periphery of white squares on the K-side, which to a great extent determines White's plan, which involves exploiting these weaknesses. Subsequently Gligoric combines play on the white squares with pressure on the Q-side, concentrating his efforts on Black's weakest point—d6.

23 Ra3 N×c4 24 N×c4 Ng6 25 Bd2 Ne5 26 Ne3 Ng6 27 Rb3 Be5 28 Nc4 Qe7 29 Rb6 Red8 30 Be1! Bf4 31 Bg3 Qf6 32 Qc3 Qe7.

Bad is 32...Q×c3 33 b×c3, when the ending is hopeless for Black. In connection with this, I should like to emphasize an important point. In situations where one of the sides must avoid going into an ending, this can be profitably exploited, and, by offering the exchange of queens, the opposing pieces can thereby be displaced from their active positions.

33 Re1 f6 34 B×f4 N×f4 35 Ne3 Rd7 36 Nf5 Qf8 37 Qd2 Rc8 38 Rc1 Rcc7 39 Rc2 Ng6 40 Qf2 Rc8 41 Qg3 Rcd8 42 Qe1 Ne5 43 Qf1 Ng6 44 b4! c×b4 45 R×b4 Ne5 46 Rb6! Rc8 47 R×c8 Q×c8 48 N×d6.

Thus the key point falls. But Black still attempts highly inventively to complicate the play, endeavouring to create threats against the white king.

48...Qc3 49 Ne8 Kf7 50 N×f6 Rc7 51 d6 Rc4 52 d7 Qd2 53 d8 = Q! Q×d8 54 Nd5 Qc8 55 Rb1 Rc2 56 Ne3 Rc3 57 f4!

A counter-attack on the black king. Bad now is 57...R×e3 58 f×e5+, when the threat of 59 Qf6! is decisive.

57...N×g4 58 f×g5+ Ke8 (or **58...Kg8 59 Nd5 Qb8 60 Rb2!) 59 N×g4 Q×g4 60 Qf5 Q×f5 61 e×f5 Rc5 62 R×b7 R×f5 63 h4 R×a5 64 R×h7 Ra2 65 h5 Kf8 66 h6 Kg8 67 Ra7! Ra5 68 Rg7+.**

The rook ending is easily won for White.

68...Kh8 69 Kg2 Ra3 70 Kf2 Rh3 71 Rf7 a5 72 Ra7! Resigns.

Here the chief threat of e4–e5 remained behind the scenes, but the concern provoked by it in Black made itself felt, and helped White to carry out successfully a plan involving the occupation of the white squares on the K-side and an attack on the Q-side and in the centre.

Modern ideas have considerably enriched this system. Here the strategical plans can have a highly unusual form, which may not stem directly from the external conditions.

We will consider one further variation: **1 d4 Nf6 2 c4 c5 3 d5 e6 4 Nc3 exd5 5 c×d5 d6 6 e4 g6 7 Nf3 Bg7 8 Bg5 h6 9 Bh4 g5 10 Bg3 Nh5 11 Bb5+ Kf8 12 e5!? N×g3 13 f×g3! d×e5 14 0-0.**

Objectively, the position on the board is balanced. But the play is highly tactical, and Black must be on the watch for all sorts of tricks.

There were interesting developments, for example, in the game **Stean–Nunn** (Birmingham, 1976), which continued **14...a6 15 Be2 Ra7 16 a4 b6 17 Qb3 f5 18 Nd2!? e4 19 g4 Bd4+ 20 Kh1 e3 21 Nc4 f4 22 N×b6 Rb7 23 a5 h5! 24 g×h5 Nd7 25 B×a6 Nf6?**

Up to this point Black has handled the tactical battle well, and had he now continued 25...R×h5, with the threat of ...Kg7 and ...Qh8, he would have retained sufficient counter-play. In this case, mind-boggling complications could have arisen after 26 g4!

26 B×b7 N×h5 27 Ne2 Bg4 28 N×d4 Ng3+ 29 Kg1 R×h2 30 K×h2 Qe8 31 Ne6+!

This cuts the Gordian knot, whereas 31 Kg1? would have been ruinous after 31...c×d4!, when it is Black who wins.

31...B×e6 32 Q×e3 Qh5+ 33 Kg1, and **Black resigned,** since after 33...Qh1+ 34 Kf2 f×e3+ 35 K×g3+, or 33...Ne2+ 34 Q×e2!, things are hopeless for him.

Switching the object of attack to the opposing king is highly characteristic of modern strategical threats. In the game **Unzicker–Fischer** (Varna, 1962) the plan of a dynamic attack on the king appeared as a secondary strategical threat.

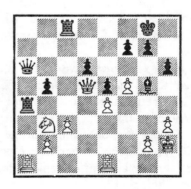

The opening struggle had developed mainly on the Q-side, but when in this position White incautiously weakened his castled position by **24 g3?** (24 Rad1 was better), Black very quickly corrected his plans, and in literally a few instants created an attack on the K-side.

24...Qa7! 25 Kg2 Ra2 26 Kf1.

26 R×a2 Q×a2 27 Re2 would have also been met by the same tactical blow 27... R×c3!

26...R×c3! White resigns. Against the threat of ...Rf3+! there is no defence.

This example shows that you should always take care about not only the tactical, but also the strategical safety of your king!

The struggle in a chess game is invariably linked with the threat of implementing this or that plan. And apart from the main strategical threat, here other threats can gradually come to the surface. In other words, there is a whole series of positions which are rich in a variety of plans. It must also be remembered that, with insufficiently energetic action by the attacking side, the main trump may be transformed into a chronic weakness. This applies especially to those positions in which the threat stems from the external contour.

Unpromising positions

Situations often arise in which, in spite of apparent well-being, one of the sides has no good strategical prospects. Such positions already bear the germ of defeat, if, of course, the opponent has an active strategic plan.

This example from the game **Portisch–Panno** (Wijk-aan-Zee, 1978) is instructive.

Black appears to have successfully overcome his opening difficulties and gained every chance of equalizing. But this is not quite so, as White's next move emphasizes.

14 Nd3!

White not only avoids exchanges favourable to Black, but also directs his knight to the important f2 square, from where it will assist in the seizing of the centre by e3–e4. Black's chief misfortune is the absence of a good plan of active counter-play. In addition, his knights are lacking in co-ordination. Black is therefore obliged to conduct a long and gruelling defence.

14...Nf6 15 Nf2 Nc7 16 e4 Ne6 17 e5 Nd7 18 Qd3 Qh4 19 Be3.

All White's subsequent moves have been links in the one chain, and have assisted the steady strengthening of his position in the centre. Note White's ruthless consistency. Thus 19 d×c5 N×c5 20 Q×d5 would have been a step in the wrong direction, and would have given Black strong counter-play after 20...Red8 21 Qc6 Qc4 followed by 22...Rac8.

19...Rac8 20 g3 Qh5 21 f4 f5 (?).

The lesser evil was apparently 21...c×d4 22 B×d4 f5 23 e×f6 N×d4, or 23 Qb5 N×d4 24 Q×d5+ Ne6 25 Q×d7 g5, and Black can still hold on. But now White inexorably increases his advantage.

22 d×c5! Nd×c5 23 Q×d5 Red8 24 Qc4 Kf7 25 B×c5 R×c5 26 Qa4 Rc7 27 Rad1 R×d1 28 R×d1 Ke7 29 Rd6 Qf3 30 Qb3 Nd8 31 Qg8 Nf7 32 Rd3 Qe2 33 Q×g7 Q×a2 34 Qf6+ Resigns.

The Hungarian grandmaster's fine positional mastery is also revealed in the following game from the same tournament.

Portisch–Timman
Wijk-aan-Zee 1978

1 d4 Nf6 2 c4 e6 3 Nc3 Bb4 4 e3 c5 5 Bd3 Nc6 6 Nf3 B×c3+ 7 b×c3 d6 8 0–0 e5 9 Nd2?! c×d4?

Black incautiously accepts the pawn sacrifice. In the spirit of the position was 9...Qe7, maintaining a solid defence in the centre.

10 c×d4 e×d4 11 e×d4 N×d4 12 Re1+ Ne6 (unsatisfactory is 12... Be6 13 Ne4 N×e4 14 B×e4 Nc6 15 Ba3, when the white bishops become enormously active) **13 Ba3 0–0 14 Nb3 Qd7.** It is apparent that Black already has a very difficult position: his Q-side is immobilized.

15 Re3! Qc6 (no better is 15...Rd8 16 Bb2 Ne8 17 Qh5 h6 18 Rae1!) **16 B×d6 Rd8. 17 Be5.**

White is complete master of the board. Black must now have fully sensed what a 'Greek gift' the pawn sacrifice was, offered by his opponent on the 9th move.

17...Nd7 18 Qh5 h6 (18...g6? 19 Q×h7+!!) **19 Bb2! Q×g2+.**

Timman once again wins a pawn, but obtains a completely hopeless ending.

20 K×g2 Nf4+ 21 Kg1 N×h5 22 Rd1! Rf8 23 Ba3 Rd8 24 Bb2.

Black is in a state of *zugzwang*. The outcome of the game is decided.

24...Rf8 25 Ba3 Rd8 26 Bf5 Nhf6 27 Be7 Re8 28 B×f6 N×f6 29 R×e8+ N×e8 30 Rd8 Kf8 31 B×c8! Resigns.

If there are altogether no strategic threats for either side, we have a position of complete static equilibrium. In such cases one has either to agree to a draw, or else resort to forceful, risky measures in order to sharpen the play.

It is on account of their strategically unpromising nature that many opening systems have gone or are going out of use, those where outwardly correct actions by the two sides lead in the end to a tedious equilibrium. Take for instance this variation of the Four Knights' Game: 1 e4 e5 2 Nf3 Nc6 3 Nc3 Nf6 4 Bb5 Bb4 5 0–0 0–0 6 d3 d6 7 Ne2 Ne7 8 c3 Ba5 9 Ng3 c6 10 Ba4 Ng6 11 d4 d5, with complete equality. Or in the Scotch Game: 1 e4 e5 2 Nf3 Nc6 3 d4 e×d4 4 N×d4 Nf6 5 Nc3 Bb4 6 N×c6 b×c6 7 Bd3 d5 8 e×d5 c×d5 9 0–0 0–0 10 Bg5 Be6 11 Qf3 Be7 12 Rae1 h6 13 B×h6!? g×h6 14 R×e6 f×e6 15 Qg3+ Kh8 16 Qg6, with a draw by perpetual check.

Here the opening resembles (of course, from the viewpoint of modern opening strategy) a battle between tin soldiers, and the wave of complications turns out to be no more than a 'storm in a tea-cup'.

These arguments also apply fully to a number of set-ups which arise in currently popular openings. It is an absence of strategical promise which explains why this or that system 'leaves the stage' (although in practice they can sometimes return). Consider one of the lines in the Open Variation of the Ruy Lopez: 1 e4 e5 2 Nf3 Nc6 3 Bb5 a6 4 Ba4 Nf6 5 0–0 N×e4 6 d4 b5 7 Bb3 d5 8 a4?!

For a certain time this was regarded as one of the most dangerous lines for Black. But as soon as Schlechter found a worthy antidote —8...N×d4!, interest in the move 8 a4 waned. Even today it sometimes occurs, but more likely for some practical reason, from a desire to avoid the main lines. That is what happened in the game Libert–Langeweg (Sochi 1966), where after 9 N×d4 e×d4 10 a×b5 Bc5 11 c3 0–0 12 c×d4 Bd6 13 Nc3 Bb7 14 b×a6 R×a6 15 R×a6 B×a6 16 N×e4 d×e4 17 Re1 Bd3 Black had no difficulties at all.

What determines the strategic promise of a position?

Strategic promise is illustrated very clearly by modern, complex set-ups, arising in the main, problem variations in the transition from opening to middlegame. Look at the standard positions which arise, for example, in the Ruy Lopez, the Sicilian Defence and the King's Indian Defence. They do not resemble one another, but, irrespective of the concrete form of the strategic 'conflict', in each individual case it will be noted that there is a promise of persistent tension, a wealth of positional and tactical motifs, and a certain 'asymmetry' in the struggle. A typical instance is the situation where one of the sides controls the centre, while the other creates piece pressure on it. With castling on opposite sides, the basic plan becomes mutual attacks on the flanks. Such situations rule out a quick compromise, leading to peaceful exchanges or tedious symmetry. And exceptions to this rule occur mainly only when both of the players are peaceably inclined.

During the middlegame, it is not essential for the strategic tension to be fierce, and constantly growing. It is sufficient merely to skilfully maintain a 'spark', out of which in time a flame will flare up!

One of the most important threats in modern strategy is the transition into a favourable ending. The diagram position was reached in the game **Karpov–Liberzon** (Bad Lauterberg, 1977) after White's 21st move. The World Champion holds a certain initiative. He has just attacked the f6 pawn, and also threatens the rook manoeuvre Rf1–f3–c3. Black's desire to create counter-play is perfectly natural.

There followed **21...d5!? 22 Nb3 Qc7 23 Bg2! d×e4 24 Q×e4.** Karpov makes a sharp turn away from a double-edged and, apparently, favourable middlegame, in favour of an ending. And although the position is considerably simplified, Black's troubles merely increase.

24...Bb7 25 R×d8+ R×d8 26 Q×b7+ Q×b7 27 B×b7 K×b7 28 c3.

A good alternative was 28 R×f6 Rd1+ 29 Nc1 Bc5 30 R×e6 Rh1 31 c3 R×h2 32 Nd3, when Black has a difficult struggle to draw. However, the path chosen by White is even more exact.

28...Be7 29 Nd4 e5 30 Nf5 Bc5 31 Kc2 a5 32 g4 Kc6 33 Ng3 Be7 34 Rf5 Rg8 35 h3 Kd5 36 Kd3 a4 37 Ne4 Ke6 38 Rh5 Rd8+ 39 Ke2 a3 (39...b4 is more stubborn) **40 b4! Kd5 41 Kd3 Ke6+ 42 Kc2 Rc8 43 Kb3 Kd5 44 Ng3 Bd6 45 R×h7 e4 46 Nf5 Rd8 47 Ra7 Bf4 48 Kc2 Kc4 49 Rc7+ Kd5 50 Rc5+ Ke6 51 Nd4+.**

Here the line could have been drawn. From 'inertia' there followed **51...Kf7 52 R×b5 Be3 53 Rb7+ Kg8 54 Nf5 Rd2+ 55 Kb3 Resigns.**

Strategically won positions

In annotations to games, we often read that one of the sides gained a 'strategically won position', and that the remainder was 'a matter of technique'. By a strategically won position we normally mean the achievement of an objectively big and very stable positional advantage, which with correct play can no longer be shaken.

However, to convert such a position into a win, as we know from numerous examples, is not always a simple matter. Accurate realization of an advantage is one of the indications of a high standard of play.

Smyslov–Rudakovsky
14th USSR Championship 1945

White played **13 f5**, to which Black, instead of the correct retreat of his bishop to d7, incautiously replied **13...Bc4**. Now White obtains by force a strategically won position. With this aim he first exchanges the white-squared bishops: **14 B×c4 Q×c4,** and then by **15 Bg5** gains lasting control of the critical central square d5.

15...Rfe8 16 B×f6 B×f6 17 Nd5 Bd8 (on 17...Q×c2 there could have followed 18 Rc1 Q×b2 19 Qg3 Kf8 20 Qh3, with the strong threat of 21 N×f6 g×f6 22 Qh6+!) **18 c3 b5 19 b3 Qc5+ 20 Kh1 Rc8** (20...f6 is more tenacious) **21 Rf3 Kh8 22 f6! g×f6.**

Also bad is 22...g6 23 Rh3 h5 (*24 R×h7+!* was threatened) 24 Qg3 Rg8 25 Qg5 Kh7 26 R×h5+, with a crushing attack.

23 Qh4 Rg8 24 N×f6 Rg7 25 Rg3 B×f6.

If 25...Be7, then 26 R×g7 K×g7 27 Q×h7+ K×f6 28 Rf1+ Ke6 29 Qf5 mate. There is also a fine finish after 25...Qf2: 26 Q×h7+! R×h7 27 Rg8 mate!

26 Q×f6 Rcg8 27 Rd1 d5 28 R×g7 Resigns.

Planning and typical strategic methods

We have already seen that the implementation of a plan each time demands inventiveness, tactical skill, and ingenuity. But along with this there are a number of approved technical methods, assisting in the realization of a plan, which one should know and be able to use. Practical experience enables a player constantly to replenish his store of such methods.

The forms of technical methods are unusually diverse: from a simple manoeuvre, favourable exchange, or, say, a pawn offensive on a wing, to highly complicated strategical operations. In the Smyslov–Rudakovsky game we have just seen a common device: the exchange of an important defensive piece of the opponent (in the given case the exchange of the bishop for the knight at f6).

A technical device of a different sort is the typical 'Sicilian' sacrifice of a piece on d5, employed so as to open the key e-file, for example: 1 e4 c5 2 Nf3 d6 3 d4 c×d4 4 N×d4 Nf6 5 Nc3 a6 6 Bc4 e6 7 Bb3 b5 8 0–0 Bb7 9 Re1 Nbd7(?) 10 Bg5 Nc5(?) 11 Nd5! with a very strong attack.

The study of technical strategic devices brings a double benefit. On the one hand, with such material the understanding of strategic subtleties is perfected, and positional feeling developed. On the other hand, the mastery of each new method adds to your practical ability, and at the same time facilitates the difficult process of thinking at the board.

A text-book example of strategic mastery was demonstrated by Black in the game **Rash-**

kovsky–Geller (Chigorin Memorial, Sochi, 1977): **1 d4 Nf6 2 c4 g6 3 Nc3 Bg7 4 e4 d6 5 h3 0–0 6 Bg5 c5 7 d5.**

Here Geller chose an interesting and very sharp plan of counterplay on the Q-side, involving the sacrifice of a pawn: **7...b5! 8 c×b5 a6 9 b×a6 Qa5 10 Bd2 Qb4!**

This manoeuvre is the point behind Black's idea. Ignoring possible danger, the black queen boldly invades the opponent's position, sowing confusion in his ranks. Black's growing initiative more than compensates for the sacrificed pawn.

11 Qc2 B×a6 12 B×a6 N×a6 13 a3 Qc4! 14 Rb1 Nb4! 15 a×b4 c×b4 16 Nge2 b×c3 17 N×c3 Rfc8 18 f3 Nh5 19 g4 Ng3 20 Rg1 Ne2!

A wonderful tactical stroke on a strategic canvas. White has clearly been outplayed, and is now forced into a hopeless ending.

21 Rg2 Nd4 22 Qd1 Qd3 23 Kf2 N×f3 24 Q×f3 Q×d2+ 25 Kg1 Bd4+ 26 Kh1 Qe3! 27 Q×e3 B×e3 28 Rc2 Rab8 29 Kg2 Rb3 30 Ra1 Bd4 31 Rac1 Rcb8 32 Nd1 Kg7 33 Rc7 Bf6 34 R1c2 Rd3 35 Nf2 Re3 36 Ra7 Rbb3 37 Rac7 h6 38 Ra7 Bh4 39 Rac7 B×f2 40 R×f2 R×e4 41 Rd2 Rbe3 42 Rb7 Rf4 White resigns.

After the game Geller asked his opponent: "I don't suppose you were familiar with my game against Mikenas from the 22nd USSR Championship in 1955? There was a similar picture there. The only difference was that I was playing White, and had an extra tempo. But in principle the manoeuvre... Qa5–b4 (or Qa4–b5) is a highly unpleasant one, and such a device should be known!"

The Geller–Mikenas game referred to developed as follows: 1 Nf3 d5 2 c4 d4 3 g3 c5 4 Bg2 Nc6 5 0–0 e5 6 d3 Be7 7 b4!? c×b4 8 a3 b×a3 9 Qa4 Bd7 10 B×a3 Nf6 11 Qb5!

0–0 (better is *11...B×a3* and *12...Qe7*) 12 N×e5 N×e5 13 Q×e5 B×a3 14 R×a3! Bc6 15 B×c6 b×c6 16 Re1 Qb6 17 Nd2 Qb4? 18 Qa5! Qd6 19 Rb3 Rfe8 20 Rb7 Re5 21 Qc7 Qe6 22 Nf3 Rh5 23 N×d4 Qe8 24 Reb1, and Black resigned.

An instructive example of a grandmaster's erudition!

However diverse in form strategic methods may be, they should normally meet the following conditions:

1. Economy of action, the maximum possible in one manoeuvre! Not a fraction of time lost. It is sometimes better to incur a slight material deficit, than to lose valuable time.

2. Purposefulness. A technical device should not transform into a purely tactical operation, but should be directed in the first instance towards the achievement of a strategic goal.

3. Effectiveness. The maximum content of tactical threats, and the tireless watching for counter-threats by the opponent.

Consider the following example.

This position arose in the game **Spielmann–Duras** (Ostende, 1907). Here White played **16 g6!**

The aim of this sacrifice is the rapid opening of lines on the K-side, where White is conducting an offensive. The move played is undoubtedly the most economic solution to the problem. After the natural 16 h5 Black could have put on a secure 'brake' by playing 16... g6 17 Bd4 d5! The g-file would have remained closed, and it would have required considerable effort on White's part to gain prospects of an attack. But now White's initiative develops much more swiftly.

16...h×g6 (in the event of 16...Nf×g6 17 Bg5 followed by h4–h5 White's attack would have been very strong) **17 h5! f×e4 18 R×f7 B×f7 19 B×e4 d5 20 Bd3 Qd7 21 Bd2 Nf5 22 Qg5 Ne7 23 Ne2 Ne6 24 Qg2 g5.**

Black no longer has any satisfactory defence. 24...g×h5 fails to 25 Nf4!

25 B×g5 B×h5 26 Bf6! B×e2 27 Q×e2 Rf8 28 Be5 Rf7 29 Qh5 Kf8 30 Qh8+ Ng8 31 Bh7 Ke8 32 B×g8 Resigns.

And now two further examples of the pawn break-through g5–g6!

Petrosian–Sidorov (Gorky, 1950): **1 Nf3 Nf6 2 d4 d5 3 c4 e6 4 Nc3 c6 5 c×d5 e×d5 6 Qc2 Bd6 7 Bg5 0–0 8 e3 Nbd7 9 Bd3 Qc7 10 0–0–0 Re8 11 g4 Kh8 12 Rdg1 b5 13 B×f6 N×f6 14 g5 Ne4 15 N×e4 d×e4 16 B×e4 Be6.**

White develops very precisely his offensive on the K-side: **17 g6! h×g6 18 Ng5 f5 19 N×e6 R×e6 20 Bf3 Rc8 21 h4 c5 22 d5 Rf6 23 h5! g5 24 R×g5 c4 25 Kb1 Rcf8 26 Rhg1 R8f7 27 Rg6 Be5 28 h6 g×h6 29 Rg8+ Kh7 30 Bh5 R7f8 31 R×f8 R×f8 32 f4 Bg7 33 Bg6+ Kh8 34 B×f5 Qc5 35 Qg2 Qe7 36 Qg6 R×f5 37 Q×f5 Q×e3 38 Rd1 Qf2 39 Qc2 Q×f4 40 d6 Qf8 41 d7 Qd8 42 Qg6 Resigns.**

Spassky–Boleslavsky (25th USSR Championship, 1958): **1 e4 c5 2 Nf3 Nc6 3 d4 c×d4 4 N×d4 Nf6 5 Nc3 d6 6 Bg5 e6 7 Qd2 Be7 8 0–0–0 0–0 9 Nb3 Qb6 10 f3 Rd8 11 Be3 Qc7 12 g4 a6 13 g5 Nd7 14 h4 b5.**

Once again the optimum way of attaining the goal is the pawn sacrifice: **15 g6! f×g6 16 h5 g×h5 17 R×h5 Nf6 18 Rg5 Ne5 19 Qg2 Bf8 20 f4 Nc4 21 B×c4 b×c4 22 Nd4.**

White has attained a strong attacking position. Black faces a difficult defence.

Many strategic methods are subject to precise systemization, and demand serious study. At the same time, it should not be forgotten that the finding of an effective technical device is a creative matter! This searching should always be closely linked with tactics, giving great scope for fantasy, and for the appearance of new methods. Until quite recently, the positional sacrifice, or the obtaining of unbalanced material (for example, queen against rook, minor piece and pawn) were considered exceptions to the rule, whereas now we constantly encounter them.

And one further important point. It is by no means always that the necessary methods for implementing a plan can be found. Therefore the value of a strategic idea depends to a great extent on the possibility of finding technical methods to embody it. It often happens that there is a slip between the cup and the lip!

In recent times interest has grown in the Sveshnikov Variation of the Sicilian Defence: 1 e4 c5 2 Nf3 Nc6 3 d4 c×d4 4 N×d4 Nf6 5 Nc3 e5 6 Ndb5 d6 7 Bg5 a6 8 Na3 b5 9 B×f6 g×f6 10 Nd5 f5.

For a long time this position was regarded as unsatisfactory for Black on general positional grounds (the 'hole' at d5, plus a whole range of pawn weaknesses). But the more now that this variation is tested in practice, the more practice and concrete analysis confirm that to get at Black's weaknesses is very difficult, if at all possible. It turns out that, on a general, logical, positional evaluation Black's position here should not be satisfactory, but the concrete approach fails to find for White any way of refuting it. And in the absence of technical means of embodying White's plan, Black can develop active counter-play with his pieces.

Typical positions

Sometimes a plan becomes a kind of model of strategy. In chess language this is called play in typical positions. An important outward indication of such positions can be provided by the pawn formation in the centre, which influences in a definite way the course of the subsequent struggle (for example, an isolated central pawn, or a pawn chain with a wedge at d5 or e5).

Of course, the struggle in each set-up with a typical formation has its individual peculiarities, but at the same time there are those characteristic features, imposed by the external contours of the position, which facilitate evaluation. Therefore a knowledge of the general character of the struggle for a particular pawn formation in the centre makes it easier to orientate oneself, and to find a plan in each specific position of this type.

Typical positions can arise not only in the transition from opening to middlegame, or in a complicated positional struggle of middlegame character. The development of chess shows that their number is growing, and that it does not depend on the stage of the game and the number of fighting units on the board. It is also becoming clearer that the study of typical set-ups has important methodological significance. Without a knowledge and correct understanding of many characteristic features, inherent in such positions, there can be no genuine mastery.

The author of these lines devoted much attention to typical opening positions in his book *Modern Chess Opening Theory* (Pergamon Press, 1965) and certain other works. But here I will dwell on typical situations of an endgame nature, which have appeared in practice and analysis comparatively recently. We will follow how typical endgame positions are reached, using the example of endings in which rook and bishop battle against rook and knight, with pawns on both wings.

Fischer–Taimanov
4th game, Candidates' Match, Vancouver 1971

In Black's position there are no marked weaknesses, and the pawns are arranged almost symmetrically. But the game is by no means over. The black pieces are more passively placed, and the white 'rook+bishop' tandem proves to be highly mobile.

24...b6?

Black apparently fails to sense the danger, and commits an imperceptible, but significant weakening of his pawns. Note that, even after the best continuation, 24...Kd6 25 b4! (but not *25 B×b7 Rb8 26 B×a6 R×b2 27 Bc4 R×c2 28 B×f7 c4*, and the worst is over for Black), it is no easy matter for Black to draw.

25 Bf1 a5 26 Bc4 Rf8 27 Kg2 Kd6 28 Kf3 Nd7 29 Re3 Nb8 30 c3 Nc6 31 a4.

Although on the board there are few pieces and plenty of space, with each move Black becomes more and more cramped.

31...Ne7 32 h3 Nc6 33 h4 h5 34 Rd3+ Kc7 35 Rd5 f5 36 Rd2 Rf6 37 Re2 Kd7 38 Re3 g6 39 Bb5 Rd6 40 Ke2 Kd8 41 Rd3!

Choosing a convenient moment, White exchanges the rooks. A minor piece ending is now reached, in which the bishop demonstrates its decisive superiority over the knight. Black soon ends up in *zugzwang*, and by sacrificing his bishop White eliminates the enemy pawns.

41...Kc7 42 R×d6 K×d6 43 Kd3 Ne7 (otherwise 44 B×c6 is decisive) **44 Be8 Kd5 45 Bf7+ Kd6 46 Kc4 Kc6 47 Be8+ Kb7 48 Kb5 Nc8 49 Bc6+ Kc7 50 Bd5 Ne7 51 Bf7 Kb7 52 Bb3 Ka7 53 Bd1 Kb7 54 Bf3+ Kc7 55 Ka6 Ng8 56 Bd5 Ne7.**

Equally bad is 56...Nf6 57 Bf7 Ne4 58 B×g6 N×g3 59 Kb5.

57 Bc4 Kc6 58 Bf7 Kc7 59 Be8 Kd8 60 B×g6!

The decisive stroke! For the bishop White gains three pawns, and, more important, the knight with its short leaps proves helpless against the pawns.

60...N×g6 61 K×b6 Kd7 62 K×c5 Ne7 63 b4 a×b4 64 c×b4 Nc8 65 a5 Nd6 66 b5 Ne4+ 67 Kb6 Kc8 68 Kc6 Kb8 69 b6 Resigns.

Larsen–Uhlmann
Candidates' Match,
Las Palmas 1971

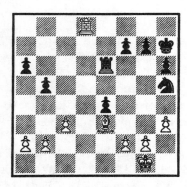

While in the previous example White's basic plan was to restrict the mobility of the black pieces, here, in a more open position,

White aims for a battle on two flanks, so as in the end to exploit his pawn majority on the Q-side.

27 g4! Nf6 28 Kg2 g5 29 Kg3 Ne8 30 h4 g×h4+ 31 K×h4 Kg6 32 b3 f5 33 g×f5+ K×f5 34 Rd5+ Kg6 35 Rh5 Kh7 36 Kg3 Ng7 37 Rc5 Kg6 38 c4! b×c4 39 R×c4.

White's threats are growing. His Q-side pawn majority is becoming more and more of a real force. At the same time Black now has three pawn 'islands', which constitute a serious weakness.

39...Nh5+ 40 Kh4 Nf6 41 Rc5 Rd6 42 Ra5 Nd5 43 Bd2 Kf7 44 Bc1 Rc6 45 Bd2 Rd6 46 Kh3 Kg7 47 Bc1 Nf6 48 Bf4 Rc6 49 Kh4 Kg6 50 b4 Ng8 51 a3 Rf6 52 Kg3 Ne7 53 Be5 Nc6 54 B×f6!

Here too there has come a convenient moment to take play into a minor piece ending, where White's bishop is clearly stronger than the black knight.

54...N×a5 55 Bd4 Nc4 56 a4 Kf5 57 a5 Nd6 58 Bc5 Ke5?

This loses quickly. 58...Nb5 was more tenacious.

59 B×d6+! K×d6 60 Kf4 Kd5 61 b5! a×b5 62 a6 Kc6 63 K×e4 b4 64 f4 Resigns.

These modern examples recall the conclusion of the 2nd game from the **Alekhine–Euwe** World Championship Match (1937).

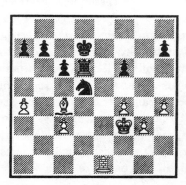

In this position each side has his pawn weaknesses. With his next move, Alekhine, who was playing White, forces a further weakening of the black pawns on the K-side, the opponent's most vulnerable sector.

32 Bd3! h6 33 Bf5+ Kd8 34 Kg4!

An instructive manoeuvre. White pays no attention to possible pawn losses on the Q-side, correctly assuming that the game will be decided on the opposite wing. If now 34... N×c3, then 35 Kh5 N×a4 36 K×h6, and wins.

34...Ne7 35 Bb1 Ke8 36 Kh5.

The decisive manoeuvre. White's king clears the way for the g- and h-pawns, the advance of which will decide the game.

36...Kf7 37 Ba2+ Kf8 38 K×h6 Rd2.

Similarly after 38...Nf5+ 39 Kg6 N×g3 40 f5 White wins easily.

39 Be6 Rd3 40 g4 R×c3 41 g5 Resigns.

And now we offer to the reader two fragments from Karpov's play. In the first of these White consistently increases the pressure, move by move restricting Black's possibilities.

Karpov–Debarnot
Las Palmas 1976

45 f5! Ke5 46 f×g6 f×g6 47 Rb4 Re1 48 Bd3 Kf6 49 Rf4+ Kg7 50 Kf3 Re5.

It was more expedient to keep the rook on the 6th rank.

51 Rb4! Re7 52 Rb5 (with the imminent threat of Rb5–c5–c6) **52...Rc7 53 Ke3 Kf6 54 Kd4! g5 55 h×g5+ h×g5 56 Ra5 Ke6 57 b3 Kf6 58 Ra1 Nd7 59 Ra5 Nb6 60 g4! Ke6 61 c4! d×c4 62 b×c4 Rd7+ 63 Kc3 Rg7 64 Bf5+ Kf6 65 Kd4 Re7 66 c5! Re5 67 Be4 Nd7 68 Ra6+ Re6 69 R×e6+! K×e6 70 Bf5+ Ke7 71 c6 Resigns.**

And in the following example, in spite of the highly limited material, Karpov concludes the game with a spectacular mating attack.

Karpov–Pomar
21st Olympiad, Nice 1974

Black's position has serious pawn weaknesses at e6 and h6, but perhaps the most vulnerable target for attack is his king.

There followed **35 Ba5+! b6 36 Bd2 Ne4 37 Bf4+ Kb7 38 Rf7+ Ka8 39 Rf8+ Kb7 40 b4 R×g4 41 Rf7+ Ka8 42 Kc2 h5 43 a4! h4 44 Kd3 Ng5 45 Rf8+ Kb7 46 Rb8+ Ka6 47 Bd2 Rg3+ 48 Kc2 Resigns.** Against the threat of b4–b5+ Black has no defence.

We will also examine some situations where, in the battle between the different minor pieces, there are two rooks on either side. In this case a direct attack on the king has a greater chance of success.

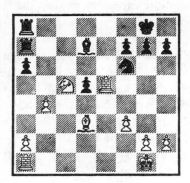

This position occurred in the 7th game of the **Fischer–Petrosian** Candidates' Match (1971).

With his last move, 21...Bc8–d7, Black developed his inactive white-squared bishop. I was a direct witness to this clash, and I must confess that I was considerably surprised when Fischer, almost without thinking, exchanged the pride of his position, his knight at c5, for the 'bad' bishop: **22 N×d7!**

But I soon realized that the path chosen by Fischer was not only non-routine, but also the most effective. The point is not just that after 22...Bb5 the bishop was 'threatening' to transform into a good one, while on 22 a4 Black had the clever reply 22...Bc6. I fancy that what was more important was something else: Fischer quickly judged that his group of pieces (two rooks and bishop) created real preconditions for an attack on the black king, to which the opponent had no counter. The game continued **22...R×d7 23 Rc1 Rd6 24 Rc7 Nd7 25 Re2 g6 26 Kf2 h5 27 f4 h4 28 Kf3 f5.**

The advance of the pawns has merely strengthened White's attack, but Black no longer had any useful moves.

29 Ke3 d4+ 30 Kd2 Nb6 31 Ree7 Nd5 32 Rg7+ Kf8 33 Rb7 N×b4 34 Bc4 Resigns.

In conclusion, here is another interesting example from Fischer's practice, in which the trio of white pieces direct their efforts towards the creation of a passed pawn.

Fischer–Taimanov
Palma de Mallorca 1970

41 Rb5 Rd4 42 c5!

Weaker is 42 h5 g5! 43 c5 Re8 44 c×b6 g4 45 b7 g×f3 46 b8 = Q f2! 47 Qg3+ Ng4 48 Rc1 Re3, when Black has drawing chances.

42...R×h4+ 43 Kg1 Rb4 44 R×b4!

Another subtle move. After 44 Rb3? R×b3 45 R×b3 Nd7 46 c6 Ne5 47 Bd5 Rc8 Black has every right to hope for a draw.

44...a×b4 45 Rc4 b×c5 (no better is 45...Nd7 46 c6 Nc5 37 a5!) **46 R×c5 Kg7 47 a5 Re8 48 Rc1! Re5 49 Ra1 Re7 50 Kf2! Ne8 51 a6 Ra7 52 Ke3 Nc7 53 Bb7 Ne6 54 Ra5 Kf6 55 Kd3 Ke7 56 Kc4 Kd6 57 Rd5+ Kc7 58 Kb5 Resigns.**

Here we can draw certain conclusions. Of course, it is by no means always that a rook and bishop (or two rooks and a bishop) prove stronger than the same set of pieces with a knight. In closed positions, especially if the knight has a good outpost, the situation may be reversed. On the whole we have been examining positions with an open centre, in which the side with the bishop has held the initiative. It is useful to remember the methods of playing such positions (as well as other typical positions).

Practice very quickly puts forward new typical positions. When analyzing them, it is very important to learn to make generalizations, to notice the most typical methods for the given situation.

8

INTUITION AND RISK IN CHESS

In this chapter I wish to dwell on certain important questions associated with the forming of chess mastery. As has already been mentioned, the 'alpha and omega' of it is the cultivation of concrete thinking, the harmonious combining of the elements of strategy and tactics.

I will begin my review with an examination of the problems of intuition, which have both practical and philosophical importance in the understanding of chess thinking.

The role and peculiarities of intuition in chess

It is unlikely that anyone will deny the role of intuition in chess thinking. A player of even the slightest skill knows from his experience that in complex situations, which do not lend themselves to logical evaluation and calculation, you regularly have to take decisions which are not precisely realized, which are intuitive. Sometimes they let you down, and prove to be cut off from the real situation. But sometimes they prove to be amazingly deep and correct.

Up till now there has been little study made in chess literature of questions of intuition. Practically no attempt has been made to create any kind of detailed generalized system of the very rich practical experience.

Of course, this is a complex problem, in particular in its philosophical aspect. To disclose it one must first of all construct a 'bridge' between the known general philosophical ideas about intuition and the specifically chess nature of this concept.

Intuition (in Latin—careful, intent scrutinization, contemplation) is "the ability indirectly, as if suddenly, without resorting to detailed, logical deduction, to find or discover the truth; an inner 'illumination', a clarification of thought, disclosing the essence of the question being studied". This is the formulation given in the Soviet *Dictionary of Logic*.

In pre-Marxist philosophy, intuition was often separated from logical thinking, and was sometimes placed above it. For example, Spinoza regarded intuition as a kind of cognition. Descartes valued intuition more highly than deduction. He wrote: "What I understand by intuition is not a belief in a shaky evidence of feelings, nor the deceptive reasoning of a disorderly imagination, but the concept of a clear and attentive mind, which is so simple and distinct that it leaves no doubt that we are thinking... and, thanks to its simplicity, more trustworthy than deduction itself".

Dialectical materialism certainly does not reject this form of cognition. It regards intuition as the ability of the brain to make a 'leap' in the process of comprehending the truth. Thinking is in its nature dialectical, and cannot manage without leaps.

The fundamental difference between the materialistic treatment of the given question, and the idealistic, is that the Marxist method does not separate intuition from the knowledge and experience already gained. Intuition is impossible without a connection with perceptible and logical cognition, and arises only on the basis of the attainment of a definite volume of concrete data, obtained in the course of experience and analysis. An idea which arises intuitively then goes through a logical checking by comparison with other ideas of a relatively studiable phenomenon.

At the same time, it is impossible to imagine the creative process without intuition, which is one of its most important components. This is confirmed more and more by the development of modern science and practice. The well-known French physicist Louis de Broglie stated that "Science, which is essentially rational in its basis and its methods, can make the most significant achievements only by dangerous sudden leaps of the mind, when there appear capabilities, freed from the heavy chains of strict reasoning, which are called imagination, intuition and wit".

These words of a scientist, in my opinion, also reflect very truly the secret aspects of chess thinking. The intuition of the practical chess player is identical in its nature and the forms of its manifestation to the general principles given above. But there are also certain essential peculiarities.

In particular, in everything, including questions of intuition, the creativity of a player is associated with a strict time control. Unlike an artist or a poet, a chess player cannot wait for the arrival of inspiration. His mastery reveals itself only in the process of play. There is also another 'dimension' of time. The intuition of a chess player operates most often in difficult, highly definite instants of the chess struggle. A player senses that the moment has arrived for the most determined measures, for example, when he has to venture upon a sacrifice, begin a counter-attack,

and so on. Moreover, none of this is subject to exact calculation or logical evaluation. Therefore the thinking of a chess player should possess great will-power and an emotional slant. Incidentally, these same qualities are also required for the calculation of variations, which is inseparably linked with creative fantasy.

In our time, when the competitive factor in chess is increasing more and more, leading players are highly unwilling to share the secrets of their thinking. And in questions of intuition, maximum frankness is required. I even gain the impression that certain of our top masters are as though ashamed of intuitive decisions, and, in the analysis of their games in print, endeavour to conceal them, explaining their thoughts, contrary to the truth, by skill in calculation or deep, conscious foresight. This is a pity. Intuitive ability is one of the most valuable qualities of chess thinking.

I am sure that many original and deep ideas are conceived intuitively at moments of great intensity. Their 'random' nature is purely apparent. They essentially occur naturally. And to share an experience of this sort is not only not shameful, but, on the contrary, is highly useful and instructive. In connection with this, I should like to present for the judgement of the reader an instance from my own practice.

Suetin–Bagirov
31st USSR Championship 1963

With his last move (*17 . . . Be7–d6*) Black appeared to have radically halted White's piece attack on the K-side. Now 18 R×f6 B×e5 19 R×c6 was unattractive because of 19 . . . Q×b2!

What was I to do? I did not wish to go in for simplification. It was here that I was attracted and as though entranced by a queen sacrifice. Feverishly I calculated the variations. The hands on my clock inexorably advanced, but the calculations became more and more complicated. I had to reconcile myself to a draw, or, relying on my intuition, take a risk . . .

18 Q×g7+ !?!

Regarding this point, Mikhail Tal wrote in his commentary: "Undoubtedly the strongest move. Of course, this sacrifice does not win by force, moreover it is probably in general insufficient to win, but even so, to such sacrifices one cannot remain indifferent."

18 . . . K×g7 19 B×f6+ .

Now came the turn for my opponent to think. As was later discovered, this was perhaps the decisive point of the game. Where should the king move to: h6 or g6? Bagirov thought for a whole hour, and also played most probably by intuition.

19 . . . Kh6.

The first analyses failed to reveal any difference between this move and 19 . . . Kg6. But when the tournament passions had died down, A. Lilienthal, in his notes to this game (*Shakhmathy v SSSR*, 1964, No.4) cast doubts on the correctness of the queen sacrifice because of 19 . . . Kg6!

Now 20 Bd3 is parried by 20 . . . Be7! Unfortunately, at this point Lilienthal and other commentators cut short their analyses. Not

without interest is the variation 21 B×e7 R×d3 22 Rg5+ Kh6 23 c×d3 Re8! (but not *23 . . . Q×b2 24 h4 Q×a1+ 25 Kh2*, or *24 Rf1 Q×c3 25 h4*, when the black king is in a mating net) 24 Bf6 Re6! White's attack is played out.

The main battle develops after 19 . . . Kg6 20 Raf1 Qe3 21 Bd3 Kh6!

Now Tal's recommendation of 22 Nd1 Qd2 23 R5f2 (on *23 Nf2* there follows *23 . . . Rg8*) fails to achieve its aim because of 23 . . . Q×f2! After 24 R×f2 Rde8 25 Bc3 f5! the game is in Black's favour.

Of interest is the variation 22 B×d8 R×d8 23 R×f7 Rd7 24 Nd5! (*24 R1f6+ Kg5 25 Rf5+ Kh4!*). Now on 24 . . . R×f7? there follows 25 N×e3, and on 24 . . . Qd2—25 R1f6+ Kg5 26 Rf5+ Kg4 27 R×d7 B×d7 28 Nf6+ Kh4 29 Rh5 mate.

If instead 24 . . . Qg5, then 25 R1f6+ Kh5 26 Be2+! Kh4 27 g3+ B×g3 28 h×g3+ Q×g3 29 Rf4+, and White is assured of a draw.

White's plans, however, are frustrated by the counter-blow 24 . . . B×d5 25 R×d7 B×g2+ 26 K×g2 Qg5+ 27 Kf3 Qf4+ etc.

After 24 . . . B×d5 White can first play 25 R1f6+ Kg5 26 Rf5+ Kh4, and only now 27 R×d7. But here too after 27 . . . Qc1+ 28 Rf1 B×g2+!, or 28 Bf1 B×g2+ 29 K×g2 Q×c2+ Black must win.

And, finally, in the event of 22 B×d8 R×d8 23 Rf6+ Black should retreat his king to g7, and if 24 R×f7+, then 24 . . . Kg8 25 B×h7+ Kh8.

The material balance is in Black's favour. This analysis is given in more detail by me in the article 'Returning to the queen sacrifice' (*Shakhmaty v SSSR*, 1965, No.2).

Thus analysis shows that Black could have parried the attack, and cast doubts on the correctness of the sacrifice. However, practical play and home analysis are by no means the same thing.

Such mysteries have a curious property. They are simple, when they are... revealed. During the course of the game, when under conditions of limited time there are difficult problems to be solved at each move, everything is much more difficult.

For Black the queen sacrifice was first and foremost an unpleasant psychological blow. And subsequently too, Bagirov feels clearly 'out of sorts'.

20 Raf1!

Threatening 21 Rh5+ Kg6 22 Rh4, with the irresistible threats of 22 Bh5+ and 22 Bd3+.

20...Qe3.

To be considered was 20...Be7, after which White could have either forced a draw: 21 Rh5+ Kg6 22 Rg5+, or could have continued sharply: 21 B×e7 f6! 22 B×f6 R×f6 23 R×f6+ Kg7 24 Rf7+ Kh8 23 Bd3 etc.

21 Rh5+ Kg6 22 Rh4! Bf4! (the only defence against mate) **23 Rh×f4.**

23 Rf×f4 appears very strong, but Black has a good reply: 23...Qc1+, and if 24 Bf1, then 24...h5! 25 Ne2 Q×c2.

23...h5.

There is no other defence against 24 Rg4+ or 24 Rh4. On 23...Qh3 there could have followed 24 Ne4!

24 B×d8 R×d8 25 Bd3+ R×d3.

Already in time trouble, Bagirov finds the best defence. Dangerous is 25...Kg7 26 R×f7+ Kg8 27 Bc4 Kh8 28 R7f5 Be8 29 Nd5, when all the same Black must give up the exchange. On 29...Qd2 there follows 30

Rf8+ Kg7 31 Nc7 Bc6 32 R8f2, and White wins. Also bad is 29...Qc5 30 b4 Qd6 31 Rf6 Qe5 32 Rf8+ etc.

26 c×d3 Q×d3 27 Rf6+ Kg5 28 R×f7 h4.

Here I could have forced a draw by 29 R7f5+, but White's position is already objectively better.

29 Kg1 Qe3+ 30 R7f2 Kh5.

The decisive mistake. Saving chances were offered by 30...h3! 31 g×h3 Bf3.

31 Ne2! Kh6 32 Nf4 a5 33 Rd1 a4 34 h3 Kh7 35 Nd5.

Having secured the position of his king, White himself turns to a decisive offensive on the K-side. Black's position is lost.

35...Qc5 36 Nf6+ Kg7 37 a3 Kg6 38 Ng4 Kh7 39 Re1 Qd6 40 Ne3 Kg6 41 Nf5, and White successfully realized his advantage.

It is difficult to convey that state of mind which seized me, beginning at the point when I decided to sacrifice my queen. Here there was both joyful creative excitement, and at the same time satisfaction and pride. After all, I had essentially taken it upon myself to solve a 'super-problem'!

A successful intuitive search is normally accompanied by fervent positive emotions.

Here is a further interesting observation. I have often noticed that intuitive decisions are taken fairly quickly. You as though see before you a high obstacle which it is essential to surmount. And you reach a state such that you forget about risk, and, casting doubts aside, you boldly proceed to surmount the 'barrier'.

Of course, genuine intuitive decisions are only in the final analysis linked with strong-willed or emotional impulses. But intuitive searchings are preceded by logical analysis and the calculation of variations. The intuitive process comes into its own in those complicated cases, when the logical course of reasoning and the calculation of variations does not enable you to penetrate into the depths of the position. At the same time it is they that create a series of preconditions for the taking of the decision. And thus intuition joins your thinking, gathering all experience as if in a focus. Intuition reflects as if in mirror the quintessence of your understanding of chess.

Academician I. P. Pavlov wrote: "I find that all intuition should be understood in the sense that a person remembers the final moment, but the whole path, by which he approached and prepared, he did not count towards the given moment". These words reflect the thinking process of a scientist on the path to a scientific discovery, where intuitive illumination represents the final, concluding act of creativity.

In the practical solving of problems facing a player, intuitive searches appear to be of a mainly problematic nature, and involve considerable risk. On the whole, they do not have the aim of solving the problem completely, but merely guess the most promising path of play, or at any rate determine the posing of new, original problems, which are difficult to solve in practice.

But this is splendid! Chess creativity can exist only if there is a constant emergence of new ideas and problems. On the contrary, their final analytical solution, even if it be of the most beautiful form, leads to an increase in the number of 'memorial plaques' in chess theory. This has manifested itself particularly strikingly in the historical development of many ancient opening variations. Irrespective of their specific evaluation, signifying a draw or an obvious advantage for one of the sides, they have ceased their existence.

Thus in the process of chess creativity, in-

tuitive decisions play the same driving, leading role as they do in science and in art. They enable new problems to be posed and discovered, which is the very core of creativity.

We will continue our discussion on chess intuition in the following example.

Valiev–Suetin
Minsk 1964

This game was played in the last round of the USSR Championship Semi-Final, and from my position in the tournament—for the umpteenth time!— I had to play for a win, and at any rate it was vital for me not to lose. I think that the reader will understand my state of mind when, in the position in the diagram I discovered a complicated combination, involving considerable risk. Overcoming my competitive fears, I nevertheless relied on my intuition, and played:

21...N×d4!

As the following move reveals, the main object of the attack becomes a concealed weakness—White's g2 square!

22 B×d4 B×g2!

The point of Black's plan. Exploiting the congestion of the white pieces, Black hurls himself at the enemy king.

How should White play now? In the event of 23 K×g2 there follows 23...Qg4+ 24 Kf1 R×d4 25 Be2! (the best defence; White loses quickly after *25 Nc5 Rf4!*, or *25 b3 Qh3+*) 25...Qe4! 26 Bf3 R×d1+ 27 R×d1 Q×a4 28 Q×c6 Q×c6 29 B×c6 Rc8, and Black has a won ending.

23 B×g7.

Possibly the best defence was 23 Be2 B×d4 24 K×g2 B×c3 25 R×d7 R×d7 26 b×c3! Rd2 27 Bf3 Rc8. Here too the position is in Black's favour, but for him to realize his advantage is still by no means simple.

23...Qg4 24 f3.

After this White ends up by force in a losing position. More tenacious was 24 Be5, after which one of the main variations of Black's combination could have occurred: 24...Bh3+ 25 Bg3 Qf3 26 Bf1 Q×d1 27 R×d1 R×d1 28 Qd3! R×d3! 29 B×d3 Rd8 30 Nc5 Rd5 31 b4 a5 32 a3 a×b4 33 a×b4 Rd4, and although the ending is definitely in Black's favour, he still has to work hard to realize his advantage.

It is interesting that, the further events in the game developed, the more I penetrated into the purely concrete aspect of the play, and relied on exact calculation.

24...B×f3+ 25 Kf2 B×d1 26 Nc5.

White is stunned by his opponent's combination, and again fails to utilize his tactical resources. Black would have had more 'reefs' to negotiate after 26 R×d1. Then, for example, 26...Q×d1? is bad because of 27 Bh6! f6 28 Qc4+ Kh8 29 Qf7 Rg8 30 Q×e7! Correct is 26...f6 27 B×f6 e×f6 28 Qc4+ Q×c4 29 B×c4+ Kg7 30 R×d8 R×d8 31 Ke3 f5!, and Black should win the resulting ending.

26...f6 27 B×f6 (no better is 27 Bh6 Qh4+ 28 Kf1 Q×h6 29 R×d1 Q×h2, when with a material advantage Black continues his attack) **27...e×f6 28 Bc4+ Kg7 29 Ne6+ Kh6 30 Q×f6.**

Both kings are in a mating net. It is the turn to move that decides....

30...Rd2+ 31 Ke3 Re2+ 32 B×e2 Q×e2+ 33 Kf4 (not, of course, 33 Kd4? Q×b2+) **33...Q×h2+ 24 Ke4 Qe2+ 35 Kf4 Qf2+ 36 Ke5 Q×b2+ 37 Nd4 Re8+.**

The conclusion of the game is accurately calculated.

38 Kd6 Qb8+ 39 Kc5 Re5+ 40 Kc4 Be2+ 41 N×e2 Qb5+ 42 Kc3 Re3+ White resigns.

As will be seen, intuition is very closely interwoven with the basic components of thinking. It follows that it is an integral and very definite factor of thinking. Besides, the range of intuitive ideas is very wide, and encompasses both combinational and positional forms of chess creativity. Above we have given examples of intuition of a combinational nature. We will now examine an example of positional intuition. As the reader will be able to see, these two varieties are not so distant from one another.

This position occurred in the game **Rauzer-Botvinnik** (8th USSR Championship, 1933).

Black continued **16...d5!**, beginning large-scale strategic play in the centre. This decision is mainly intuitive, although it reflects in concentrated form both a very deep understanding of the position, and calculating ability. But even so, such moves cannot be checked to the end by calculation. Here one needs a creative impulse, going beyond the limits of usual thinking norms, and demanding tremendous effort.

17 e×d5 e4! 18 b×c4.

The following variations were also possible:
18 B×e4 N×e4 19 N×e4 B×d5 20 Qd3 Qc6 21 Bf2 Re8;
18 N×e4 N×d5 19 Kh1 N×e3 20 Q×e3 Bd4 21 Qd2! Bb2 22 Qb4 B×c1 23 Nf6+ Kh8! 24 Qc3 Bd2 25 Qb2 Be6! 26 Nd5+ Bc3 27 N×c3 Kg8 28 Ne4 Q×f4 29 Nf6+ Kf8, with advantage to Black (analysis by A. Bekker).

18...e×f3 19 c5 Qa5 20 Red1.

This loses quickly. 20 Qd3! was essential, to which, in turn, Black should play 20...b6! 21 c×b6 a×b6 (or *21 g×f3 b×c5*), with good counter-play for the pawn.

20...Ng4! 21 Bd4.

21 Ne4 is slightly better, although even here after 21...Q×d2 22 B×d2 Bd4+ 24 Kh1 f×g2+ 24 K×g2 R×d5 Black has every chance of winning.

21...f2+ 22 Kf1 (on 22 Kh1 there follows 22...R×d5! 23 N×d5 f1=Q+!) **22...Qa6+ 23 Qe2 B×d4 24 R×d4 Qf6! 25 Rcd1 Qh4 26 Qd3 Re8 27 Re4 f5! 28 Re6 N×h2+ 29 Ke2 Q×f4 White resigns.**

Up till now we have given illustrations demonstrating the strength of intuitive decisions

(at any rate, their successful role in the outcome of the game). In the Suetin–Bagirov game we saw the objective risk which such experiments sometimes involve. I should now like to share with the reader one unsuccessful experiment.

In the diagram is a position from the game **Suetin–Kuzmin** (Sochi, 1970).

White had at his disposal a simple plan: 21 a4 Qb8 22 Qa3 followed by b2–b4, which would have enabled him to strengthen his position, without hastening with any radical measures. But I was attracted by a sacrifice of the exchange. I must frankly admit that, when considering the move **21 R×d6!?**, I was unable to reach any definite results by calculation, and took the decision mainly by intuition. All that was clear was that for the exchange White would gain two pawns, although Black's pieces would be markedly activated. Jumping ahead, I should mention that, on the whole, intuition did not let me down here. The misfortune lay elsewhere. In the subsequent play I did not display sufficient energy, and move by move let my chances slip.

After **21...B×d6 22 R×d6 Qb8 23 Qb4 Rc8 24 B×b6 N×b6** White should have played not 25 R×b6, but 25 Q×b6, retaining the better chances. What I did't like was the simplification: 25 Q×b6 Rd7 26 R×d7 N×d7. But then after **25...Rd7**, now by 'bad' intuition (here it was necessary to calculate variations exactly), White played **26 e5**? For some reason I gave least consideration to Black's main reply—the capture of the pawn: **26... Q×e5!** After all, White had the move **27 R×b7**, when I considered 27...Rd2 to be impossible because of 28 Nd5 R×c2 29 Ne7+ Kh8 30 N×c8 with the threat of 31 Qf8+, while the variation 27...R×b7 28 Q×b7 Rb8 29 Q×a6 Nh5 30 Qa7 followed by 31 Qe3 confirmed for me the correctness of e4–e5.

But when Black nevertheless played **27... Rd2**, I noticed that 28 Nd5 R×c2 29 Ne7+ Kh8 30 N×c8 did not work because of 30... Rc1! 31 Qf8+ Ng8, when it is White who is mated. I was forced to play **28 Qb3**, but after **28...h5 29 Ne4 N×e4 30 f×e4 Qf4!** I was no longer able to 'repair' the position.

Yes, on intuition alone you will not go far. Incidentally, the fading of a chess player's talent is reflected equally in graphical thinking and in intuition. From a certain age a player loses the ability to surmount high barriers.

In addition, it must not be forgotten that intuitive searchings are experimental, and are constantly accompanied by risk. To this the words of Emanuel Lasker are fully applicable: "The chess player may bear responsibility for his work, but not always for his results!"

The field for study of a player's intuition is very wide. Krogius correctly remarks in his book *O Psikhologii Shakhmatnovo Tvorchestva*: "Despite the supposedly general nature of the origination of intuitive decisions, in chess practice they manifest themselves... highly individually". Indeed, the positional 'flair' of Capablanca, Botvinnik, Smyslov, Petrosian and Fischer has become proverbial. At the same time, brilliant combinational 'flair' distinguishes the games of Anderssen, Chigorin, Alekhine and Tal. I think that, in the final analysis, such a distinction is determined by the entire aggregate of natural abilities and understanding of chess. Thus Petrosian always

believes subconsciously in the logical course of the struggle, while Tal, on the contrary, builds his intuitive searchings on exceptions.

To conclude this section, let us sum up.

The taking of intuitive decisions is a thinking process which is equally as necessary as logical analysis. It is employed in complex situations, which do not lend themselves to calculation and to the normal rules of evaluation. And although this sort of position is not encountered 'at every step', it is nevertheless embodied in the very nature of the game.

As a method of thinking, play by intuition, like others, has its virtues and drawbacks. It normally involves some risk, and demands enormous thinking energy. The practical aim of it lies mainly in the setting of difficult problems, by which the creative potential of a player is tested. Intuition is mainly individual, but at the same time one can distinguish in it certain basic types, each of which, in turn, has its advantages and drawbacks.

Intuitive abilities can and must be developed. To this aim it can sometimes be useful to 'run through' the pages of a chess periodical, so as to look through as many tournament games as possible. In doing this you will not delve into all the intricacies of the variations, but will simply pick up new ideas. This will considerably enrich your creative potential.

Broad aspects of intuition

Intuitive searchings accompany not only the immediate creative activity of the practical chess player. They also play an important role in the historical development of chess. As has already been mentioned, the evolution of visual ideas leads in the end to the creation of new verbal ideas. And in this process, intuitive creativity also appears. When Steinitz, Chigorin and Lasker began carrying out in practice their complicated thinking conceptions, in many respects they were intuitively posing and solving the advanced questions of their time.

All this did not always occur smoothly and without conflict. The new was normally conceived (and is conceived) in a heated dispute with the old, established ideas.

In connection with this, let us recall one of the pages of chess history. We have in mind the period when, after Alekhine's defeat in his match with Euwe in 1935, his creative conceptions were subjected to scathing criticism.

It has to be said that, roughly from the beginning of the 1930s, Alekhine became more and more dissatisfied with purely classical forms of chess (of which, incidentally, he had a complete mastery). Already at the tournament in Bled (1931), and especially in his match with Bogoljubov (1934), he embarked more and more firmly along the path of new, highly complicated and risky creative searchings. In his games there regularly began to appear strategic methods which were unusual for that time: positional sacrifices of a pawn (or pawns) for problematic advantages of better piece play, an obvious disregard for positional weaknesses, and so on. In other words, there was observed in his play a striving to revise the still popular teachings of Steinitz, which he tried to oppose with his dynamic searchings.

It is now clear that this was the quest of a true artist, who intuitively sensed the necessity for a renewal of chess ideas. But even a great master cannot fully detach himself from his time. In those years the number of sharp opening systems, providing wide scope for fantasy, was very inconsiderable. He was forced to operate by guess-work, at times trying to vindicate rather eccentric ideas. Here is an example, which, incidentally, drew sharp criticism.

In the 7th game of his 1935 match with Euwe, Alekhine, playing White, after **1 e4 e6**

2 d4 d5 3 Nc3 Bb4 4 Ne2 d×e4 5 a3 Be7 6 N×e4 Nc6 made the eccentric pawn advance **7 g4!?**

Regarding this, he wrote: "I decided to try this at first sight paradoxical pawn move, the obvious idea of which is to combine the flank development of the bishop with a possible K-side pawn storm...". And then: "This move was criticized too severely, and should by no means lead to a bad position".

In practice the innovation proved highly effective, and straight away Euwe did not choose the best reply: **7...b6** (stronger is 7...Nf6! 8 N×f6+ B×f6 9 Be3 Qd5, with a good game for Black) **8 Bg2 Bb7 9 c3 Nf6 10 N2g3 0–0?**

A further inaccuracy. Euwe fails to sense the danger of White's subsequent attack. After the simple 10...Qd7 followed by Q-side castling Black could have successfully deployed his forces.

11 g5 N×e4 12 N×e4 Kh8 13 Qh5! Qe8.

Black overlooks a purely tactical blow. 13...Na5 was essential, avoiding immediate danger.

14 Nf6! B×f6.

After 14...g×f6 15 g×f6 Na5 16 f×e7 Q×e7 17 B×b7 N×b7 18 Bg5 f6 19 Bh6 Rg8 20 0–0–0 Nd6 21 Rhe1 White has an obvious advantage.

15 g×f6 g×f6 16 Qh4 Qd8 17 Bf4! e5 18 Bg3 f5 19 d×e5, and White confidently converted his advantage into a win.

I think it unlikely that the innovatory nature of Alekhine's searchings was fully understood by even the very best methodologists of that time. Thus in an article in *Shakhmaty v SSSR*, 1937, No. 3, the well-known player and theorist Romanovsky, who, incidentally, always stood up for lively chess creativity, sharply criticized Alekhine's experiments. Here is what he wrote: "After winning his celebrated match against Capablanca, in his work *Auf dem Wege zur Welt-meisterschaft** Alekhine publicly declared that there had begun for him 'an era of new tasks and new responsibility'. What these new tasks comprise, Alekhine did not explain, but on the other hand he clearly demonstrated in a number of the games from the match with Euwe (1935) that the new responsibility consisted mainly of his Champion's irresponsibility... Alekhine displayed to the dumfounded, and then indignant chess world such 'creative specimens' that his supporters could only spread their hands".

Romanovsky goes on to criticize a whole series of Alekhine's strategic innovations, in particular his sacrifice of a pawn for good piece play (in our time one of the most common and effective devices). Let us examine one of the criticized examples, from the viewpoint of modern chess understanding.

In this position from the game **Alekhine-Fine** (Hastings, 1937) White went in for a rather risky sacrifice of a pawn for the initiative.

15 Nf5!?

Quieter was 15 c×d4 e×d4 16 Nf5 Q×c2 17 N×e7+ Kh8 18 Nf5, with slightly the better game for White.

15...d×c3 16 Q×c3! Rfc8 17 Qg3 (nothing is gained, of course, by 17 N×e7+ Q×e7 18 Q×a5 R×c2) **17...Bf8 18 Bd3 Nc6 19 Bg5 Ne8 20 Rac1 Qb7 21 a3 g6 22 Nh6+ B×h6 23 B×h6 Nd4 24 Rcd1 b4 25 f4! e×f4 26 Q×f4.**

Alekhine persistently seeks ways to gain the initiative. At the moment the position is balanced, but Black faces a gruelling defence, and constantly has to reckon with White's concrete threats.

26...b×a3 27 b×a3 Rc3 28 Qf2 Ne6?

Black fails to withstand the intensity of the struggle. After 28...Nc6 29 Bc1 Ne5 30 Bf1 Ng4 he would have had a sound enough position, although White's two active bishops would have almost compensated for the opponent's extra pawn.

29 a4 Rac8 30 Rf1 R3c7 31 Rb1 Qc6 32 a5! Nc5?

And this is a decisive error. The lesser evil was 32...Ra8.

33 Bc4 Qd7 34 Qa2! N×e4 35 R×f7 Q×f7 36 B×f7+ R×f7 37 Qe6 Resigns.

An excellent production, wouldn't you agree? The game was conducted by White with great style and inventiveness.

It should also be mentioned that, already in his return match with Euwe, Alekhine demonstrated the correctness and practical effectiveness of his innovatory conceptions. And in our time the dynamic treatment of chess has completed its triumphant path from an intuitive experiment to a scientifically based method.

Basic indications of a player's strength

We often speak of the strength of a player in set terms, many of which have long become part of everyday chess journalism (for example, deep positional understanding,

*Translated into English as *On the Road to the World Championship 1923–1927*, (Pergamon, 1984).

depth of calculation, combinational scale). But each of these qualities in isolation does not yet say anything about the strength of a given player.

A characteristic feature of modern high-class chess mastery is its universality. It has become an axiom that, in our time, the standard for each young player, who is aiming for competitive heights, is to possess the arsenal of all fighting means. Does not this signify that what should be regarded as of paramount importance is the development of chess strength—a synonym for universality?

The concept of chess strength contains a whole series of interesting, and at times highly subtle nuances. Still topical in this respect is the article by Tartakover 'What constitutes chess strength' (*Shakhmatny Listok*, 1929, No.4). In it the author concentrates his attention on questions of chess technique, placing it in direct dependence on playing strength. "A big role in the revelation of chess strength is played by the principle of will", wrote Tartakover, "and for the attainment of success, especially important are such qualities as the cool implementation of one's plan, the stubborn organization of defence, and the timely identification of a crisis".[1]

I should like to draw particular attention to this last point.

Black appears to be close to equalizing. He only needs to play, for example, 14... Be6, and the game will be almost completely level. But it is White to move, and Tseshkovsky not only correctly senses the moment of crisis, but also finds a way to increase his advantage.

14 Qd5! Bb7 (it is easy to see that otherwise Black cannot avoid loss of material) **15 Q×d8 B×d8 18 Nd6! Bc8 17 Ne5 N×e5 18 B×a8 Bg4 19 f4! Nd7 20 Bf3,** and the remainder became a matter of simple technique.

Of course, it is by no means always that one can catch so precisely the crisis points of a game. In modern dynamic play, such points are normally linked with tactical subtleties.

Gligoric–Sax
Vrbas 1977

By playing here 22...R×c1 23 R×c1 Qd7 followed by ...Rc8, Black would have had at least an equal game. But Sax lost his sense of danger, and continued **22...R×a2?**

There followed **23 e6! Qd6 24 d5! Be5.**

After 24...f×e6 25 d×e6 Qe5 26 h×g6 h×g6 27 N×g6 Q×g3 28 N×e7+ Kh7 29 f×g3 B×e6 30 R×f8 B×f8 31 Rc7 White has a big advantage.

25 Rc6 B×f4 26 e×f7+ R×f7?

This is the last point when Black could have

Tseshkovsky–Savon
Ljubljana/Portoroz 1977

saved the game. Necessary was 26...K×f7 27 B×f4 Q×d5 28 Rc7 Re2. Now the attack on the king is decisive.

27 B×f4 Q×d5 28 Rfc1! Rc2 29 R6×c2 B×c2 30 Bh6! e5 31 Qc3 Resigns.

Every strong player has his own idea about the most important factor of playing strength. For me this was always associated with the ability imperceptibly, move by move, to outplay the opponent. In this respect, many of Karpov's outwardly unstriking games are remarkable.

Hübner–Karpov
Tilburg 1977

1 c4 Nf6 2 Nc3 c5 3 Nf3 d5 4 c×d5 N×d5 5 g3 g6 6 d3 Bg7 7 Bd2 b6 8 Qa4+ Bd7 9 Qh4 Bc6 10 Bg2 e6!?

An instructive point. For the moment White still retains an opening initiative, and Karpov chooses the simplest way of neutralizing it—the method of simplification. But doesn't this signify that already here he is ready to agree to a draw? No! This question must be regarded in a different light. Karpov first and foremost plays chess, proceeding on the basis that, even in positions lacking in sharpness, there are usually still considerable resources left to play for a win. And in a prolonged manoeuvring game the stronger player has greater chances of success. After all, mistakes lie in wait not only in sharp combinational skirmishes.

11 Q×d8+ K×d8 12 Rc1 Na6 13 N×d5 B×d5 14 Bc3 f6!

Up till now Karpov has happily gone in for simplification, but here he shows that he

has no intention of giving his opponent an easy draw. By retaining the black-squared bishops, Karpov maintains the necessary tension of a persistent nature.

15 a3 Ke7 16 0–0 Rhc8 17 Nd2 Nc7.

This position, if it is evaluated on general grounds, must be considered level in the first, and, probably, the second approximation. But even so the struggle is far from over. Black threatens in time to cramp White's forces on the Q-side and in the centre. Realizing this, Hübner attempts to activate his pieces.

18 b4?!

This undermining move is typical for such formations, but it is normally recommended in the transition stage from opening to middlegame, when the queens are still on the board. In the endgame its strength is markedly reduced, and moreover, here the weakness of the isolated Q-side pawn may reveal itself. This move cannot, of course, be classed as a mistake, but it is a symptom that White has lost his correct bearings.

18...B×g2 19 K×g2 c×b4 20 B×b4+ Kd7 21 Bc3.

A further inaccuracy. Better was 21 Ne4, and on 21...Nd5 – 22 Bd2, although in this case Black could in time create a passed pawn on the Q-side.

21...Nd5 22 Bb2 Bh6 23 e3 B×e3!

And here is a tactical blow, leading by force to a technically won ending for Black. Jumping ahead, we would mention that Karpov conducts the ending of the game with the utmost accuracy.

170

24 f×e3 N×e3+ 25 Kf3 N×f1 26 N×f1
R×c1 27 B×c1 Rc8 28 Bb2 Rc2! 29 B×f6
Ra2 30 Ke3 R×a3.

Black has acquired a pair of connected
passed pawns, which in the end decide the
game.

31 Nd2 b5 32 Ne4 b4 33 Kd4 a5 34 Kc4
Ra2 35 h4 Kc6 36 Bd4 Re2 37 Be5 Re1 38
Bf6 Rb1 39 Be7 e5 40 g4 Rc1+ 41 Kb3 Kd5
42 Bg5 Rb1+ 43 Kc2 Rh1 44 Kb3 Rh3 45
Nf6+ Kd4 46 N×h7 R×d3+ 47 Kc2 a4
48 Be7 Rc3+ 49 Kb1 Rc7 White resigns.

Those young players are mistaken, who
think that it is sufficient to survive a tactical
storm or overcome their opening difficulties
and obtain a stable position, in order to feel
secure against defeat. Even a small source
of lively play will always set the players serious problems. One can cite a truly countless
number of examples of how quickly the
balance can be disturbed in very quiet situations. Normally, players who are unsuccessful in such instances are highly annoyed,
and endeavour to explain their defeats as
being due to purely random causes. How
often one hears this: "I myself don't know
why the rook went to the wrong square...",
or "While the game was complicated I held
my own, but when in an equal ending I
simply had to bring my king to the centre,
and make two elementary moves, the devil
took a hand. I was unlucky!"

I advise you not to get excited, but to think
more deeply. And then behind the game of
chance you will see your fundamental deficiency—weakness of technique. Or, to put
it simply, you will realize that you still have
much to learn about playing chess more
securely (and this means more strongly).

Fischer was once asked whether he had
devised some hitherto unknown method of
play.

"No", Fischer replied, "it is mainly a matter of the mistakes committed by the losers.
I merely successfully exploited them."

It can be asserted that, irrespective of style,
playing strength is mainly associated with
the degree of 'sinlessness' of a chess master,
with his ability to make the minimum of
mistakes.

Thus, he who makes the fewer mistakes is
the stronger player! It often happens that
such an obvious truth is forgotten in serious
discussions on different styles of play.

I on no account wish to belittle the importance of the creative range, the wealth of ideas
of a player. One must distinguish superb
technique from dryness and narrowness of
creativity. Thus Capablanca, Smyslov, Petrosian, Fischer and Karpov are united first
and foremost by their possession of an amazing technique. Many of their games seem so
understandable and strategically clear, that
one gains the impression that such a manner
of play is accessible to anyone. But it is not
by accident that they say that the truth of
genius is simple. To gain a mastery of such
technique is very difficult, and by no means
accessible to everyone.

But in general the creativity of every outstanding master is exceptionally rich in content. And behind meticulous technique is
concealed enormous combinational talent.

Restrictive play and 'pressurizing'

One of the signs of a player's practical
strength is his ability to direct the play along
the necessary lines, and to inflict his will on
the opponent.

Situations of various types can arise in
tournaments. It may happen that, having
already acquired a reasonable number of
points, you meet an opponent who is eager
only for victory, and is aiming at any price
to complicate the game. Here you sometimes

have to turn to severe 'pressurizing', not allowing the opponent to draw you into a heated skirmish.

There is a rich arsenal of such 'retarding paths' in literally every opening. Yes, along with systems revealing broad scope for creativity, theory also knows of many quiet variations (especially for White), leading in the middlegame to very solid set-ups.

Take, for example, the most 'asymmetric' semi-open game—the Sicilian Defence. Along with truly fantastic paths of creative struggle, there are also many means of playing to restrict the opponent's possibilities. One such instructive means is the 2 c3 variation.

This at one time unfashionable variation has in recent times become a frequent guest in master games. And it is employed mainly in those instances when the player with White wishes to avoid double-edged play in favour of reliable 'pressurizing'. At the same time his opponent is not only restricted in the creation of counter-play, but must also play very accurately to equalize. Interesting in this respect is the following game.

Hort–Polugayevsky
'Match of the Century', Belgrade 1970

1 e4 c5 2 c3 Nf6 3 e5 Nd5 4 d4 c×d4 5 Q×d4 e6 6 Nf3 Nc6 7 Qe4 d6 8 Nbd2 d×e5 9 N×e5 Nf6 10 Qa4 Qd5 11 Ndf3 Bd6 12 Bf4 Qe4+ 13 Q×e4 N×e4 14 Bd3 N×e5 15 B×e5 B×e5 16 N×e5 Nc5 17 Bc2 f6 18 Nc4 Ke7 19 0-0-0.

A symmetrical ending has been reached with a small 'plus' for White. Black appears to have no grounds for concern, but danger in such instances is not always sensed by the most circumspect of players.

19...Bd7 20 b4 Na6 21 Nd6 b6 22 Rhe1 g6 23 Bb3 Rad8?!

A more exact way to equalize was by 23... Nc7! 24 f4 Rhd8!

24 f4 Nc7 25 f5 g×f5 26 N×f5+ Kf7 27 Rd3 Bc8 28 Rg3 Ne8 29 Nd4 Nc7 30 Nf5 Ne8 31 Nd4 Nc7 32 Re4 Rdg8 33 R×g8 R×g8 34 Nf5 Rd8 35 Rg4 Ne8 36 Rh4 h5?! 37 R×h5 Kg6 38 Ng3 Ng7 39 Rh4 Bb7 40 Rg4+ Kf7 41 Ne2 f5 42 Rc4 Ne8?

The difficult defence would appear to have exhausted Polugayevsky. Essential was 42... Rd7! 43 Nf4 Kf6 44 Rd4 Bc6, retaining drawing chances. Now Black cannot save the game.

43 Rd4! Rd6 44 Nf4 Bc8 45 Ba4 R×d4 46 B×e8+ K×e8 47 c×d4 Ke7 48 Kd2 Kf6 49 Nd3 Kg5 50 Ke3 Ba6 51 Nf4 Bc4 52 a3 a5 53 g3 Kg4 54 Kf2 Kg5 55 h4+ Kf6 56 Ke3 a×b4 57 a×b4 e5 58 Nd3 e×d4+ 59 K×d4 b5 60 Nf4 Bf1 61 Kd5 Bc4+ 62 Kd6 Bb3 63 Nd5+ Kg6 64 Ke5 Bc2 65 Ne7+ Kh5 66 N×f5 Resigns.

Thus strategic 'brakes' can give considerable practical effect. Without taking account of this, incidentally, it is difficult to penetrate into many of the subtleties of tournament and match struggle between leading grandmasters.

Risk and 'second order' mistakes

As we have already seen, risk in chess has a very wide range. The most dangerous, of course, is tactical risk. It is an extreme measure, and can be justified only in time trouble conditions, or in special instances of a psychological nature. But intuitive risk is not only an expedient, but even at times an essential method of playing.

In this interpretation, risk is not limited only to dynamic situations, but involves many purely positional set-ups. Remember the method of studying typical positions, first employed by Botvinnik back in the early 1930s. For a long time no one was able not only to discover the darker sides to certain of his favourite set-ups, but also to guess at the magnitude of their practical danger. And this enabled Botvinnik, exploiting the routine play of his opponents, regularly to make considerable gains right from the opening stage.

It may be that, objectively, certain of the strategic positions put forward by Botvinnik were dubious. What is more important is the fact that he was ahead of his time, and had a complete mastery of the arsenal of his fighting means.

In our time the 'stonewall' system in the Dutch Defence is considered difficult for Black, and has practically gone out of use. But at that time its problems had been little studied, and Botvinnik, regularly adopting it as Black and being much better prepared than his opponents, achieved great practical success.

Among those to suffer at the hands of it was Salo Flohr, one of the most promising young grandmasters of that time.

Here is how the opening developed in the game **Flohr–Botvinnik** (match, 1932):

1 d4 e6 2 c4 f5 3 g3 Nf6 4 Bg2 Be7 5 Nc3.

In our time the development of the knight at d2 is rightly considered more promising, with the two knights moving according to the scheme: Ng1–f3–e5–d3, and Nb1–d2–f3, keeping control of all the most important points in the centre. The game Petrosian–Bondarevsky (18th USSR Championship, 1950) went 5 Nf3 0–0 6 0–0 c6 7 Qc2 Qe8 8 Nbd2 d5 9 Ne5 Nbd7 10 Nd3! Ne4 11 Nf3 Nd6 12 b3 b5 13 c5 Nf7 14 a4! b×a4 15 R×a4 Bf6 16 Bb2 a6 17 Nfe5 Nf×e5 18 d×e5 Be7 19 f4 Rb8 20 Rfa1 Rb5 21 b4, with a marked positional advantage to White.

5...d5 6 Nf3 c6 7 0–0 0–0 8 b3.

And here 8 Bf4 is more accurate. In this position the development of the bishop at b2 weakens the important f4 square.

8...Qe8 9 Bb2 Nbd7 10 Qd3(?).

Better is 10 Ng5 Bd6 11 f4, and in general the queen is better placed at c2.

10...Qh5 11 c×d5.

A further inaccuracy, after which the bishop at c8 is markedly activated, and the e-file is advantageously opened for Black.

11...e×d5 12 Nd2 (it was essential to play 12 Ne1 followed by f2–f4 and Nf3–e5).

Now Black mounts a massed offensive on the K-side.

12...Ne4 13 f3 N×c3 14 B×c3 f4! 15 Rfe1 Bd6 16 Nf1 Rf7 17 e3 f×g3 18 N×g3 (18 h×g3 R×f3!) **18...Qh4 19 Nf1 Nf6 20 Re2 Bd7 21 Be1 Qg5 22 Bg3 B×g3 23 N×g3 h5!** Black has won the opening battle, and White faces a gruelling defence.

Even so, the development of theory showed that for Black in this system there are more 'thorns' than 'roses'. But while the roses fell to the lot of Botvinnik, the thorns began painfully to prick his imitators. Botvinnik in the meantime had prepared for himself a new 'bunch of roses' which he was able to enjoy sooner than his opponents could find a counter to them.

A healthy degree of risk is an essential factor in the modern chess game, and its chief effect lies in its practical unexpectedness.

Constantly associated with risk are so-called 'second order' mistakes. We include in these inevitable errors during complicated play, which, however, do not entail forced consequences. Such mistakes can be highly diverse in character. At the same time there is no division into 'black' and 'white', as is the case with obvious blunders or serious positional errors.

Out of a number of examples of complex, dynamic play, it can be seen that certain games are literally 'woven' out of individual slight mistakes. It should be said that to avoid such mistakes is almost impossible, and that in practice they are a perfectly normal phenomenon.

'Play without rules'

As practice shows, each stage of a chess game is subject to its own laws. At first (and sometimes for a very long time) the players follow theoretical recommendations. Often the first section of the game they do not play, but simply reproduce a well-known variation up to the 15th, or even the 20th move. Then begins play following the laws of strategy and tactics in accordance with the tastes of the players. If the opening is of a quiet nature, the logical course of events often results in a conflictless middlegame. Then, however one plays, a draw ensues.

It cannot be denied that this is a tedious story. But suppose that, even in such unfavourable creative conditions, it is nevertheless necessary to play for a win? And sometimes an even sharper competitive situation can arise, when, in spite of the quiet situation in the game, both sides must play for a win.

It is here that there begins 'play without rules'. In it the war of nerves assumes the leading role, leading to surprising turns, and also sometimes to amazing collapses. From the logical point of view, such phenomena, especially when the game is studied from its bare score, appear absurd. In order to understand the content of such chaotic duels, which are not subject to the direction of any rules, one must look into their 'heart'.

I will give another example from my own practice. This was in the 11th Chigorin Memorial Tournament in 1977, when my opponent, playing White, was the Rumanian master **Suba.** The game was twice resumed after adjournments: firstly on the eve of the last round until deep into the night, and then on the morning of the next day. In the event of a win I would move up to second place.

In this game there was a sharp contrast between its first part, which was very quiet, and the second, which at times resembled a kind of jazz cacophony.

This position was reached after 47 moves, during the course of which there had been a purely positional battle. Black has an insignificant advantage, since the white pawns at b4 and d3 are slightly weakened. But White has a sound defensive position, and under other circumstances I would have agreed to a draw. But competitive considerations, to which were added vexation, resulting from the fact that in another game the previous day I had gained a won position, only to let slip the win, strongly affected my mood. Hence the subsequent miraculous happenings on the board. They reflect as though in a distorting mirror the subjective nature of certain decisions.

48 Rd1 Qd8 49 Qb3 Rd6 50 Qa3 Qd7 51 Ra1 a6 52 Rd1 Kg7?

The king should not have been placed on the dangerous a1–h8 diagonal.

53 Qb2 Qd8 54 f4!

And here is the reaction! White's hitherto 'silent' centre suddenly sets decisively into motion. It becomes clear that Black has not only lost the slight advantages of his position, but has also allowed his opponent to seize the initiative.

54...Re6 55 f×e5 R×e5 56 Bd4.

Not, of course, 56 B×h4? because of 56... g5 and ...R×e4.

56...Re6 57 e5 Bg5 58 Be2.

With the unequivocal threat of 59 Bg4 and 60 e6+. Black is forced to mobilize all his defensive resources. Nevertheless, the psychological burden of extraneous thoughts was discarded. Willy-nilly I was forced to think only of the events happening on the board.

58...Kg8 59 Bg4 Rc6 60 Bf2.

It was probably better to parry the threat of ...Rc2 by 61 h3.

60...Ba4.

There was no time left for doubts: an open battle is in progress, where it is essential immediately to create concrete threats.

61 Re1 Rc2 62 Qa1 Bc6 63 e6?!

A tempting move, especially in approaching time trouble. But here White should have thought in terms of stabilizing the position. In this respect either 63 Bd1 or 63 d4 deserved consideration.

63...f×e6 64 B×e6+ Kh7 35 Bh3 Bf6 66 Q×a6.

At this point I was firmly convinced that Black must have a forced win, but alas, despite all my efforts, I was unable to find it. Fatigue resulting from the tense struggle was having its effect. Literally up to the last minute before the time control I was working out the variation 66...Bd4 67 B×d4 Q×d4+ 68 Kh1 Qf2 69 Rg1 Re2, but the simple 70 Qa7+ Kh6 71 Qa1 invariably left me at a loss. I should remark that it is mainly combinational vision and calculating ability, in my opinion, that become dulled through fatigue. This is why a player, irrespective of his standard, requires a clear head just as much as a knowledge of theory and the principles of conducting a positional struggle.

Failing thus to find a win, with my flag now poised to fall I decided to sacrifice the exchange: **66...R×f2?!**

And even so after 66...Bd4 there was a forced win. It is achieved by 67 B×d4 Q×d4+ 68 Kh1 B×g2+! 69 B×g2 h3! 70 B×h3 Qf2!, and White has no defence against the mating threats. I tried the idea of ...h4–h3! in many variations, but failed to find the correct form. Meanwhile the battle continued...

67 K×f2 Bd4+ 68 Ke2 Qe7+ 69 Kf1 Qf6+ 70 Ke2 Qe7+ 71 Kf1 Qf6+ 72 Ke2 Bd5 73 Qa4 b5 74 Qc2 Qf2+ 75 Kd1 Qf7.

76 Qe2?

Up to this point White has defended very accurately, but here he makes a decisive error.

76 Kc1 was essential, and if 76...Bb3, then 77 Re7! Q×e7 78 Q×b3 Qe1+ 79 Kc2 Qe2+ 80 Kb1. The white king is under close arrest, but it is not apparent how Black can strengthen his attack. But now follows a dramatic finish, which I was able to anticipate in my adjournment analysis.

76...Bb3+ 77 Kc1 Qc7+ 78 Kb1 Qc3!

It is this move that wins the game. I discovered the manoeuvre ...Qc7–c3 literally just before the start of the morning adjournment session.

79 Qe7+ Kh6 80 Q×h4+ Kg7 81 Qe7+.

White appears to have the menacing move 81 Re7+, but it is parried by the simple 81... Kf8!, when Black wins.

81...Bf7 82 Re2 Bf6 83 Qc5 Q×d3+ 84 Qc2 Qa3 85 Qc5 Qd3+ 86 Qc2 Qd4! 87 Qd2 Qa1+ 88 Kc2 Bb3+! White resigns.

Thus I nevertheless succeeded in gaining a won position (this occurred for the first time on the 66th move), but for this it was necessary, so to speak, to lure the opponent out of his defensive 'armour', by tempting him to play for a win. Such a subsidiary method has existed for a long time in chess strategy. Each time it must be based on psychological calculation, and involves considerable risk.

There is one further conclusion to be made from this story. It is very important, on the threshold of a storm, to retain reserves of fresh inner strength. In practice it is not so annoying to fail to achieve one's goal, as to let slip an apparently certain win.

9

THE VARIOUS STYLES AND SCHOOLS OF CHESS CREATIVITY

These interesting and very important questions still demand a deep study. Although the terms 'style' and 'school' have long been current in chess literature, here there is no generally accepted and precise systemization.

Problems of classifying styles

Before making a necessary excursion into the history of the problem, we should mention that what is meant by style in its general meaning is a device, means or method of work. In its application to various spheres of skill, it is the unity of basic ideological artistic peculiarities, which appear in the works of writers, artists, composers and others. This definition also applies equally to the concept of chess style.

Even the most inexperienced enthusiast is well aware of the generally accepted division of styles into combinational and positional. Until recently it was the basic one. The sign of a combinational style is a striving towards the creation of very sharp tactical situations, sacrifices of material, and fascinating attacks on the king. It is here that the greatest scope is revealed for combinational creativity.

A positional style places in the foreground a rigid scale of material and strategical values, teachings about strong and weak squares, and the dominant elements are those of logic and rationalism.

At the present time such a division, of course, appears too schematic, although it has a perfectly sound basis.

As yet there have been very few serious attempts in chess literature to create a more differentiated division of styles. For a long time virtually the only classification was the one made by Emanuel Lasker in his book *Common Sense in Chess*, published at the end of the last century.*

Lasker picked out the following playing styles, accompanying them with brief descriptions, the essence of which are given below:

1. The style of the automaton. The 'automatically' thinking player finds a move without any special searching or expenditure of energy. He as though takes it from his 'reserves', a kind of prepared pattern, and in similar positions reproduces from memory identical ideas.

Note that subsequently this method of thinking became known as routine.

2. The solid style. It is based first and foremost on the avoidance of danger. Active 'sorties' are permitted only in the event of an obvious mistake by the opponent.

3. The decoy style. This is a rather risky manner of play: the player voluntarily places himself in a dangerous position, where there is apparently no salvation, but where in fact he is still very close to the almost imperceptible drawing verge. And on the first exces-

*Neither this classification nor the citation on p 180 appears in the original English editions of Lasker's book (Translator's note).

sively risky manoeuvre by the opponent there follows a furious counter-attack. (In our time this method has become fairly common. Examples of it can be found, for example, in the games of Petrosian and Polugayevsky).

4. Combinational style. Lasker limits this style only to the calculation of endless variations and the non-acceptance of any rules.

5. The style following the laws of the struggle, or the classical style. Here Lasker had in mind the positional style based on the theory of Steinitz.

In our time this undoubtedly interesting classification attempt, which was innovatory for its time, nevertheless has the appearance of an anachronism. Nowadays we no longer give the name style to individual methods of strategic thinking, such as decoy or the cautious construction of a fortress. Sentence was passed long ago on harmful 'weeds' such as routine thinking, or the blind calculation of variations without evaluation criteria.

It will not be without interest to mention that in the mid 1930s an interesting discussion took place in our chess press on the theme of basic chess styles, in which, however, the main participants were not practical players, but journalists. For example, a division was suggested into classical and psychological styles. The first of these was characterized by objective logic, for which the personality of the opponent was totally irrelevant. For the second type the main criterion was deemed to be the practical struggle, the sense of which depends largely on the individuality of the opponent.

A rather different approach to this problem was made by the Soviet theorist Rauzer. In a small discussion article he stands up for the classical style, which he defines as a synthesis of positional and combinational play, which he contrasts with the 'vulgar practical' style, the style of complications 'with the draw in hand' (cf. *Shakhmaty v SSSR*, 1934, No.8.).

However, interest in the discussion quickly waned, and for a long time the question of styles was again pushed into the background.

Quite recently the problem was referred to by grandmaster N. Krogius in his book *Lichnost v Konflikte* (The Individual in Conflict). He proposed the following rather detailed systemization of the basic syles. :

1. Practical (a tendency towards the attainment of immediate practical gain).

2. Logical and systematic (first and foremost consistency, a reliance on typical positions).

3. Theoretical (relying on the principles of strategy and tactics).

4. Critical and analytic (careful concrete analysis, searchings for exceptions, belief in the lengthy calculation of variations).

5. Artistic (creative fantasy, a tendency towards the original).

6. Combined (a combination of the characteristic peculiarities of the first five styles of play).

7. Harmonious (many-sided, with a wide range).

Such at the present time is the picture of style classification.

For my part, I should like to add the following: the attitude to this or that style, and even its very content, are by no means constant, but depend on new achievements and trends of theory and practice. Take for instance the classical style. Lasker in his time gave this name to the positional style, based on the theory of Steinitz. It was allotted a quite different content in classifications in the 1930s. In our time the concept of classical style has altogether gone out of use, it being too general.

Playing practice has put forward and continues to create a whole series of new, more and more complete chess styles, in which a prominent place is occupied, for example, by the dynamic and universal styles, which originate from the various strategic playing methods examined by us.

In addition, practice confirms more and more that the strict contrasting of styles has long been discarded. In actual fact, there is a constant inter-penetration of the various strategic and tactical methods, which creates additional gradations in the classification of styles.

It would seem that the positional methods of the Steinitz theory were crystal clear, but even here there were considerable differences in the leading representatives of this style. There is no doubt, for example, that Tarrasch and Pillsbury were faithful devotees of the positional style, but a comparison of their games demonstrates eloquently just how different and diverse were its forms.

This applies even more to modern styles of play. Each of them has a number of striking, sometimes eccentric shades. What a wide range is revealed by the dynamic style, which has advanced such a very sharp and extravagant method as the method of ultra-dynamism, with its brain-racking complications and cascades of positional sacrifices!

It has to be said that the problems of modern playing styles still await their large-scale research and a complete, differentiated classification. And even so it would seem that the basic modern varieties of chess styles should be a sound starting-point for analysis. The development of theory shows that it is out of playing styles that the great historical schools of chess creativity have grown and continue to grow.

A little on the historical schools of chess creativity

Turning to chess history, in the first instance, of course, we remember such schools of chess creativity as the romantic and the positional. Each of them can be regarded as a whole era of theory development! Reflected in them was not only a sum of individual practical methods, but first and foremost a system of theoretical views on the conducting of a strategic struggle.

It is interesting that the development of the ideas of each of these schools found its reflection in the national schools, at the time of hegemony in the chess world of the representatives of this or that country.

The cradle of romanticism in the 16th century was Italy, and then it flourished here with new strength in the 18th century, subsequently finding new impulses of development in the French, English and German schools of the 18th–19th centuries. At the same time the forerunner of the great German positional school of Steinitz and Tarrasch must rightly be considered to be the French positional school of the 17th century, originating from Philidor, and, to a certain extent, the English school of Staunton.

An enormous role in the modern development of chess is played by the Soviet chess school. It is this school that has promoted the emergence and detailed analysis of leading styles such as the dynamic and universal.

At the same time, at its roots the Soviet chess school is closely linked with the Russian chess school, which was led by such chess innovators as Chigorin and Alekhine.

Individual playing styles

One should distinguish this or that general style (as a method of strategic thinking!) from the individual style of a specific player. General style (say, positional or combinational) is to a certain extent a collective concept. When it is said that this or that master is a player of combinational style, one has in mind the main direction of his ability. But in reality a player does not, and, it would seem, cannot have any general style in its pure form. His manner of play is 'interfered' with by his character, tastes and inclinations (strangely enough, it is not often that there is harmony between a player's style and his temperament!), and finally, practical necessity.

An example of disparity between method of thinking and human character is to a certain extent provided by the chess career of the outstanding Soviet grandmaster I. Boleslavsky. By the nature of his thinking Boleslavsky was a fervent representative of the combinational style, which determined the enormous activity of his strategy. In his youth he created a series of amazing examples of attacks on the king, which entered for ever into the treasury of chess art. But with the years, Boleslavsky, who was of an amazingly peaceable disposition, began more and more to lose the necessary competitive ambition. And his combinational style began to fade, giving way at times to routine play, which told even more on his tournament successes.

At the same time it is hardly necessary to demonstrate the practical necessity for a player, wishing to attain the heights of mastery, not only to develop his strong points, but also to work constantly on the universalization of his play. From the analysis of the games by the great masters, it can be concluded that there are a great number of positions which, irrespective of their style, they solve in identical fashion. The main role in such cases belongs to the necessary knowledge and general fundamentals of mastery, i.e. to the culture of a player.

Let us therefore try to work out what should be understood by individual style of play. Numerous arguments may be provoked by this question: at what level of qualification (master, candidate master, first category) can it be said that a player has his own style of play?

Until recently it was considered axiomatic that one could speak of a style of play (as in many other fields of art) only in application to genuine masters. In his book *Common*

Sense in Chess, Emanuel Lasker wrote: "...only the maestro possesses a style. I have never seen a player who was not a maestro even once in his life conduct a game consistently. During his lifetime a maestro creates a small number of games which from beginning to end are imbued with one and the same thought, which is completely perfected by him, but even this alone is sufficient to justify the claims of the maestro to a definite style, characteristic of himself alone... If, in order to become a maestro, it were sufficient to be a master of calculation, there could be no question of the style of a maestro. But the logic of chess is by no means of a calculating nature. For the adding machine $2+2$ will always be 4, but a master move in chess is rarely the only correct one. It is determined only after weighing up everything 'for' and 'against', and moreover the most insignificant factors can give the advantage to one side or the other; a considerable role is also played by personal inclinations, and, what is most important, a very active part is played by the fantasy inspiring the player".

The presence of a style is undoubtedly one of the true signs of mature mastery. But at the same time it seems to me that the broad development of chess teaching in our country, which often enables all the development stages of young players to be followed, gives the possibility of examining this question 'in the second approximation'.

From almost its first steps we are fairly well acquainted with the career of Mikhail Tal, and I fancy that the basis of his style was laid down long before he became famous. As long ago as 1954, the strong master Saigin, who to the surprise of many had lost to the 17-year-old Tal a qualifying match for the master title, said: "Tal has a 'terrifying' style. Soon even grandmasters will know of this".

In front of my eyes began the chess career of the striking and original master Viktor

Kupreichik. I am becoming more and more convinced that Kupreichik's style (I have in mind his entire approach to the game, and not only his combinational inclinations) was formed very early, back in the period of his chess youth. Once I was talking to him on this topic. The conversation was about how his play, for all its energy and inventiveness, suffered from annoying inconsistency, for which his extreme uncompromisingness was to blame. "That's right, of course", said Viktor after some thought, "but even so I can't do anything about it. I am convinced that my entire career can only be this way. Otherwise I would cease to be myself".

And even so, playing style can change fundamentally even for a fully developed and strong master. If we follow, for example, how the style of grandmaster Bondarevsky developed, we see that up to roughly his mid-forties he was in his element in combinational play, but then he sharply changed his role, and began playing much more rationally and dryly. And, it would seem, he was wrong to do so.

Although style is one of the indications of mastery, by no means every master has complete possession of some style. This is becoming even more marked in our time, when competitive factors in chess acquire ever greater importance, which also has its darker side. The practical playing strength, technique and knowledge of many talented young players develop' quickly enough, but at times there is a lack of distinctive and original play.

This directs me more and more strongly to the thought that an individual playing style is not only a function of mastery, but in particular a property of the nature and education of a person. A style can be formed by various ways and means, but it is always linked to the natural intellect of the player. In other words, style is character.

Playing style and chess practice

What connection nevertheless exists between mastery and playing style? In order to answer this question, let us turn to the games of some great players. And then we will inevitably come to the conclusion that genuine mastery presupposes the possession of a variety of methods of play (of which, strictly speaking, the reader may already have repeatedly become convinced).

What universally recognized masters of positional play are, for example, grandmasters Tigran Petrosian and Svetozar Gligoric! And even so in their practice there are double-edged, truly irrational games, fantastic combinations and simply reckless attacks, which defy sensible logic.

As illustrations we will use two of their games played against each other. In both of them Petrosian had White, and Gligoric as Black employed the King's Indian Defence. Incidentally, Petrosian and Gligoric have played so many interesting King's Indians, that on this material one could make a special study of the subtleties of this popular opening (I should mention that such a method of studying an opening is one of the most effective).

As a rule, in the majority of these duels, Petrosian, playing in strict positional style, attempted to 'press' on the opponent's position on the Q-side, while Gligoric sought counter-play on the K-side.

Petrosian–Gligoric
Los Angeles 1963

In this game, however, a tactical battle developed in the centre. The first to disturb the balance was Petrosian. Perhaps this was influenced by the competitive situation, which demanded that he play for a win? At that point the Yugoslav grandmaster was leading the tournament.

17 e5!? N×e5!? (blow for blow! 17...
d×e5 is unpleasantly met by 18 f5!) **18 f×e5
B×e5 19 Rf3 Nc7 20 Qd2 Qe7 21 Bg2 a6 22
Rb1 b5 23 a×b5 a×b5 24 b3 B×e2 25 N×e2
b4 26 Rbf1 Ra1 27 Nc1 Nb5 28 R×f7! Q×f7
29 R×f7 K×f7 30 Bf1 Nd4 31 Kg2 Nf5 32
Bd3 Kg7 33 B×f5 g×f5 34 Qd3 Rf8 35 Bd2
f4 36 Kf3 Ra7 37 Qe4 Ra3 38 Qc4 Ra7 39
Qc2 Re7 40 Nd3! Bd4 41 Qc4 Be3 42 B×e3
R×e3+ 43 Kf2 Rh3 44 Kg1 Rf5 45 Qe4
R×g5+ 46 Kf1 Rg6 47 N×f4 Rf6 48 Kg2
Resigns.**

Here Petrosian literally snatched victory
in a tense tactical battle, and, moreover, in
the course of the struggle he had to display
exceptional combinational perspicacity.

Throughout his career Gligoric has stubbornly upheld the King's Indian Defence.
Sometimes he suffers setbacks in it. The question arises: perhaps his style would be closer
to the purely defensive classical opening systems? But on a careful examination of his
games, such a question no longer arises.
How many excellent examples of counter-
attack has Gligoric created in this sharp
opening!

Petrosian–Gligoric
Zagreb 1970

White has just attacked the black knight.
After 14...Ng6 White has an obvious advantage, while in the event of 14...Nh3+

15 Kg2 N×f2 16 K×f2 g4 17 B×g4! Black's
attack is repelled. And even so, Gligoric
finds an original way to develop his attack,
and does not stop short of making sacrifices.

**14...Nd4! 15 g×f4 N×f3+ 16 Q×f3 g4
17 Qh1?**

A serious mistake. After 16 Qd3 e×f4 17
f3 Bf5 18 Nde4 g×f3 19 R×f3 B×c3 20
Q×c3 B×e4 21 R×f4 Qg5+ 22 Qg3
Q×g3+ 23 h×g3 R×f4 24 B×f4 a5 25 b×a5
R×a5 26 Re1, White, according to analysis
by Petrosian, should be able to save the game.

17...e×f4 18 Bb2 (18 Ra3 is slightly better) **18...Bf5 19 Rfe1 f3 20 Nde4 Qh4 21 h3
Be5.**

In spite of his extra piece, White's position
is indefensible. We have an example of positional *zugzwang* with the board full of pieces.

**22 Re3 g×h3 23 Q×f3 Bg4 24 Qh1 h2+
25 Kg2 Qh5 26 Nd2 Bd4 27 Qe1 Rae8 28
Nce4 B×b2 29 Rg3 Be5 30 Raa3 Kh8 31
Kh1 Rg8 32 Qf1 B×g3 33 R×g3 R×e4
White resigns.**

Gligoric conducted this game like a striking representative of the combinational style.

Are not these examples of genuine mastery? Although, I repeat, by nature both of
these outstanding grandmasters are adherents
to and innovators in the positional style.

I should add to this that any great master of a combinational tendency also has a number of examples of excellent positional play.

The individuality of chess creativity

The individual playing characteristics of a great player are always wider than that style to which he belongs. Remember, for instance, that leading light of positional play, Carl Schlechter. In the memories of the majority of chess players there now remains only the basic aspect of his style. But meanwhile the genuine characteristic of his style was much more complex and interesting.

Let us begin with the assessment given of him by Emanuel Lasker in 1909: "Schlechter evaluates a position completely objectively. If it is good, he attacks consistently, persistently and intelligently. If it is level, he plays carefully, cautiously, without false illusions. If his position is dangerous, he becomes desperate: he sets the opponent cunning traps, and undertakes desperate attacks or defends with unusual tenacity—according to circumstances. He is an example of a genuine fighter".

Here is an example of his defence in a difficult position.

Chigorin–Schlechter
Ostende 1901

White has a won position, but a certain accuracy is still required of him. With the aim of escaping as soon as possible from the checks, White is very anxious to exchange the queens. Realizing this, Schlechter set a cunning trap: **1...Qc7+ 2 Qb6+??** (2 b6 is correct) **2...Ka8!!**, and White was forced to agree to stalemate.

Somewhat later, after losing to Schlechter in one of their games for the World Championship, Lasker wrote: "Even the prospect of victory does not divert him, and does not shake his caution. How can one win against a player who reacts with equal coolness to the delusion of success and to the threat of an imminent attack; who regards safety as of paramount importance, and who proceeds towards his goal most scientifically, or when it is necessary, with guile and flair? The answer to this question is not yet known. For the moment the following can be said. If Schlechter's strategy were combined with the initiative in the appropriate place, we would have a complete style, and Schlechter would be invincible. On the other hand, it is not granted to anyone to be absolutely faultless. Every kind of virtue in a chess player is always, in the end, merely an approximation to an ideal. Everyone has some kind of concealed weakness, and most often this is an illness, excessive boldness or inexact observation". This pronouncement, in my opinion, is of general methodological interest, and retains its topicality to this day.

Schlechter was primarily a strategist. The predominance of the strategic principle was especially noticeable in his handling of the opening. It is interesting that Schlechter was the editor of the 8th edition of Bilguer's *Handbuch*, that encyclopaedia of opening variations. He introduced many valuable ideas into the theory of closed openings. To this day his system in the Slav Defence is popular: 1 d4 d5 2 c4 c6 3 Nf3 Nf6 4 Nc3 g6. It was Schlechter who in 1908 first employed the system 1 d4 d5 2 c4 e6 3 Nc3 c5 4 c×d5 e×d5 5 Nf3 Nc6 6 g3!, which was subsequently analyzed in detail by Rubinstein.

Schlechter had excellent combinational vision, but his combinations, as a rule, played a subordinate role in the overall strategic plan. At the same time he was one of the founders of the positional sacrifice.

Schlechter–Gunsberg
Monte Carlo 1901

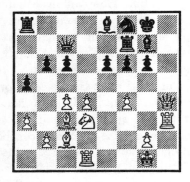

With the aim of developing his attack, Schlechter resorts to a subtle positional sacrifice of a pawn: **28 d5! e×d5 29 c×d5 c×d5 30 Nf2! Rd8** (30...f5? 31 Qh8+!) **31 Ng4 Rd6 32 Bb3 Bc6 33 Rdd3 Qd8 34 f5! g5** (34...g×f5 35 Rdg3! f×g4 36 R×g4) **35 Qh5 Be8 36 Ne3! Rfd7 37 N×d5! R×d5.**

White's queen is taboo. On 37...B×h5 there would have followed 38 N×f6++ Kh8 39 R×h5+ Bh6 40 R×h6+ Kg7 41 N×e8++ K×h6 42 Rh3 mate!

38 R×d5 Bf7 39 R×d7 Q×d7 40 Rd3, and White won.

This game was highly rated by Chigorin, and there were a number of examples of this type in Schlechter's practice. They show that he was not averse to a certain degree of risk, which, however, was based on sound intuition (this was his strong side).

At the same time the opinion grew up that Schlechter did not fully disclose his talent. As Réti rightly remarked, Schlechter displayed his full strength only in bad positions. Strangely enough, his crystal-clear style with its fine technique as though hindered the disclosure of his great and diverse talent.

In connection with this, I should like to conclude this description of Schlechter with another pronouncement by Lasker: "Schlechter may perhaps be sufficiently talented to battle for the World Championship, but he values too highly a quiet life and... is evidently not capable of that determined effort of will, which is necessary so as to snatch from the hands of another player the World Championship".

As you see, an evaluation of the strength of a great master inevitably includes psychological factors.

And now, from the same point of view, let us attempt to look into the creative laboratory of our contemporary, grandmaster Lajos Portisch. Who can deny that Portisch possesses an amazingly complete style, which embodies all the best traditions of the classical positional trend? And the question inevitably arises: why has Portisch, for all his colossal purposefulness and capacity for work, nevertheless not achieved the highest successes? After all, in contrast to, say, Schlechter or Boleslavsky, he is not lacking in fighting qualities or good competitive fervour.

I think that the causes here are mainly of a creative nature. In my opinion, there is no other modern top-class player, and Portisch is undoubtedly one of them, with whom there is such a marked difference between the playing of analyzed stratagems, where he feels very much at home, and variations which he has not anticipated in his home preparation—in these Portisch feels unsure.

As I see it, it is Portisch's colossal analytical

work which sometimes dulls his ability to improvise.

For comparison, let us examine two of his games.

Portisch–Minic
Ljubljana/Portoroz 1973

1 d4 g6 2 e4 Bg7 3 c4 d6 4 Nc3 Nc6 5 Be3 e5 6 d5 Nce7 7 g4! f5 8 g×f5 g×f5.

The players have chosen one of the modern variations of the Pirc-Ufimtsev Defence, one which is assessed by theory as difficult for Black. The subsequent course of the game shows how, with amazing accuracy and ease, Portisch directs his strategical play on the weakened white squares in Black's position. One senses that he has polished this plan very smoothly.

9 Qh5+ Kf8 10 Bh3! Nf6 11 Qf3 f4 12 Bd2 c6.

It is interesting that Portisch already had experience of playing this variation. Thus the game Portisch–Ree (Amsterdam, 1967), which up to Black's 12th move developed in similar fashion, went 12...h5 13 B×c8 Q×c8 14 0-0-0 Bh6 (the transition into the ending also favours White: *14...Qg4 15 h3 Q×f3 16 N×f3 Bh6 17 c5*) 15 Qd3 Rg8 16 Nf3 Rg2 17 Qf1 Rg7 18 Kb1 c5 19 d×c6 b×c6 20 Qe2 c5 21 Nb5 Ne8 22 Bc3 Qe6 23 Rhg1, with a positional advantage for White.

13 Nge2 B×h3 14 Q×h3 Qd7 15 Q×d7 N×d7 16 Nc1 Rc8 17 Nb3 c×d5 18 c×d5 a6 19 Ke2 b6 20 Nc1!

In spite of the exchange of queens, Black is faced with a very difficult defence. White begins a vigorous offensive on the Q-side.

20...Bf6 21 Nd3 Nc5 22 N×c5 b×c5 23 Na4 Rb8 24 Rab1 Nc8 25 b4! c×b4 26 R×b4

R×b4 27 B×b4 Be7 28 Rc1 Na7 29 Nb6 Kf7 30 Rc7 Nb5 31 Rb7! Re8 32 Kd3.

White's plan proceeds without a hitch. Black's position is strategically lost.

32...Kg6 33 Nc4 Bh4 34 a4! Nd4 35 N×d6 Rg8 36 Nc4 B×f2 37 N×e5+ Kf6 38 Rb6+ K×e5 39 Bd6+ Kf6 40 Bc5+ Kf7 41 B×d4 B×d4 42 K×d4 Rg2 43 Ke5 Resigns.

Before turning to the analysis of the following game, I should mention that one can most surely discover a weak point in the play of a great master by the analysis of his lost games. In connection with this, we will follow the course taken by the decisive, 13th game of the Candidates' Match **Spassky-Portisch** (Geneva, 1977). In this clash, Spassky, playing White, wanted first and foremost to deviate from the well-trodden paths, and played the opening in fairly original fashion.

1 e4 c5 2 Nc3 Nc6 3 g3 g6 4 Bg2 Bg7 5 d3 d6 6 f4 e5 7 Nh3 e×f4 8 B×f4 Nge7 9 0-0 h6 10 Rb1 0-0 11 a3 Be6 12 Be3 Ne5 13 Nf4 Bd7 14 Kh1 Rc8 15 Qd2 Kh7 16 h3 Bc6.

Objectively Black has handled the opening quite well, but in the middlegame he begins playing indecisively, and is obviously too slow in building up his Q-side counterplay. One senses that Portisch has little feel for this system. (Namely 'feel'. Here a general knowledge of it is inadequate.) The result is that White soon dominates the position.

17 g4 Qd7 18 Rf2 b6(?) 19 Rbf1 Bb7 20 Qe2 Rce8 21 Bc1 Kg8 22 Qe3 b5 23 Qg3 b4 24 a×b4 c×b4 25 Nd1 d5 26 d4 N5c6 27 e×d5 N×d4 28 c4 b×c3 29 b×c3 Nb3 30 Ba3 Rc8 31 c4! Na5 32 Re2 Rfe8 33 Rfe1 Bf8 34 Nh5!

A tactical blow prepared long ago. The attack on the king quickly leads White to his goal.

34...N×d5 35 c×d5 g×h5 36 g×h5+ Bg7 37 Bb2 f6 38 B×f6 R×e2 39 R×e2 Qf7 40 Re6 Resigns.

The individuality of a player manifests itself even more among the representatives of the combinational trend. The play of such a striking master of combination as Grandmaster Alexandr Tolush was noted for its strength of intuition, and its boundless belief in fantasy. The young players of ours who are most richly endowed with these qualities are Rafael Vaganian and Vitaly Tseshkovsky.

Here is a wonderful example of Tolush's mastery.

Tolush–Kotov
14th USSR Championship 1945

22 N×g7!

The main motif of this sacrifice is the lack of harmony among the black pieces, and their remoteness from the trouble spot.

22...B×e2.

In the event of 22...K×g7 23 Nd4 Bc4 24 B×e4 Kh8 25 Qh5 Bc5 26 g×f6 Bd5 27 f7! Nf6 28 Q×h7+! White gives mate.

23 Q×e2 K×g7 24 B×e4 Nd5 25 Qh5 Rfd8 26 Rg1 Bc5 27 g×f6++ Kf8 28 R×g8+! K×g8 29 B×h7+ Kf8 30 Qg6, and White's attack quickly decided the game.

Sometimes, however, players of this type believe too much in their combinational feeling, and commit oversights when in their very element. Thus, for example, the game **Tolush–Smyslov** from the same tournament is instructive. After playing the opening in interesting fashion, and gaining an excellent position after **1 d4 d5 2 c4 c6 3 Nf3 Nf6 4 Nc3 d×c4 5 e4 b5 6 e5 Nd5 7 a4 Be6 8 a×b5 N×c3 9 b×c3 c×b5 10 Ng5 Bd5 11 e6! f×e6 12 Qg4 h5 13 Qf4 Qd6 14 Qf7+ Kd7 15 Ba3 Qc7 16 Be2 Nc6,** instead of the natural 17 0–0 White played the rash **17 B×h5.**

There followed a 'knock-out' counter-blow: **17...Ne5! 18 d×e5 Q×e5+ 19 Kf1 Q×g5 20 Bf3 Qf6 21 B×d5 Q×f7 22 B×a8 a5,** when White was left in a hopeless position.

Also instructive is the following example.

Vaganian–Suetin
Kaliningrad 1972

With his next move White began a highly original combination: **19 N×e5! f×e5 20 f4! B×h6 21 f×e5+ Kg8 22 Q×h6 Be6.**

I must confess that at this point I was in a bad frame of mind. My vigilance became sharply keener, and I saw the very strong move 23 Rf6!!, after which it is difficult to find a good defence. But the continuation chosen by my opponent showed that, in beginning the combination, he had relied exclusively on intuition, which at first had not deceived him, but now had badly let him down.

23 Rd6? Nc8 24 Bd4 Qg7 25 Qd2 Nd7 26 Bc3 N×d6 27 e×d6 Ne5 28 c5 a4, and soon Black easily realized his advantage.

All this once again shows that even intuitive searching demands checking with variations (within the greatest possible limits). The importance of deep and exact calculation is clearly demonstrated by the evolution of modern chess, which is becoming more and more concrete and being reinforced by precise analyses.

A striving towards a detailed calculation of variations is precisely what distinguishes the representatives of another group of players of combinational tendency. The range of their ideas may not be as sweeping and original as with supporters of combinational intuition. But in the games of the greatest players, combinational ideas and the accurate calculation of variations are harmoniously inter-connected, which is the ideal combination to be aimed for.

On the pages of this book we have already examined a number of examples of accurately and deeply calculated combinations. Here we will give a further few illustrations on the theme of accuracy of calculation, inspired by brilliance of fantasy.

The diagram shows a position from the game **Keres–Raud** (Pjarnu, 1937).

23 Qb6!! The start of a combination which wins by force.

23...Nc6.

In his notes to this game, Keres gives the following variations, which he had to calculate before deciding on the combination:

23...g6 24 Qd8+ Kg7 25 R×f7+ K×f7 26 Ng5+ Kg7 27 Ne6+;

23...Qc8 24 Rc7 Qe8 25 Ng5 Nh6 26 Q×d6+ Kg8 27 Q×e5 (if *27...Qf8*, then *28 Ne6!*);

23...Nd7 24 Q×d6+ Kg8 25 Q×d7.

24 Qc7! Nh6 25 Q×d6+ Kg8 26 d×c6 Kh8 27 Rb8+ R×b8 28 Q×b8+ Ng8 29 c7! Bb5.

No better is 29...Q×c2 30 h4! Qc1+ 31 Kh2 Qf4+ 32 g3! Q×f3 33 Q×g8+!

30 Qd8! Q×c2 31 Kh1 f6 32 c8 = Q Qb1+ 33 Ng1 Q×a2 34 Qf8 Resigns.

And now another fragment from the play of this outstanding grandmaster.

Keres–Unzicker
Hamburg 1956

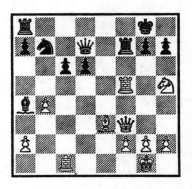

23 N×g7! R×g7.

Other variations also lead to an elegant finish:

23...K×g7 24 Bh6+;

23...Raf8 24 Ne6! R×f5 (*24...Q×e6 25 Qg4+ Qg6 26 Rg5*) 25 Qg4+ Kh8 26 N×f8!

187

24 Bh6 Qe7 25 B×g7 Q×g7.

25...K×g7 is met by 26 Qc3+ Kg8 27 Rf3, with the decisive threats of 28 Rg3+ and 28 Re1.

26 h4 h6 27 Rc4! Resigns.

In the examples given, beautiful combinations were associated with an attack on the king. In the position in the following diagram, Black carried out a spectacular combination, utilizing geometrical motifs.

Polugayevsky–Petrosian
Tbilisi 1956

17...N×e4! 18 B×d8 N×d2 19 B×c7 N×c4 20 B×b8 B×d5 21 Ba7 e4! 22 Ng5 h6 23 Rb3 Bc6.

By means of exchanges and temporary sacrifices, Petrosian has rid himself of his inactive pieces. On the other hand, all Black's remaining forces are operating at full power, and are coordinating excellently. White is forced to return his extra material, but even this does not help.

24 N×e4 B×a4 25 R×b4 a×b4 26 b3 B×b3 27 Rb1 Nb2! 28 Nd6 Re7 29 Bc5 Bc2 30 Ra1 Na4!

As a result of his multi-move combination, Black has gained a won position.

To conclude this chapter, we have a little more to say about schools of mastery, on this occasion about the purely practical significance of this concept. We know that for a long time the teaching of chess was of a strictly individual, spontaneous nature. Players were basically self-taught. Only under socialist conditions in our country has chess teaching, for the first time in history, become a widespread and systematic process. This began with the opening of chess circles in the Pioneers' Palaces, and now chess is already knocking at the doors of general educational schools. In our time the forms of instruction have undoubtedly become broader, and the quality has reached a high level. Specialized chess sections have been opened in many top sports schools.

Also very important is the fact that, nowadays, our famous players have the opportunity of generously sharing their experience with young chess enthusiasts. The foundation was laid by the famous school of Mikhail Botvinnik. Recently its initiative has been maintained by the schools of two other former World Champions: Tigran Petrosian and Vasily Smyslov. For our chess youth there has indeed been opened every possibility for improvement!

POSTSCRIPT

Thus, the path to chess mastery presupposes steadfast work on the cultivation of a whole number of components of thinking and character. First and foremost, it is very important at an early stage of your development to concentrate your efforts on the mastery of concrete methods of thinking, assuming a harmonious combination of visual and verbal ideas. This process is linked with the overcoming of 'catching', 'infectious' thinking deficiencies. At the same time you should learn how to use certain secondary methods, like, for example, thinking by analogy, partly by 'negative' means, and so on. In a number of cases they can prove a valuable support to the basic creative process.

At the same time you should work purposefully on gaining a certain chess culture, including a knowledge of opening and end-game theory, and an understanding of a whole series of typical positions and methods. All this together creates the pre-conditions for acquiring the technique of thinking.

The growth of a player should be based on a practical foundation. And in order to develop his practical strength successfully, he must play regularly and fairly often. Play in tournaments can be combined in a certain dosage with training and friendly games.

A player who has set himself the aim of achieving mastery must constantly widen his horizons. In this respect it is very useful to study psychological and intuitive factors of the struggle, which assumes considerable independent work. The author has seen one of his chief problems to be precisely to arouse the independent thinking of the reader. Seek your own playing style, your own attitude to chess creativity, and don't be afraid to try and to experiment!

The path to mastery is difficult and lengthy, and requires enormous enthusiasm. But in this lies its attraction. If you genuinely love chess, it will disclose to you its amazing secrets.

INDEX

Index